Solomon Northup's Kindred

The Kidnapping of Free Citizens
before the Civil War

David Fiske

PRAEGER™

An Imprint of ABC-CLIO, LLC
Santa Barbara, California • Denver, Colorado

Library of Congress Cataloging-in-Publication Data

Names: Fiske, David, author.
Title: Solomon Northup's kindred : the kidnapping of free citizens before the
    Civil War / David Fiske.
Description: Santa Barbara, California : Praeger, 2016. | Includes
    bibliographical references and index.
Identifiers: LCCN 2015037767 | ISBN 9781440836640 (hard copy : alk. paper) |
    ISBN 9781440836657 (ebook)
Subjects: LCSH: Free African Americans—History—19th century. |
    Kidnapping—United States—History—19th century. | Free African
    Americans—Legal status, laws, etc. | African Americans—History—
    To 1863. | Slavery—United States.
Classification: LCC E185.18 .F54 2016 | DDC 973/.0496073—dc23
LC record available at http://lccn.loc.gov/2015037767

ISBN: 978–1–4408–3664–0
EISBN: 978–1–4408–3665–7

20 19 18 17 16   1 2 3 4 5

This book is also available on the World Wide Web as an eBook.
Visit www.abc-clio.com for details.

Praeger
An Imprint of ABC-CLIO, LLC

ABC-CLIO, LLC
130 Cremona Drive, P.O. Box 1911
Santa Barbara, California 93116-1911

This book is printed on acid-free paper ∞

Manufactured in the United States of America

Contents

A photo essay follows page 112.

Introduction

This book is intended to build upon Carol Wilson's study of this topic, *Freedom at Risk: The Kidnapping of Free Blacks in America, 1780–1865*.[1] That work provides an overview of how free blacks were kidnapped and sold into slavery, assistance the government provided to free blacks, and how black citizens and abolitionists responded to crimes of kidnapping. It also includes a significant amount of information on the operations of one of the most notorious kidnapping operations, the Cannon-Johnson gang, which was responsible for numerous abductions along the Pennsylvania-Delaware border in the early nineteenth century.

In the process of doing research on the life of Solomon Northup (now one of the most well-known victims of kidnapping, thanks to the Academy Award–winning film *12 Years a Slave*), I stumbled onto many more cases of kidnapping—some, such as that of Eli Terry, with similarities to the experience of Northup. Sadly, our national history includes many instances of citizens stealing the liberty of fellow citizens. It will never be known precisely how many free citizens were kidnapped and enslaved, but it seems clear that it took place with relative regularity.

Undoubtedly, most people who have seen the film *12 Years a Slave* come away thinking about how terrible it was that a free man of color was hoodwinked, kidnapped, and sold into bondage. But the experience of Solomon Northup was by no means unique. The same thing happened to many others. Some were rescued before their kidnappers were able to complete the process of selling them into slavery, while others became slaves for months or years before their releases were accomplished.

Kidnapping is an atrocious crime by any standard, and whatever the motive behind it. But kidnapping with the intent and result of "stealing" a person's ability and right to pursue a life of his or her own choosing—for the remainder of the person's life—seems especially cruel and reprehensible. By taking away a person's freedom, kidnapping is just one step below the taking of his life. Consider also the disruption and heartbreak suffered by the victim's family and friends, the fear that such crimes instilled among free black populations, and the loss to communities in free states of the talents and abilities of some of their neighbors. "Free coloured [*sic*] citizens," read an 1840 report on the kidnapping problem in New York State, "occupy places and discharge duties, important to the interests and essential to the comfort and convenience of society."[2] The loss of these fellow citizens, to the vile institution of slavery, was of consequence to everyone.

Even in free states, African Americans often enjoyed less than full civil rights. This probably made it easier for kidnappers to commit their crimes, and it surely allowed them to justify their actions in their own minds. Laws affecting black citizens only (such as the "black codes" in Ohio, Indiana, and Illinois),[3] and other discriminatory legal provisions—such as, in New York State, the requirement that free blacks own real property in order to vote, and their exclusion from jury and militia service—fueled racial attitudes and stereotypes. Such feelings led, in some cases, to the lack of concern when crimes were perpetrated against African Americans.

Though slavery had been abolished in the northern states long before the Civil War, the kidnapping issue helped give the horror of slavery a presence in those states, since free people could be cast into bondage. The fact that kidnappers were able to operate with a certain level of efficiency and success, and that some of those who were detected received only light punishment (or even none at all), is a reminder that, even in free states, slavery had those who supported (or at least tolerated) it.

Somewhat counterbalancing the repugnance of the crimes related here, there remains the fact that noble efforts were often made by citizens determined to assist victims. People from the neighborhoods where victims had lived in freedom undertook rescue missions that sometimes involved lengthy and inconvenient journeys. Attorneys came forward—in both free and slave states—to help victims seek their release according to law, and some individuals who believed in justice listened to victims and conveyed information about them as a first step in getting them released. A chapter of this book is devoted to some of those who provided assistance to victims in various ways.

As someone who specializes in uncovering lost history, I feel proud to be able to tell the tragic stories of some of these victims. Though I find it unsettling to have learned that so many crimes were committed, that feeling is partially offset by the satisfaction of being able to recover the stories of people whose lives have otherwise been long overlooked. Their stories are a stain on our national history; a stain that—given social prejudices, governmental actions, and a system of slavery that gave some people nearly total control over the minds and bodies of others—was bound to appear. I have tried to keep the focus of this book on the victims, in order to tell their stories as well as they *can* be told.

In addition to telling the stories of several dozen victims of kidnapping, this book also provides some historical context to help explain why and how these kidnappings occurred.

Kidnapping's prevalence can be attributed, at least in part, to various factors that served as motivation for the crime, and which made it an attractive activity for criminals to pursue. The very active internal slave trade in the United States meant that a commercial network was readily available for marketing and transporting people illegally sold into slavery. Although financial gain was a major motivator for kidnappers, some were induced to abduct free blacks in order to replace slave labor, which they were denied after slaves they owned ran away. Resistance in free states to returning fugitives from bondage led owners of absconded slaves to seek a remedy outside the legal system, which they believed had failed them.

Kidnapping was common enough (and of enough concern) that efforts were made to prevent and deter it. Laws were enacted, but were not entirely effective. Personal liberty laws were also put in place, to provide some guarantee, via court proceedings, that persons alleged to be fugitive slaves were not free persons who had simply been grabbed off the streets. Cases of kidnapping were publicized in the antislavery press, and in regular newspapers, as a way of creating awareness of the crimes—as well as building antipathy toward slavery generally.

Victimized individuals found that the deck was largely stacked against them when it came to getting released. Coercive measures—including physical and psychological abuse—served to stifle their resistance, and those who refused to give up on their claims to freedom usually found that their protestations fell on deaf ears. In the slave states, social and legal barriers hindered their efforts to rejoin the free population. Lack of communication with friends and relatives who might have been able to help them, along with miles and miles of distance that lay between them and the communities they had been torn from, added additional barriers to the chances of rescue.

Despite the hurdles, some rescues were accomplished. Those who regained their freedom had often not been enslaved for long, but there were cases where victims were located and taken home after years of involuntary servitude.

Certain difficulties confront the researcher of this topic. The word "kidnapping" implies forcible abduction, but this was not always the case. Persuasion was often used by criminals who were more con artists than violent offenders. They took advantage of the desire almost all human beings have of improving their personal situations.

In her book, Carol Wilson noted that the study of kidnapping is complicated by "several other historical uses of the term," including the removal of people from Africa, impressment of men for military service, people who became involuntary colonists, and the "stealing" of slaves by abolitionists.[4] In nineteenth-century America, the word "kidnapping" was also used in reference to the apprehension of runaway slaves by slavecatchers. This practice is also of historical importance, but it is not the topic of this book. I have confined my research to individuals who were enslaved counter to the law of the time. Today, we understand that no one should have been a slave to another person, but in antebellum America, the fact was that, by accident of birth, some people—born to free parents—enjoyed freedom, while others—born into slavery—were likely to be lifelong bondsmen or bondswomen.

Further adding to the complication of research is the fact that some of the best contemporary sources for information on cases of kidnapping are publications that promoted antislavery views. Consequently, some exaggeration or misrepresentation appeared in their pages as they attempted to sway the public. As much as possible, I have not relied solely on such sources.

Some scholars have referred to the kidnapping phenomenon as the "reverse underground railroad." I do not, because, for one thing, it puts the cart before the horse. The organized system of aiding runaway slaves arose in the nineteenth century, though surely, there were scattered assisted escapes prior to that. Kidnapping came first—there were instances even in colonial America.

The approach taken in the current volume has been to research a number of cases of kidnapping—documenting them as well as possible—and to draw from them some observations about how kidnappers operated, various factors that allowed them to operate with a certain amount of ease, and how the problem was dealt with socially and politically. Additional research was carried out in order to help explain why kidnapping occurred, the efforts used to fight it, and the impact that actions of governmental bodies had on it.

Criteria I applied for including specific case studies were: that the victims' names were given in newspaper accounts or other documents (many, many cases were noted in the press where the victims were not identified by name—such cases are difficult to confirm without doing significant additional research), and that there was some credible source of information indicating that a victim was in fact free (and not a runaway slave—stories of fugitive slaves represent an interesting, but distinctly different topic).

Slavery is now largely viewed as a southern institution, but there were many ways that northern states benefited from it.[5] Many kidnappers were northerners—sometimes neighbors of their victims—looking to profit from their crimes. A general lack of respect for the rights of African Americans, even in free states, allowed kidnappers to carry on their filthy business without a great amount of interference. Even in those cases where the perpetrators *were* brought to justice, they sometimes were not heavily punished. Wilson has noted that: "Since kidnapping was a crime usually committed by whites against blacks, a large segment of the white population did not find it particularly troubling."[6] Racial attitudes toward blacks—based on stereotypes—were such that, even in the North, some people believed that blacks were better off as slaves. Those holding this belief would not be expected to feel too badly about the fate of free citizens whose liberty had been stolen, possibly dooming them to lives of miserable servitude.

ACKNOWLEDGMENTS

Many people have, directly or indirectly, encouraged me in the writing of this book. Individuals I would like to specifically thank include: Craig Lukezic (who shared some material relating to Aaron Cooper); Gary L. Knepp (whose insights on the Vincent Wigglesworth family were helpful); the Library of Virginia (which helped me find and obtain interesting and important documents relating to the cases of Sidney O. Francis and Nahum Gardner Hazard); and the Indiana Historical Society (which provided me a photocopy of a rare pamphlet about the rescue of Eli Terry, whose case rivals that of Solomon Northup). I am also grateful to the numerous libraries, historical societies, and commercial services who have made historical newspapers and publications available in digitized format; having access to such information was incredibly helpful to my research. As always, my wife Laura patiently looked over early drafts, catching a number of typographical errors. The cover illustration, "A Northern Freeman Enslaved by Northern Hands" (American Anti-slavery Almanac, 1839), depicts the kidnapping of Peter John Lee.

1

Factors That Led to and Enhanced the Business of Kidnapping

A sequence of factors contributed to the prevalence of the crime of kidnapping free people and profiting from their sale as slaves. Measures undertaken for political reasons added to the profitability of such crimes, as well as to the relative safety that kidnappers enjoyed. Economic development in the South escalated the value of kidnappers' ill-gotten "merchandise." Legal protection available to victims was limited by court decisions. Over time, kidnapping became a lucrative business for immoral individuals to pursue, generally with little accountability for their actions.

THE CONSTITUTIONAL PROVISION FOR RETURN OF FUGITIVE SLAVES

A number of northern states had abolished slavery prior to the drafting of the U.S. Constitution, and, out of concern that these states would become places of sanctuary for slaves who had deserted their masters in the south, a clause was included in the Constitution to satisfy the slaveholding states that escaped slaves would be returned.[1]

Thus, Article IV, Section 2, includes the following clause, which was added "without debate or formal vote."[2] "No Person held to Service or Labour in one State, under the Laws thereof, escaping into another, shall, in Consequence of any Law or Regulation therein, be discharged from such Service or Labour, but shall be delivered up on Claim of the Party to whom such Service or Labour may be due."

Kidnappings of free persons were in no way authorized by this provision of the law of the land, but they certainly occurred in the years following the adoption of the Constitution. Owners of slaves who had escaped often offered rewards, hoping that they would be returned to them. Owners also sometimes hired others to go to other states to find and retrieve their "property." This provided monetary incentives for slavecatchers, who might not have felt the need to carefully verify that the person they brought back was in fact the person who had escaped (so long as the person was considered an acceptable replacement by the owner).

THE 1793 FUGITIVE SLAVE LAW

Clarification of the legal process for returning fugitive slaves was sought after the governor of Virginia refused to honor a 1791 request from the governor of Pennsylvania, who sought the extradition of three men who had allegedly kidnapped a black man named John Davis. These three Virginians were not kidnappers, according to Virginia, but merely men who had, according to law, recaptured a runaway slave.

The squabble between the two states dragged on for some time, with Virginia eventually arguing—as justification for not turning over the kidnapping suspects—that citizens of Pennsylvania had been "seducing and harboring" slaves that belonged to her citizens.[3] President George Washington apprised Congress of the matter, and Congress eventually acted. During the legislative process, versions of the bill contained wording that would have provided some protection for free blacks wrongly accused of being fugitive slaves, but in the end, these measures were dropped from the law that was enacted and signed in 1793.[4] The northern legislators "appear to have failed to appreciate the dangers that slavehunting posed to both free blacks and antislavery whites."[5]

A person apprehending a slave could go before a federal or state judge, or a mere magistrate of a municipality. Minimal proof that the seized person in fact was the property of the claimant was required; an oral statement to that effect was adequate.[6] In an ultimate irony, even John Davis, the man whose claim to freedom had some validity, and whose case had prompted the federal legislation, was not saved from slavery. He lived in bondage for the remainder of his life.[7]

With minimal obligation on the part of slaveowners (or those working on their behalf) to prove that a captured person was actually an escaped slave (and, in fact, the slave being sought), and given the prospect of financial gain, either from the restoration of a piece of valuable property, or the receipt of a reward or payment for slavehunting services, there was certainly adequate incentive to encourage the kidnapping of free persons. Clearly, it took place. Some states enacted "personal liberty laws" to provide some measure of protection against such abuses, by giving individuals accused of being fugitives their day in court.[8]

THE 1808 BAN ON IMPORTING SLAVES INTO THE UNITED STATES, AND ITS EFFECT ON THE SUPPLY OF SLAVE LABOR

Article I, Section. 9 of the U. S. Constitution reads:

"The Migration or Importation of such Persons as any of the States now existing shall think proper to admit, shall not be prohibited by the Congress prior to the Year one thousand eight hundred and eight, but a Tax or duty may be imposed on such Importation, not exceeding ten dollars for each Person."

It is not at once evident, thanks to its couched wording, that this constitutional language is about slavery, but the "such Persons" referred to included slaves. By this provision, the southern states were assured of being able to bring slaves into the country for 20 years: Congress could not ban the trade during that period. Congress could, and did, restrict other aspects of the slave trade. In 1794, it prohibited exporting slaves from the United States to other countries, and in 1803, it forbade the importation of slaves into states where slavery had been abolished.[9]

Finally, in 1807, as the constitutional time constraint expired, the importation of slaves into any of the United States was prohibited: after January 1, 1808, it was against federal law to bring slaves into the country, "under heavy penalties." This major step forward in the elimination of slavery in America had an unfortunate side effect, however. In a description of an 1817 kidnapping case, a legal publication provided this historical background:

> The importation of slaves into the United States being thus prohibited, and, in many of the states, slavery having been in a measure abolished, and high rewards being offered for slaves in the southern states, the practice of kidnapping was commenced, and has been carried to an alarming height. Fraud, force, and cunning, on the part of the kidnappers, have been successively employed in procuring persons of colour for the southern market, from the middle and northern states. Persons of colour, whether slaves, servants, or freemen, have been forced, stolen, or inveigled, and carried in droves, manacled with fetters, to the southern states. On the lines between the southern and middle states, free people of colour have frequently by stratagem, or force, been dragged away from their relations and friends, carried into a foreign land and made slaves.[10]

Though slaves were still brought in, contrary to law,[11] the ban on importation surely had some impact on the supply of slaves. With downward pressure on supply, upward pressure would be expected on the prices of slaves. "The ban increased the value of slaves ... and encouraged kidnappers from the Border South to prey on free African Americans in the Lower North."[12]

INVENTION OF THE COTTON GIN

With the 1793 invention of the cotton gin, and its adoption in many southern states, the cultivation of cotton expanded into interior areas where cotton had not previously been grown. With this expansion came increased demand for labor, and slave labor was preferred. The willingness of buyers in the Deep South to pay high prices led to an influx of enslaved African American laborers into the region.[13]

Between 1820 and 1860, there was an involuntary migration of nearly one million blacks from states in the upper South to the Deep South, a migration that was supported by "a well-organized internal slave trade."[14] Some of the increased demand for forced labor was no doubt met by natural reproduction among slaves, perhaps with encouragement of this trend by slaveowners.[15]

These developments added to the practice of kidnapping free blacks in several ways. Prices for slave labor rose (making illicit slavetrading more enticing),[16] the system for moving slaves from place to place enabled surreptitious transportation of kidnapped individuals away from areas where they were known or could be located, and the increased value of a slave made it less likely that a purchaser would readily give up a person whom he might suspect (or know) had been enslaved and sold contrary to law.

THE *PRIGG V. PENNSYLVANIA* DECISION

States in the North, having observed that federal judges would permit slaveowners or their agents to take persons claimed as runaways out of their jurisdictions, had enacted personal liberty laws. Such laws made it illegal for fugitives to be removed without following proper state judicial procedures. Though such procedures surely prevented many free citizens from being sent into bondage upon little firm evidence, they also frustrated efforts by legitimate owners to reclaim their property. "Despite their rights under federal law, slaveholders found it virtually impossible to recover their runaways through state court proceedings."[17]

The U.S. Supreme Court decided the case of Edward Prigg in 1842. Prigg had been hired to find and return a fugitive to a Maryland slave-owner, but was arrested and convicted when he removed the person from Pennsylvania without following the process called for by the laws of that state. The Supreme Court's ruling bore on the issue in two ways: the states had no role in returning fugitives, as the Constitution clearly placed that function in the hands of the federal government; and, because it fell under the jurisdiction of the federal government, states could not be compelled to use their resources— policemen, magistrates, and judges—to support the process of capturing, detaining, and returning fugitives.

The Pennsylvania statute under which Prigg had been convicted[18]— and similar personal liberty laws in other states—was therefore unconstitutional. Tossed out along with these laws was the protection that they had offered to free people who were either misidentified as runaways or who were kidnap victims held out as fugitives. This made the work of kidnappers that much easier.

Because the Supreme Court's decision also said that it was the federal government's responsibility to see that escaped slaves were restored to their owners, the states could not be compelled to use their own resources in connection with this function.[19] Those states in the antislavery camp could complicate (if not prevent) slave renditions by forcing slavecatchers to do their own work in locating and apprehending missing chattels.[20]

State and local officials—who were in better positions to have local knowledge that alleged fugitives were actually free persons (who may have been born free or manumitted)—were not to be involved in the whole process. People accused of being runaways would be taken before harried federal officials, who might not have the time, inclination, or community knowledge to do anything other than accept the word of the claimants—and to ignore the protestations of those individuals on the verge of being wrongfully enslaved.

THE 1850 FUGITIVE SLAVE LAW

The passage of a new Fugitive Slave Law, as part of the Compromise of 1850, added to the hurdles faced by free blacks who wished to retain their liberty. In theory, it merely built upon the Constitutional provision for the return of runaways and the 1793 law. Though defenders of the new law pointed out that safeguards were available to keep kidnapped freemen from being enslaved, the language employed in the statute was open to a different interpretation.

With state and local courts having been removed from dealing with fugitive slave matters by the *Prigg* decision, the 1850 law spelled out how federal officials would proceed in these cases. A slaveowner seeking the return of a runaway began by swearing out an affidavit that a particular slave had escaped, and that the owner actually had a legal right to the slave. This was to be done in the place where the owner resided, before officials possibly known personally by the owner, and who surely were interested in supporting the legality of the concept of slaveownership.

The paperwork was to include "a general description of the person so escaping, with such convenient certainty" as possible. The owner, or an agent working on behalf of the owner, was then to travel to the state where the runaway was thought to be, and to pursue one of two options: to present the paperwork to a federal commissioner or judge and obtain assistance in apprehending the escapee, or to seize the person and then go before a federal official. The official could accept the paperwork (referred to as "the record") and turn the person over to the claimant, or could request "other and further evidence if necessary, either oral or by affidavit," in order to establish "the identity of the person escaping."

When the claim was substantiated to the satisfaction of the official, the claimant could go home with his recovered property and could even, if he feared an attempt to rescue the slave was imminent, have the person transported back by the federal government.

Despite the relatively low standard of proof necessary to establish that the person apprehended was indeed the escaped slave, the claimant was not absolutely required to produce a "record," as the law provided that, if he did not, "the claim shall be heard and determined upon other satisfactory proofs, competent in law."

There was no requirement for a *habeas corpus* hearing, nor any sort of trial before the person was delivered up to the claimant. U.S. Senator Stephen A. Douglas (a proponent of the 1850 law) claimed that such protections were not ruled out, but that such procedures could be carried out in the slave state to which the fugitive was being returned.[21]

The law stacked the deck against an alleged fugitive in other ways. The person himself could not testify: "In no trial or hearing under this act shall the testimony of such alleged fugitive be admitted in evidence." If the accused had to be detained for a time while an official considered his case, various expenses including those for "keeping the fugitive in custody, and providing him with food and lodging" could be run up, and these were payable by the claimant—who therefore had an interest in keeping the proceedings as brief as possible.

Financial inducements could have influenced decisions in these cases. The federal officials—commissioners or judges—were paid for handling cases of fugitives. They received $5 for cases where the accused person was released, and $10 when the person was restored to the owner, creating at least the semblance of "bribing" officials to decide against the fugitive. Federal marshals, if brought in on a case, were personally liable for the value of any fugitives who escaped their custody for any reason.

The new law was detested by many. At a Whig convention in 1850, it was called the "law for the encouragement of kidnapping." That phrase was also used by a Michigan antislavery society, who also noted that "in its execution, the liberties of all our citizens, irrespective of color or condition, are endangered, wherever an individual can be found base enough to commit perjury."[22]

In 1852, the Democratic Party Convention was criticized for pledging to "abide by a law that abolishes jury trial, allows *ex parte* evidence, creates swarms of petty officers to enforce it, gives a double compensation to find every claim set up in favor of the master, and pays the expenses of returning fugitives from the public Treasury."[23]

The 1850 law meant, according to scholars James Oliver Horton and Lois E. Horton, that: "Any black person could be judged a fugitive, taken south and sold into slavery." The law encouraged slave hunters who "worked alone or in gangs to make easy money by kidnapping blacks and selling them south." One criminal, who kept a diary, "had little regard for whether his victim was truly a fugitive or simply an African American who might be accepted by a slaveholder."[24]

Under the act, "nothing could prevent a slaveowner or his agent from coming up to any Negro on the streets of any Northern city and accusing him or her of being a sought runaway," and the person could be taken based on evidence in "certificates . . . issued by state courts in the South to claimants without the slightest evidence."[25] One example of how easily a free person could be identified as a runaway can be seen in the case of Adam Gibson, who was taken up—not long after the 1850 law took effect—as a fugitive in Philadelphia. A commissioner surrendered him "with indecent haste" to a slavecatcher. Gibson was delivered to his supposed owner in Maryland, who "refused to receive him, saying he was not the man."[26]

The Fugitive Slave Law had its defenders, who minimized the consequences it might have for free citizens. Senator Stephen A. Douglas claimed that "When he [a fugitive] returns [to the south], or is surrendered under the law, he is entitled to a trial by jury of his right of freedom, and always has it if he demands it." The new law was necessary "to carry into effect, in a peaceable and orderly manner, the provisions of the law and the Constitution on the one hand, and to protect the free colored man from being kidnapped and sold into slavery by unprincipled men on the other hand." Douglas stated that "The slaveholder has as strong a desire to protect the rights of the free black man as we have," because abuses would not bode well for the future of the institution of slavery.[27]

A New York City newspaper commented on the case of a local man who had been sent back to Virginia, "where, if he is not a slave, a thousand lawyers stand ready to serve him for nothing, and to secure him just as fair a trial by jury as a white man can have there." Disagreeing with another paper that had called for new personal liberty laws because of fraudulent apprehensions of supposed runaways, it stated that laws in southern states were adequate to protect victimized freemen: "If mock master kidnaps, the Virginia law to protect the free negro is, head and shoulders, above any New York city negro law."[28]

Though it is true that some who had been wrongfully enslaved could, and did, initiate "freedom suits" (sometimes successfully), the barriers were significant, especially since a person considered to be a slave ordinarily could not testify against white people, and the legal process required the assistance of a white person in the place where the person was in bondage, which could not always be readily obtained.

THE *DRED SCOTT* DECISION

The March 1857 decision of the U.S. Supreme Court in the *Dred Scott* case (*Dred Scott v. Sandford*) seriously muddied the waters relating to the legal status of Americans of African descent. Scott had been a slave in Missouri, but then lived for years in Illinois (a free state) and in a part of the Louisiana Territory where slavery was against the law. After returning to Missouri, he unsuccessfully sued for his freedom in state courts, and then commenced an action in federal court. His argument was that, having lived in places that were free of slavery, he had become a freeman.

The Supreme Court ruled that free negroes were not entitled to any standing in federal courts, and therefore Scott had no right to bring a lawsuit. This decision—that blacks had no rights under federal law—detracted from whatever protection might be afforded them under state statutes. The Court's opinion, written by Supreme Court Chief Justice Roger B. Taney, was very likely a factor in the abortive prosecution of the kidnappers of Solomon Northup in New York.[29] The decision was also alleged to have been the cause of numerous assaults on the rights of African Americans, in various states.[30]

To would-be kidnappers, any qualms about selling free blacks into slavery could be allayed by the *Dred Scott* ruling, since the victims could be considered not to be citizens at all. They were free to "mix free blacks with slaves in one legal category based on race," as it has been said Taney had done.[31]

2

The Kidnappers and Their Methods

What were the motivations of kidnappers, who intended to deprive others of their freedom, probably for the remainder of their lives? For although some victims were miraculously rescued,[1] these were the exceptions. More typically, a victim's experience was similar to a case described by a war correspondent in Alabama at the end of the Civil War: "One old man ... born in the North, a freeman, had been kidnapped at the age of 15, and had been held in slavery 63 years."[2] Monetary gain is an obvious answer to the question, and it undoubtedly motivated most of the perpetrators to carry on their miserable business. Others engaged in the activity as a means to replace slaves who had escaped or had been helped to escape. They did not necessarily care that they got back the same person who had run away, just so long as they obtained the equivalent services of *some* person.

FINANCIAL GAIN

The money that could be made by a kidnapper was substantial. In a speech in 1854, Abraham Lincoln observed that the value of the nation's 430,000 free blacks would amount to over $200 million if they were instead slaves. "Slavery," he said, "is founded in the selfishness of man's nature."[3] Lincoln used $500 as the average value of a slave for his calculation—kidnappers typically received a much larger sum for a victim—making Lincoln's estimate a low one. Perpetrators of kidnappings incurred certain necessary expenses: transporting, lodging, and feeding themselves and their victims. A kidnapper stood to earn, say, on the order of $500 or more in profit per victim. Using this basic assumption, the per-victim "take," in the 1850s, equated to at least the amount of pay a carpenter in New England would receive for almost one year's labor, and an amount that it would take over four years for a southern farm worker to earn.[4] A successful kidnapper would not have to work for probably several years after completion of his caper.

Some people—even in the North—believed in the stereotype of the indolent black, who was so incapable of providing for himself that he was better off as a slave.[5] Such beliefs mitigated any compunction kidnappers might feel—they were (they could imagine) doing their victims a favor, and, happily, enriching themselves at the same time.

In light of these considerations, one author noted that it was almost surprising that so many blacks escaped being victimized: "[I]n view of the seeming ease of its accomplishment and the potential value of the victims it may well be thought remarkable that so many thousands of free negroes were able to keep their liberty."[6]

RESTORATION OF SLAVE LABOR LOST TO ESCAPES

Complaints by slaveowners about the difficulty or impossibility of regaining slaves who had escaped to free states were numerous, and they led to squabbles between state governments.[7] If a particular escaped slave could not be found or returned, an owner might be willing to settle for anyone who could be seized and brought back to him, in order to perform the services of the actual fugitive. Slavecatchers hired by owners were aware of this. One slavecatcher "had little regard for whether his victim was truly a fugitive or simply an African American who might be accepted by a slaveholder."[8] In Missouri, a so-called *anti*-abolition society was even formed to recapture fugitives, and it resolved to see that "a free citizen of Illinois be kidnapped for every slave that escaped."[9]

This sort of kidnapping often took the form of cross-border incursions from a slave state into a free state. One example was the armed attack on a party of free blacks whom Dr. John Doy was helping to relocate out of Kansas. After being forced into Missouri at gunpoint, the "slaves" were parceled out to owners who had had servants run away (the victims were apparently allowed to choose who their "owners" would be). Doy (and for a time, his son also) were imprisoned for weeks until he was rescued by friends from Kansas.[10]

METHODS USED BY KIDNAPPERS

In some instances, kidnappers used physical force to take their victims,[11] sometimes during "home invasions." These incidents tended to be staged during the night, when victims probably had been sleeping and were less likely to resist being dragged away, and when the crime was not likely to be witnessed by neighbors. A certain amount of resistance could be expected when seizing adults, but children could be more easily subdued and borne away out of sight of bystanders. When young Isaac Moore could not be cajoled into leaving his neighborhood in New York City, he was grabbed, carried aboard a ship, and locked up below decks for days before seizing an opportunity to escape.[12]

In many cases, though, kidnappers were accomplished con artists. Using deception to trick a victim into going off with the abductor (or to convince a parent to allow a child to leave home) was a method that avoided the messiness of forcibly removing a person. Victims (or parents of victims)—seeking to improve the situations of themselves or their children—were enticed with offers of good pay for positions in another state, and they left their neighborhoods voluntarily. Arrangements made with a child's parents might include promises of schooling as well as earnings from work. The legal term used to describe such crimes was "inveigling."

Such trickery was even attempted in Canada, a place without slavery, where blacks might have felt safer than in the United States. In 1851, a Canadian newspaper noted that "parties are at present in Toronto, endeavoring to induce colored persons to go to the States in their employ as servants. From the character of the propositions, there is reason to believe that 'foul play' is intended."[13] In 1855, the newspaper warned blacks that "hopeless slavery" could result from agreeing to "enter service at a distance from their homes," thereby becoming victims (like Solomon Northup) as a "result of listening to fair offers of excellent pay and easy position from rogues."[14]

Some kidnappings quite obviously took a significant amount of planning. The two men who inveigled Solomon Northup probably knew the time of year when a potential victim would be low on funds in the resort community of Saratoga Springs, and they were aware of a hotel in Washington, D.C., that was handy to the taverns where slave traders conducted their business—a hotel from which a victim could quickly and stealthily be led through the nighttime streets of Washington to a nearby slave pen, just a few blocks away.[15]

The men who bamboozled the parents of Sidney O. Francis had their stories in sync: one claimed to be seeking a young boy to do light work in his store several towns away, and the other chimed in, saying that he himself had been working for the storekeeper for several years and that he was a very nice person. They had traveled around central Massachusetts for several days, seeking the right type of child, especially one who had not been away from home before and who therefore would not understand where he was actually being taken.[16]

Other times, a kidnapper was someone with "larceny in the heart," who chanced upon a person who constituted a "target of opportunity." John Adams, a teenager, disappeared after he was left alone for just a few minutes at a busy marketplace in Washington, D.C., in a neighborhood where slave traders conducted their business. Isaac Moore (mentioned above) was simply walking along a street near his home in Manhattan; his taking was in all likelihood a crime of opportunity.[17]

Individuals who were actively involved in kidnapping sometimes made use of accomplices who assisted with their dirty work. A neighbor of the Dredden family helped kidnappers by encouraging both parents to leave home for a day, and by delivering some of their children to a kidnapper in a secluded spot in nearby woods. Joel Henry Thompson's mother (a woman who was a fugitive) was encouraged by an African American friend to visit with her free-born baby—and both were led into the waiting arms of a slavecatcher.[18]

Kidnappings were also carried out by criminal rings. Elisha Tyson, a Maryland abolitionist, wrote a letter to Congressman Alexander McKim in 1811 in which he detailed several cases of free persons being kidnapped and sold as slaves. Tyson observed that "This trade is conducted by a chain of individuals of the most unprincipled and profligate characters, whose connection extends from Orleans to New York."[19] There were family connections between several parties involved in the kidnappings of Sidney O. Francis and Nahum G. Hazard in central Massachusetts.[20] A notorious gang, headed up by husband and wife Jesse and Patty Cannon, operated in Maryland and Delaware, near the border with Pennsylvania.[21] In New York City, police officials Tobias Boudinot and Daniel D. Nash often recaptured fugitive slaves and also dipped their toes into the muddy waters of kidnapping.[22]

PRETENDED FUGITIVE SLAVE APPREHENSIONS

One way in which a kidnapping could be accomplished was by claiming that the victim was not a free person, but an escaped slave.[23] Minimal proof was required to identify a particular person as a specific runaway. Physical descriptions were often not very detailed, and numerous individuals could easily be found who bore at least a vague resemblance to a missing slave. Identification often relied on the memories of people who had not seen the runaways for years. For example, in 1835, Robert Aitkins claimed that a woman known as Mary Gilmore was a slave who had run away from him 10 years earlier. His evidence that Gilmore was the runaway consisted mainly of the testimony of a black woman, who had had a run-in with Jacob Gilmore, a black man with a successful bakery in Philadelphia. Jacob Gilmore testified that Mary had been left in his care by her white mother, prior to the year that Aitkins's slave had escaped. The court ruled against Aitkins's claim, and it was later determined that the mother of Mary Gilmore was actually an Irish woman named O'Connor.[24]

Similar cases included that of "an old man, named Harper, a Methodist preacher" who was seized at gunpoint by three men, one of them declaring that Harper was his slave. At a hearing before a magistrate, "such proof was presented of his right to freedom" that Harper was released, and the men were indicted for assault and battery; only one of them was arrested, and he was acquitted at a trial.[25] In Indianapolis, Indiana, John Freeman was seized by a preacher who claimed him as his escaped slave. Freeman produced some evidence of his free status and was granted time to obtain more. His supposed owner, Rev. Pleasant Ellington, brought witnesses from Kentucky, who viewed Freeman's stripped body, and identified him as Ellington's slave Sam, despite the absence of specific scars on Freeman's body which Ellington had said Sam bore. In time, the actual Sam was located in Canada, and he proved to be "a tall, straight negro; jet black, full chest," while Freeman was "a low heavy-set man, muddy brown, by no means black like Sam, and at least six inches shorter." When additional, incontrovertible evidence surfaced that supported Freeman's case, Ellington made a furtive departure, presumably seeking to avoid being held accountable for his seemingly intentional and fraudulent misidentification.[26]

Even though the standard of proof for identifying a runaway was low, a kidnapper could make sure of a positive match by using the following technique: "Having selected a suitable free coloured person, to make a *pitch* upon, the *conjuring* kidnapper employs a confederate, to ascertain the distinguishing marks of his body and then claims and obtains him as a slave, before a magistrate, by describing those marks, and proving the truth of his assertions, by his well-instructed accomplice."[27]

Possession of free papers was no guarantee that a person would not be falsely accused of being a fugitive. Solomon Northup had free papers (his kidnappers had even helped him obtain them before they left New York), but they were taken from him after he became ill—not long after he consumed liquor given him by his kidnappers. Dr. John Doy recounted an incident of a freeman's papers being taken from the man, torn up, and burned by a slave trader.[28]

Pretending that a free person was actually a runaway slave in the process of being reclaimed was also useful for maintaining custody of a victim. Once a victim had been taken into a slave state, any suspicions could be allayed by explaining that the victim (despite what he or she might say) was not free at all, but rather an escaped slave who belonged to the kidnapper. Thus, when authorities in Virginia began looking into the case of George Anderson, his abductor explained that the man was his slave whom he had located in New York City, to whom he had made a false offer of employment in order to get Anderson to go away with him quietly.[29]

Napoleon Bonaparte Van Tuyl, who inveigled John Hight and Daniel Prue, explained to southern men he met on board a train in Ohio that he had located his former slaves and was taking them back to Tennessee. After Prue became uneasy and got off the train, Van Tuyl called on his new friends for assistance, and one took charge of Hight and continued on to Kentucky, while another got off the train and spent substantial effort helping to locate Prue, and trying to recapture him.[30]

PRETENDED CRIMINAL APPREHENSIONS

Similar to the previously described method of kidnapping was the taking of a person for a crime that had allegedly been committed. Under the Constitution, fugitives from justice were to be turned over from one state to another upon request. An indictment could be obtained in the state where the crime had been committed, along with an affidavit of flight, and these forwarded to the state where the person was thought to be living. There, "the constable may pick up the first likely negro he finds in the street, and ship him to the south; and should it be found, on his arrival on the plantation, that the wrong man has come, it will also probably be found that the mistake is of no consequence to the planter."[31] The technique could also be used to apprehend an actual fugitive, since an owner "wishes to recover him with as little noise, trouble, and delay as possible."[32] On being delivered up to the state requesting him, the person might be tried for the alleged crime (or not), and then given over to the supposed owner. Peter John Lee,[33] along with others, was captured in New York State in this way. Charged with having stolen the boat in which they fled Virginia, some of them were tried and sentenced to death. Instead of being executed, they were pardoned and turned over to their owners.

Identification in such cases was as imprecise as for fugitive slave apprehensions. David Ruggles suspected that Tobias Boudinot had hoped to kidnap him in this manner, making use of an open arrest warrant "by which he can arrest any colored person that Waddy [a sheriff from Virginia] may point out to him named 'Jesse,' 'Abraham,' 'Peter,' or 'Silvia,' and send him or her South, without taking such person before a magistrate."[34]

In Pennsylvania in 1838, two men who had an African American in custody attracted the attention of the public. Asked why they had arrested the person, they at first said he was a runaway slave and displayed a runaway slave ad, but after an attorney pointed out that it was not adequate proof and that they were violating Pennsylvania law, they instead said they were arresting him for having stolen the jacket he was wearing. The men were arrested, and the fact that they had told various inconsistent stories "tended strongly to excite suspicion that their objects were lawless and mercenary."[35]

Interaction of Kidnappers and Slave Traders

Once a kidnapper had managed to get custody of a victim—whether via abduction or deceit—it was not difficult to find a buyer and thereby reap the rewards of his criminal activity. Though not all slave traders were involved with kidnappers, "all kidnappers utilized the interstate trade since they eventually had to sell their victims."[1] Professor Robert H. Gudmestad has noted that: "The growing number of abduction stories firmly linked slave traders with kidnappers in the public's mind." One person in Baltimore who saw a group of slaves being led through the streets assumed (probably incorrectly) that it was entirely composed of abducted freemen.[2]

ADVERTISING BY SLAVE TRADERS

Slave traders routinely placed ads in newspapers in cities where there were active slave markets. They were anxious to obtain additional human product to add to their inventories. Judging by the wording of these types of ads, the field was very competitive. "CASH FOR NEGROES," they often blared, as in the following ad in the *Daily National Intelligencer*, placed in 1838 by James H. Birch (the District of Columbia trader who would later purchase Solomon Northup from the men who had decoyed him away from New York State in 1841): "CASH FOR NEGROES.—I will give cash and liberal prices for a number of likely Negroes, under twenty-five years of age, families included. I can be found at B. O. Shekell's Tavern, a few doors below Lloyd's Tavern, opposite the Center Market. JAMES H. BIRCH, Washington City."[3]

Immediately below Birch's ad was one for Jilson Dove, who sought "young and likely negroes of both sexes." Dove conducted his business at "Thomas Lloyd's steamboat hotel, on Seventh street, opposite the Center Market House." (The close proximity of these two slave dealing businesses probably resulted in very competitive prices being offered to individuals with slaves to sell.)

The casual nature of such ads astonish the modern reader. In another ad (on the same page as those for Birch and Dove), directly beneath one for "L. Galabran, Confectioner and Restaurateur," was one in which Thomas M. Jones offered cash for "any number of negroes, including both sexes, up to the age of thirty." He advised "persons having likely servants for sale" to go see him, "as I will give the highest prices, in cash." Sellers could find him at "Levy Pumphrey's tavern" or at the "Farmers' and Citizens' hotel"—both were located at the back of Gadsby's hotel (where Solomon Northup would be lodged by his kidnappers). Also among the traders operating in the area of the national capital were Franklin and Armfield, George Kephart (who took over the former's establishment in Alexandria, Virginia) and William H. Richards, who did business opposite the Williams slave pen (where Northup was confined prior to being sent south).[4]

In New Orleans, James White informed the public that he "Will constantly purchase NEGROES," and a competitor, Elihu Creswell, was looking to purchase "100 SLAVES, for which the highest cash prices will be paid." Creswell advised, "Citizens and merchants who have Slaves for sale ... [, to] please call before leaving their Slaves with other persons."[5]

In Richmond, A. C. Pulliam and William H. Betts made it known that as auctioneers they would "sell NEGROES both publicly and privately." Those with slaves to sell could meet representatives of the firm, who were "always at each depot and at boats on their arrival."[6] Dealers in slaves advertised their firms in cities other than where they conducted business, and Franklin and Armfield had a network of agents to solicit customers for them.[7]

PUBLIC PERCEPTIONS OF SLAVE TRADERS

Though some people—even in slave-trading cities—viewed kidnapping with disdain,[8] it does not appear that kidnappers generally would have encountered much difficulty finding traders willing to buy merchandise of doubtful origin. In general, dealers in human flesh were understood to be somewhat disreputable.[9] Abraham Lincoln, in an October 1854 speech, described the slave dealer as the man who "crawls up to buy your slave at a speculating price." He was someone to be despised: "you do not recognise [sic] him as a friend, or even as an honest man. Your children must not play with his." When business with a trader was unavoidable, "you try to get through the job without so much as touching him."[10]

The temptations for slave dealers to become involved in kidnapping were significant. "Around the trader," observed Harriet Beecher Stowe, "are continually passing and repassing men and women who would be worth to him thousands of dollars in the way of trade—who belong to a class whose rights nobody respects, and who, if reduced to slavery, could not easily make their word good against him."[11]

Some who were in the slave business were able to rise above such portrayals, attaining social status and holding important positions,[12] and some even made efforts to improve the industry's image in various ways, including deemphasizing its profit aspect.[13] To make the business "more palatable" to the public, they kept from view certain seamy elements: "coffles, kidnapping, and the separation of slave families."[14] More reputable dealers sought to keep the trade honest, by keeping kidnappers out of it. The major firm of Franklin and Armfield actively discouraged kidnapping,[15] and Petersburg, Virginia, trader Thomas H. Lipscomb even traveled all the way to Massachusetts to testify at the trial of a kidnapper he had helped to apprehend.[16]

But even defenders of slavery blamed traders for tending to put the institution in a bad light: "[T]hey stood outside of respectable society, and as such, they became the perfect target for all of the criticisms that the domestic trade produced."[17] Not all traders were overly concerned about their reputations, when there was money to be made. "At the lowest fringes were those who everyone despised: kidnappers, thieves, and crooks."[18]

With an abundance of traders—ranging from individual proprietors to large firms—and with potentially large profits, the temptation to buy suspect goods from strangers was often not shunned. Kidnappers did not seem to have encountered great difficulty disposing of their victims. As Jesse Torrey wrote in the early nineteenth century, "several hundred people, including not legal slaves only, but many kidnapped freemen and youth bound to service for a term of years, and unlawfully sold as slaves for life, are annually collected at Washington (as if it were an emporium of slavery) for transportation to the slave regions."[19] Accosting some men who were conveying a group of slaves through the streets of Washington, bound for the Georgia market, Torrey asked: "Have you not . . . enough such people in that country yet?" He received the answer: "Not quite enough."[20]

There is little question that some slave dealers knew full well that some of the people they bought had been abducted. Jesse Torrey applied the term "man-dealers" to "those speculators in human flesh, who purchase free people as well as slaves, without discrimination."[21]

In 1838, when three sailors were led from a docked steamship into the city of New Orleans, George A. Botts met with them after they were placed in a slave jail. Botts, a trader, asked if they were free and inquired about their lives back in New York. After they responded truthfully, they were each given 35 lashes and told that, if they ever mentioned the ship, its captain, or New York again, they would get a similar beating.[22]

Solomon Northup, when told by trader James H. Birch that he was his slave, "asserted, aloud and boldly, that I was a freeman." Birch told him he was not free, but a slave from Georgia. Northup repeated "again and again" that he was a freeman, which enraged Birch, who: "With blasphemous oaths, ... called me a black liar, a runaway from Georgia, and every other profane and vulgar epithet that the most indecent fancy could conceive." When Northup persisted in his contention that he was free, a series of beatings was inflicted upon him, leaving him, finally, too weak and demoralized to protest. He was then informed by Birch "that if ever I dared to utter again that I was entitled to my freedom, that I had been kidnapped, or any thing whatever of the kind, the castigation I had just received was nothing in comparison with what would follow."[23]

In Richmond, when a Maryland law enforcement officer tried to obtain evidence relating to a kidnapping, the Pulliam firm refused to turn it over to him, instead offering to sell the papers to a lawyer representing the kidnappers. The evidence—and the victim—were turned over to the policeman only after court proceedings were instigated. The kidnappers were apprehended, in spite of the firm's deliberate efforts to help them.[24]

It is evident that traders carried on much of their business in taverns and hotels.[25] A victim of kidnapping, taken into such establishments, would not be aware that he was being showcased rather than being treated to a libation. Northup records that the two men who took him to Washington "[at] several times during the afternoon, entered drinking saloons, and called for liquor. ... On these occasions, after serving themselves, they would pour out a glass and hand it to me."[26] His kidnappers may have displayed him to various slave traders, doing business in different taverns, in order to surreptitiously shop him around to obtain the highest price.

Once a victim had been purchased by a trader, it was typical for him to be sent out of the area relatively quickly,[27] given a new name, or resold to another party at once.[28] Such practices, or course, made it less likely that the crime would be discovered. The victim would often have disappeared before authorities, friends, or relatives could show up looking for the abducted person. Men who had pursued the kidnappers of Aaron Cooper from Delaware to Maryland barely missed catching them there, and after learning that Cooper had already been shipped off to Norfolk, Virginia, regretfully gave up the chase.[29]

4

Ways Kidnapping
Was Fought

Combating kidnappers was accomplished in a number of ways. Legislative measures included the passage of criminal laws making it a crime, laws meant to guarantee the personal liberty of free blacks, and mechanisms to encourage the rescue of kidnap victims. Antislavery activists, journalists, and authors strove to inform and educate the public about the problem, hoping to garner their support in preventing kidnappings and in assisting victims or potential victims.

USING THE LAW TO PREVENT KIDNAPPING

Provisions under common law that protected *any* person from being kidnapped applied equally—at least, in theory—to blacks as well as whites.[1] Ordinary legal processes could be utilized in cases of kidnapping: "[E]xisting state procedures, such as *habeas corpus* and *homine replegiando* [a writ seeking the release of a person held in custody], could be used to free a person from an unlawful detention."[2]

These provisions proved inadequate, however, in view of the level of victimization experienced by blacks, and specific criminal laws were passed to expressly address the problem. In 1788, Connecticut offered a fine of 100 pounds for anyone who "shall kidnap, decoy or forcibly carry off out of this State, any free Negro, Indian or Mulatto, or any person entitled to freedom at the age of twenty-five years." Judges were also empowered to award damages to the victim.[3] Massachusetts recognized that common law protection was available to kidnap victims, but, since the victim might well be outside the Commonwealth's jurisdiction, in 1788, it specifically allowed friends and relatives to seek damages on behalf of people "carried off by force, or decoyed away under various pretences [*sic*], by evil-minded persons, and with a probable intention of being sold as slaves." Any such payments recovered were to be paid to the victim if he had returned to

Massachusetts, and, if not, they were to be devoted to the "use and maintenance of the wife, children or family, of the injured party."[4] A 1788 Pennsylvania law was passed with provisions to "correct kidnapping and other abuses that had arisen."[5]

In New York, a statute was enacted in 1813, titled "an act to prevent kidnapping of free people of colour." This law made it a criminal offense for someone to "seize and forcibly confine, or inveigle, or kidnap, any negro, mulatto, mestee, or other person of colour, not being a slave, with intent to send him out of the state against his will." Revisions made in 1817 removed the words "not being a slave," and additional language was added making it illegal to send out of the state "any slave or servant."[6] By use of words such as "decoyed" and "inveigle," anti-kidnapping laws recognized that victims were subjected not only to forcible seizure, but also to being tricked into going away.

Laws against kidnapping of blacks were not limited to the northern states. In North Carolina, for example: "In 1779 the Legislature made the act of taking a free Negro out of the State with intent to sell him punishable by death without benefit of clergy, and in 1800 made the act of stealing a free Negro, carrying off, or appropriating his services within the State punishable by heavy fine and imprisonment, changed later to a death punishment."[7] A Virginia statute in 1787–1788 outlawed the kidnapping and selling of free persons, and it was followed up by a 1792 statute that provided for the death penalty for offenders as a means to "protect that liberty which the Laws had extended to them, and which from their weakness might be easily wrested from them by the arts, or violence of unprincipled men."[8]

In the slave states, however, protection under the law was complicated due to the assumption that blacks were slaves unless proven not to be. In North Carolina: "In 1802 the Court held that presumption of freedom depended upon a man's color. If he was black, he was presumed to be a slave; if he was yellow, he was presumed to be free."[9] In Maryland, a law dating back to 1715 said that negroes who could not positively prove they were free were assumed to be runaways, subject to being detained as such, and sold as slaves to cover the costs of their incarceration. Free blacks might enjoy some security when in their own neighborhoods, but "once outside the circle of such acquaintances they were liable to be suspected and to be treated as fugitive slaves."[10] In the case of Charles Covey, a slave tried in Mississippi for having stolen a horse, his effort to get off because it had not been specified whether he was free or a slave were stymied because under Mississippi law: "All Africans or negroes are presumed to be slaves till the contrary appears."[11] Overall, anti-kidnapping laws in the South were ineffective.[12]

Consequently, the difficulties encountered by victims seeking legal recourse in southern states were immense, since they usually found themselves some distance from their homes, where the crime had actually occurred, and were someplace where—before they could even initiate any sort of legal recourse—they had to somehow prove they were not slaves. Ordinarily, they also needed to find some white person to press their cases in court as a "next friend," because the victims could not institute court proceedings on their own.[13]

PERSONAL LIBERTY LAWS

As incidents of kidnapping continued to occur, northern states tried to enhance the protection of their black citizens under their legal systems. Notable among such "personal liberty laws" was the rather involved statute passed by Pennsylvania in 1826. It dealt with kidnapping in considerable detail, and also spelled out precise procedures to be followed by slaveowners seeking to reclaim runaways in the state.[14] The U.S. Supreme Court's 1842 decision in the case of *Prigg v. Pennsylvania*, which made the apprehension of fugitive slaves (as well as protection for those wrongfully claimed as fugitives) a strictly federal matter, removed nearly all the clout from the states' personal liberty laws. (Pennsylvania passed a new version in 1847, trying to work around the *Prigg* decision.)[15]

Following the passage of the Fugitive Slave Law in 1850, protection available to blacks taken under the guise of runaway reclamation was greatly reduced. Not surprisingly, kidnapping continued apace in the late 1850s. The state of Connecticut attempted to hinder questionable fugitive renditions—as well as combat kidnapping—with an 1854 law whose drafters "were careful in the use of language not to interfere with the constitutional requisitions upon the subject, but to clothe the whole process with as many difficulties as not only to prevent false claims or to hinder the prosecution of doubtful cases, but to discourage the southern masters from entering the State to pursue his runaway slaves without the most complete proof of their identity."[16] Though it was claimed that this law was intended to nullify the Fugitive Slave Law, a northern newspaper pointed out that: "Surely it will not be contended that the Law of 1850 was *intended* to enable people to kidnap persons born free?"[17]

Though some people called for strengthened personal liberty laws,[18] the political climate was not conducive to this. Calls were also made for the repeal of those laws that were already on the books, which were widely considered to be unconstitutional.[19]

LAWS TO ALLOW FOR RESCUE OF KIDNAP VICTIMS

In addition to creating laws intended to deter kidnappers and to guarantee the personal liberty of citizens, free states began to acknowledge the plight of kidnapped freemen who had been taken to distant states. In slave states, victims' access to the courts to regain their freedom was problematic.

Massachusetts, which years earlier had made provisions for friends and relatives of absent victims to take legal action in their interests, established in 1839 a means by which kidnapped citizens could be rescued. The governor was empowered to appoint an agent who could travel to another state to locate and bring back a victim, with expenses to be reimbursed by the state.[20] When noting how this procedure had been used to rescue a young Massachusetts boy, a New York newspaper asked: "Why should not New York have such a law[?]"[21]

The following year, New York *did* have such a law. Its title alone indicated that the criminal law against kidnapping had not been enough to prevent occurrences of the crime: it was titled "An act *more effectually* to protect the free citizens of this State from being kidnapped or reduced to slavery" (emphasis added).[22] Its most notable application was in the rescue of Solomon Northup, but the statute was also used in connection with several other kidnapping cases later on.[23] Illinois, a state that suffered a number of kidnappings, adopted a measure very similar to New York's in 1855.[24]

Though rescues under such laws were not frequent, they were important—especially for those who regained their freedom. Victims in far-flung slave states could do so little to help themselves that their best hope for salvation lay in getting assistance from afar. If rescuers were not able to make the trips to retrieve victims, they could sometimes help by forwarding documents showing that the enslaved victims were indeed free.

EDUCATION AND PUBLICITY

Another way in which kidnapping could be fought was by increasing public awareness. Even people who supported, or at least tolerated, slavery, could see the inhumanity of seizing or duping free people and casting them into bondage. As one newspaper remarked, in relation to the kidnapping of several children in Illinois, people who showed indignation regarding slavery were called fanatics, but: "Is not a little indignation allowable towards such frightful wrong?"[25]

Vigilance Committees

Vigilance committees, in addition to providing legal support for kidnapped freemen, sought to inform the public via meetings, reports, and letters published in newspapers. They also sometimes played roles in rescues. In New York City, the Manumission Society took an early role in thwarting kidnappings. In an 1817 case, intervention by some of its members prevented the departure of a schooner with a number of people of color on board, bound for slave markets in the South. Though there was some confusion about whether the people were slaves or free, subsequent court proceedings determined that at least some *were* free.[26]

In New York on November 20, 1835, a meeting of the "Friends of Human Rights" was held, with the stated purpose of discovering the prevalence of "the cruel practice of kidnapping men, women and children" in the city, and determining ways to "aid such unfortunate persons as may be in danger of being reduced to slavery." This meeting resulted in the formation of the biracial "New York Committee of Vigilance," which monitored cases where blacks were accused of being fugitives and provided them as much legal assistance as it could. (It also provided assistance to fugitive slaves.) David Ruggles, the black publisher of an antislavery journal called *The Mirror of Liberty*, was a vital and active member of this committee, and his activities led to his being jailed more than once.[27] In its first annual report in 1837, the committee noted that various city officials were sometimes complicit in misidentifying free citizens as escaped slaves. Another ploy used by kidnappers, wrote Ruggles, was to "lure by a thousand false pretenses their victims from all the endearments of their homes to a life of toil and misery."[28]

Members of some vigilance committees were directly involved in some kidnapping cases. The indefatigable David Ruggles made a trip from New York to New Bedford, Massachusetts, in order to effect the arrest of Thomas Lewis, a man involved in the enslavement of Stephen Dickinson, Robert Garrison, and Isaac Wright.[29] Nahum Gardner Hazard, a young Massachusetts boy, was ultimately rescued after a member of a vigilance committee in Virginia contacted key antislavery people in Hazard's home state.[30] In 1858, the Pennsylvania Anti-Slavery Society's Passmore Williamson prevailed upon George C. Morgan to go south to effect the rescue of Frank Jackson.[31]

Antislavery Books and Abolitionist Publications

A number of publications were issued that provided a significant amount of background on the kidnapping problem. Jesse Torrey's works, published under various titles and imprints in the early nine-teenth century, offered substantial information on the practice, includ-ing his personal encounters with some victims.[32] Kidnapping was discussed in other materials published throughout the period of American slavery, including reports by the New York City vigilance committee,[33] reports issued by the American Anti-Slavery Society,[34] a publication by the British and Foreign Anti-Slavery Society,[35] and books by authors Harriet Beecher Stowe and Mary Langdon (whose novel *Ida May*, about an enslaved white girl, was subtitled "A Story of Things Actual and Possible").[36] One widely read book, *Twelve Years a Slave*, published in 1853, presented an exceedingly objective and factual account of Solomon Northup's kidnapping and enslavement.[37] A book published in 1856 told the story of Levin and Peter Still, who had been kidnapped as children.[38] (Years later, Peter found another brother, William Still, who was active on the Underground Railroad. William Still wrote that their mother had actually been a slave at the time the boys were taken, however, so that they had not strictly been kidnapped.)[39]

Government Reports

A number of reports issued by government bodies dealt specifically with kidnapping of northern citizens, and in Massachusetts and New York, they led to measures intended to improve the chances that vic-tims would be rescued. These included a report that George Bradburn, a member of the Massachusetts legislature, sent to that body on March 6, 1839. Titled "On the Deliverance of Citizens Liable to Be Sold as Slaves," it detailed a number of cases ("a few out of a VAST MULTI-TUDE")[40] of residents of the Commonwealth wrongfully enslaved in southern states. In relation to cases given in the report: "It would be easy to fill scores of pages with details similar to the preceding. We have furnished enough, however, to show, that, in all probability, *each* United States' census of the *slave* population, is increased by the addi-tion to it of *thousands* of free colored persons, kidnapped and sold as slaves."[41] The legislative committee concerned with the matter dis-tanced itself from the report, which was signed only by Bradburn him-self. It fell to him to convince the whole legislature to adopt the resolves providing a legal mechanism for rescuing victims, which his report had been written to support (as Bradburn said, "The mass of its members needed but the facts in the case.").[42] Bradburn delivered an impassioned speech, which led to passage of the resolves, which were signed into law by Governor Edward Everett.[43] (The rescue of Nahum Gardner Hazard, that same year, was aided by this measure.)[44]

Similar efforts were made in the state of New York. A report was prepared there also (using information probably supplied by the New York Committee of Vigilance).[45] Legislation that was championed by Assemblyman Victory Birdseye was passed in 1840.[46] This law—as with the Massachusetts resolves—provided that the governor should appoint an agent to collect proof of the free status of an enslaved citizen, and to undertake a rescue mission at the expense of the state. (The law was apparently first applied years later, when Solomon Northup was rescued from Louisiana in 1853.)[47]

Antislavery and Abolitionist Periodicals

In addition to books and reports, kidnappings were routinely reported on in various antislavery or abolitionist periodicals, including newspapers like the *Liberator, Emancipator, Anti-Slavery Bugle,* and the *Philanthropist.* The *National Anti-Slavery Standard* printed a series of articles by Isaac T. Hopper, with the running title "Tales of Oppression." A number of these tales were about victims of kidnapping.[48] Quaker periodicals also often told of kidnappings.[49]

General Interest Newspapers

Because kidnappings were crimes, they were also often covered by local newspapers, especially if the perpetrators were caught and put on trial. Coverage in regular newspapers would spread information on the kidnapping problem to the general public, as opposed to only the slavery-opposing readers of antislavery publications. In several cases notices were printed in newspapers seeking the public's assistance in tracking the criminals or in gaining the return of victims of kidnapping. Sometimes rewards were even offered.[50]

Antislavery Meetings and Lectures

Information on kidnappings was sometimes presented at conventions or meetings of organizations opposed to slavery. At a meeting of the New York Committee of Vigilance, the wife of Peter John Lee was present, and she addressed the attendees, explaining that, though her husband had been said to be an escaped slave, in fact he had been a free African American in Virginia, who had come north due to harassment he had encountered in Virginia.[51] Solomon Northup, undeniably the most well-known victim (both then and now), traveled widely throughout the northeastern states. By attending lectures and even some plays,[52] audiences learned how he had been tricked into leaving his home in upstate New York, the way in which he had been sold as a slave in the nation's capital, and how he had endured nearly 12 years as a slave in Louisiana. Perhaps the story of how he had been rescued (which was related on several occasions by his rescuer, Henry B. Northup)[53] encouraged members of the public to be willing themselves to assist victims in some way, should an opportunity ever arise.

5

How Victims Were
Kept Enslaved

Once victims had been kidnapped and sold as slaves, various techniques were used to keep them in slavery. Although they had the capability to communicate their situations and explain that they had been kidnapped and enslaved counter to the law, various obstacles made it extremely difficult for them to do so. Victims could be subjected to physical and mental abuse that served to break their spirits. Even if they had the mental fortitude to continue to tell about the circumstances that had resulted in their servitude, their stories were often met by deaf ears, since the rights of African Americans were not always respected. To gain release from slavery, victims were dependent on friends and relatives, who typically were in distant regions and had little information on the whereabouts of those who had gone missing. Those in free states who were interested in traveling to rescue victims faced arduous and expensive journeys, and could expect a less than welcoming reception upon reaching their destinations.

PHYSICAL AND PSYCHOLOGICAL SUBDUING OF VICTIMS

In a report prepared by a select committee of the New York State Assembly in 1840, the observation was made that victims could be "brought under the dominion of persons accustomed to the unscrupulous exercise of the most arbitrary means to subdue persons in their condition, [and that] they are scourged and otherwise punished, until they are deterred from disclosing their claims to freedom; then transferred to the slave markets of the south, cut off from all means of communicating with friends, and reduced to a life of degrading and hopeless bondage."[1]

Both physical and psychological coercion were commonly used to subdue and intimidate enslaved free men and women. Both were effective ways to break down the resistance of a recalcitrant victim.

Beatings

To keep victims from persistently asserting their actual status as free people, and to keep them from speaking about how they had come to be enslaved contrary to law, physical force was sometimes used. In America in the nineteenth century, corporal punishment was for the most part a socially accepted manner of maintaining control within families and communities, and this was even more true (and more severe) where slavery was concerned.

Solomon Northup and Stephen Dickinson provided firsthand accounts of such use of physical coercion, as inflicted upon themselves.[2] Dr. John Doy described the terrible punishment he saw visited upon Wilson George Hays and Charles Smith,[3] as a result of their refusal to be cooperative by saying that they were slaves. Though they still insisted they were free—despite the treatment meted out to them—they were taken away, and were sold as slaves anyway.

Psychological Methods

Various psychological methods were used to keep victims in a state of subjugation. Sometimes they were duped into saying they were slaves, and techniques were used to hide their real identities and geographical origins, making rescue attempts extremely difficult, if not impossible.

In several cases, victims were told that, for purposes of expediency, they must pretend to be the slaves of those who were in the process of reducing them to slavery.[4] A person who had acknowledged being a slave—particularly in front of witnesses—would find it that much harder to assert a credible claim to freedom afterward. Such a claim would then be seen by third parties as simply a feeble effort by an unhappy slave to gain release.

Victims would often be given new names ("slave names," if you will). Allowing a victim to use his or her real name would make it easier for the person to be located by friends, relatives, or law officers who might be searching for the person. At the time that Solomon Northup's narrative was published in 1853, a newspaper observed that: "Northup's sad experience shows how difficult it is for kidnapped persons to regain their Freedom. They are taken far into the interior where they are only known by an arbitrary name."[5] Thus, Northup, as a slave, was known as Platt (the surname Hamilton—the alias used by one of his kidnappers—was given on the manifest of the ship that carried him to New Orleans).[6] Eli Terry (who as an enslaved freeman was rescued—as was

Northup—after years of bondage) was called Jack.[7] Young Sidney O. Francis became Franklin—a name similar to his own, perhaps to make sure that, being a young boy, he would easily become accustomed to it.[8]

Assigning a victim a new name probably also served to distance the person from his pre-slave sense of self. It undoubtedly helped instill the message that the person's life as a free person was over, and their life as a slave had begun. Rather than hope for or effect rescue, the newly enslaved might as well accept the situation and make the best of things.

Allegations That Victims Were Runaways

In order to belay suspicions by members of the public, kidnappers sometimes held out that their victims were runaway slaves who had been found and who were being returned. George Anderson's kidnapper used this ploy to allay suspicion by others,[9] and the man who lured John Hight and Daniel Prue out of New York State was able to enlist the help of others in handling his alleged runaways.[10] Should a victim claim to be free, his or her statement could be countered by explaining that the person was in the habit of falsely saying that he was free.[11]

Serial Selling

In some cases, victims were sold and resold over a short period of time. This reduced the chances that they would be located by any parties looking for them and also allowed buyers who had suspicions that the person might actually be free to shift their liability onto another buyer.

John Hight was purchased by a new acquaintance of his kidnapper at a bargain price, in return for assistance the buyer had provided on the way to Kentucky. Hight's new owner immediately sold him to another man, who, having no need for him at that time, placed him in a slave pen in order to find yet another buyer for Hight. "It was reported that he had been 'shoved' through several hands in Kentucky in order to thwart any efforts that might be made for his recovery."[12] Dimmock Charlton was sold a number of times, sometimes after telling an owner the story of how he had been wrongfully enslaved.[13] Three seamen were sold several times; in at least one instance, after an owner got an inkling they were free.[14] Frank Jackson—who had a propensity to run away (attempting "self-rescue")—had perhaps a dozen different masters.[15]

LACK OF REGARD FOR THE LAW

The prevailing notion in slave states was that blacks were commodities, regardless of whatever legal status might apply to individual men or women. Sometime around 1859, Fort Sumter at Charleston, South Carolina, was used to temporarily house some blacks whom the government had rescued from a ship that had illegally brought them from Africa. Though they were not slaves (thanks to the capture of the slave ship), "there was an eager desire on the part of all the people around us to seize these negroes, and distribute them among the plantations." Had the federal government not sent them back to Africa, it was believed by one army officer that local citizens would have taken them by force, with the excuse that the blacks had violated a state law.[16]

In the early 1800s, Jesse Torrey was informed of a former southern congressman who had among his slaves a man whom he believed to have been a freeman, kidnapped from New England. Torrey asked "how he could bear then to retain him" and was told that "the customs of his part of the country were such that these things are not minded much."[17]

Torrey confronted a man who expressed sympathy for the buyer of an enslaved freeman, because he stood to lose his investment: "I asked him whether he considered it worse for the trader to lose a few hundred dollars in money, than for the mulatto man to be transported to a strange country, and be deprived of his liberty for life. To which he replied, after a short pause, that he did not know as there was much difference!"[18]

In New Orleans, in the 1830s, Jacob Barker, a transplanted New Englander, intervened in a number of cases where people who were not slaves were confined in a local jail and forced to work on road gangs. Barker was sometimes criticized for assisting such victims. A New Orleans newspaper said that "Mr. Barker ought to know that he is making himself very obnoxious to every citizen, by this course of his. Does he suppose that he can come forward with impunity, and act as the counsel for every black vagabond who may land on our shores?"[19] Barker's efforts also prompted threats: "It is said that Jacob Barker, Esq. a lawyer of some note in New Orleans, who has been extensively engaged in suits for free negroes, has received a notice from a committee that unless he quits the State, he will be taken before his honor Judge Lynch."[20] Responding to such attacks, Barker noted that he was acting pursuant to Louisiana law, and asked: "Why pass laws protecting free men of color, if it is to be considered wrong for counsel to appear in their behalf?"[21]

Barker found that some of the enslaved men appeared to be white, and in one case, a Native American. Some men were immediately released after Barker complained to the Recorder, who "pronounced five of them free from their complexion, without argument and without requiring any other testimony." When asked "why they had not been liberated the morning after their arrest ... his honor replied that they had been placed in the chain gang by the officers of the prison without having been brought up before him for examination."[22] In an especially egregious incident, Barker told of a man, born in Maine of free parents, who was on the chain gang for nine months, even though "the driver of the gang knew him to be free, was born in the same town, went to school with him, and had known him from childhood."[23]

Rules by which a freeman's status could be proven were inconsistent. Barker advised any free blacks intending to go to Louisiana to procure freedom certificates from the governors of their states; "protection" papers, usually carried by seamen, were not honored there. In the course of his efforts in gaining the release of numerous freemen seized illegally, Barker observed that: "At one time, the Recorder said the witness must be white, at another, that one respectable witness was insufficient, at another, that a person who had been (improperly) confined and released was not a competent witness. &c., &c."[24] Officials at a jail at first denied even having in custody two men about whom Barker inquired, even though: "There was not any pretence [*sic*] that either of these men were slaves." Both were released.[25]

Though there could be exceptions (such as in the case of George Anderson, whose continual insistence that he was free prompted a southern mayor to look into his case),[26] a victimized person's claims to freedom were often ignored. Dimmock Charlton, wrongfully enslaved after being taken as a prisoner of war during the War of 1812, eventually told the story to one of his masters—who quickly sold him to someone else.[27] Solomon Northup, held in a slave pen in the District of Columbia, asserted his free status, but his demands to be released were ignored—and earned him beatings.[28]

The owner of a slave with a legitimate claim to freedom stood to lose a valuable piece of property if he acknowledged the claim and liberated the person. Thus, Edwin Epps, upon learning that Solomon Northup was actually free and liable to be taken away from him, "swore that if he had only had an hour's notice ... that he would have run me [Northup] into the swamp, or some other place out of the way, where all the sheriffs on earth couldn't have found me."[29] Northup's decision to remain silent for years concerning his earlier life as a freeborn New Yorker was surely a wise one. "Northup owes his deliverance, finally, to the fact that during his long and severe ordeal, he kept the secret of his being a Free born Man locked up in his own bosom. For this the Master whom he served for ten years, when his Deliverers came, reproached him. Had the truth been known he would have been out of the reach of Friends and Laws."[30]

In providing for a legal mechanism for freemen to gain their release from slavery, the Georgia legislature recognized that claimants were "liable to be removed, whenever an effort is made to redress their grievances."[31] In 1816, Dr. Jesse Torrey, having taken down notes of what several kidnap victims had told him, returned to the house with a deputy marshal, and learned from the landlord that "the person who saw me writing, suspected some difficulty, and had directed him to conceal the Negroes, and that he had done it."[32]

For this reason, those victims whose claims seemed to have some validity could be sequestered—often placed in jail as a form of protective custody—until the matter could be resolved in court. Thus, Northup was taken into custody by the sheriff—his case was to have been heard at a court session in the spring of 1853, but Epps gave him up voluntarily upon advice of counsel: "the defendant's [Epps's] counsel stated to the client that the case was a plain one, and the man should be at once given up without further legal proceedings, or expense. This advice was followed."[33] Likewise, William Houston was sequestered in a New Orleans jail until his status was resolved—in his favor. He was released and put aboard a ship that returned him to his native England.[34]

INTIMIDATION OF POTENTIAL RESCUERS

Individuals who might be willing to undertake a long and possibly arduous journey to a distant southern state to try to rescue a kidnapped freeman had also to consider the type of reception they might get upon their arrival. In 1844, the Massachusetts legislature decided to dispatch some agents to South Carolina and Louisiana for the purpose of guaranteeing the freedom of its seafaring free African American citizens. Black seamen who were free were typically jailed while in ports in these states, with the possibility that they might end up as slaves for life. Samuel Hoar and Henry Hubbard were sent to Charleston and New Orleans, respectively.

Though neither man had any intention of interfering with slavery— being occupied simply with the rights of *free* blacks—both were hounded out of the cities to which they had been sent. Hoar's hotel-keeper kicked him out of his lodgings, and the South Carolina legislature called on the governor to expel him.[35] Hubbard, in New Orleans, went out of his way to make it clear that his objective was not to challenge slavery in any way. He was "careful to disclaim all connection with abolitionism" and explained that his purpose was only "to enable the citizens of that State [Massachusetts], imprisoned without crime, to avail themselves of all lawful means for their liberation."[36]

Despite his avowed pledge not to interfere with slavery, it was to no avail, as "the murmurs of hostile intent grew louder, and threats of lynching were freely circulated." Hubbard was urged to leave by local officials, and, upon his refusal to do so, was informed by the City Recorder that: "If you do not promise to leave the city immediately, your life is not safe this night; and if I should take you into custody, I could not protect you, for they would murder me in a moment. If you stay here another night, your life will certainly be taken."[37] Jacob Barker, a former Massachusetts resident, also warned him that he was in peril, and Hubbard at last realized it would not be possible for him to carry out his mission, and he went home to Massachusetts.

Following the failed missions of Hubbard and Hoar, both South Carolina and Louisiana passed laws that forbade any future expeditions of that sort.[38]

Responses such as this—to men who merely sought to guard the rights of free African Americans—must surely have had a chilling effect on any northerners who might contemplate going to a southern state in order to gain the release of an enslaved person. Three men who set out for Texas to find and rescue Eli Terry anticipated encountering trouble, and considered arming themselves (but ultimately decided it would be too confrontational to do so).[39] A party who went to the assistance of Kitty Payne, an emancipated slave who had been abducted back into slavery, were subjected to an "attempt made by a pro-slavery mob to drive [away] a number of benevolent minded gentlemen who went to the rescue ... for the purpose of seeing justice done to the alleged slaves." During the process of getting Payne and her family members free, some people had tried "with the cry of 'abolitionist' and the like, to render them [the rescuers] odious."[40]

DENIALS OF KIDNAPPING

There were cases where, apparently to minimize the extent of the kidnapping problem, or to reduce culpability for it, victims were accused of having collaborated with their kidnappers. The victims, so these stories went, had made arrangements with other individuals such that they allowed themselves to be sold into slavery, with the intention of either running off afterward or of obtaining evidence of their free status that would allow them to be released. After regaining their free-dom, they would connect up with their partners in crime and receive their share of the profit earned from their sale.

Solomon Northup, within weeks of his release from slavery, was accused of having collaborated with his abductors in order to share in the profits from his own sale. These stories—though vehemently denied by Northup—surfaced from time to time for years afterward.[41] In the case of Eli Terry, a Texas newspaper at first "blamed the victim," saying Terry had never voiced any claim that he was free. Later on, he also was accused of having allowed himself to be kidnapped.[42]

Confirmed cases of such collusion are hard to come by, but in one such case, Abram Hiter, a free mulatto, allowed himself to be sold by Abner W. Mercer (also known as William Wilson). It was shown by evidence that Hiter "was sold by his own consent, to the purchaser, under a collusive contract between the prisoner and the person sold, that they should divide the proceeds of the sale between them." Virginia judges, in 1818, determined that this was "an offence not likely to happen often."[43] In another case, two men sold Mary Whiting, a free black from Chambersburg, Pennsylvania, in Baltimore. It turned out that she was actually in the employ of one of the men, who had intended to defraud her purchaser of $500.[44] However, all evidence points to such examples being extremely atypical. The majority of kidnappings discovered through research appear to have been crimes perpetrated by money-motivated individuals upon unsuspecting and unwilling victims.

6

Honest Men, North and South

People in both the North and South enabled kidnapping. Kidnappers in free states abducted or inveigled their neighbors; the legal and social system in slave states made it difficult for victims of kidnapping to regain their freedom; and citizens all across the nation gave short shrift to the rights of free African Americans. But some individuals—on both sides of the Mason-Dixon Line—behaved nobly, by spreading the word about the kidnapping problem or by providing assistance to victims in their quest for liberty.

EDUCATORS AND CRUSADERS

Many individuals who were opposed to slavery helped to inform the nation of the dangers of kidnapping. This undoubtedly was a good strategy to pursue in addressing the general public—not all of which was opposed to slavery. Citizens who were supportive of it, or who were ambivalent to it, could yet see the injustice and evilness engendered by robbing free persons of their liberty and subjecting them to an unwarranted lifetime of servitude.

Elisha Tyson, a Quaker from Baltimore, was a key member of the "Maryland Society for promoting the abolition of slavery, and the relief of poor negroes and others unlawfully held in bondage." Tyson, who was involved in the liberation of hundreds of wrongfully enslaved individuals (African Americans, and also Native Americans), pursued—nearly single-handedly—the goals of that society after its dissolution in 1798.[1] Tyson was one of several people who testified about kidnapping before a congressional committee in 1817.[2]

New York City's Committee of Vigilance did a great deal to interfere with kidnappers, and to assist their victims. For example, they provided them with legal representation at court hearings. It seems likely that the committee was instrumental in the passage of the 1840 law in New York that provided a mechanism for the rescue of victims.[3] David Ruggles, one of the most active members of the committee, was especially active in fighting kidnapping and even traveled to Massachusetts to see that charges were brought against one of the perpetrators in one case.[4]

Another organization that did a great deal was the Pennsylvania Abolition Society.[5] One of its members, Isaac T. Hopper, a Quaker, actively assisted victims and helped unveil the practice of kidnapping in a series of newspaper items called "Tales of Oppression."[6] Hopper was involved in the rescue of kidnapping victim Ignatius Beck.[7]

NEWSPAPERS AND OTHER PUBLICATIONS

Details of kidnappings that occurred all over the nation were reported in antislavery newspapers, such as the *Liberator*, the *Emancipator*, the *Anti-Slavery Bugle*, and the *Philanthropist*. Articles in papers such as these spread the word to their slavery-opposing readers. But when kidnappers were apprehended and put on trial, incidents were covered in local newspapers as crime stories.

An early book that dealt with kidnapping and other aspects of the slave trade was Jesse Torrey's *A Portraiture of Domestic Slavery in the United States*, first published in 1818.[8] In addition to describing how kidnappers operated, Torrey came across several victims in Washington, D.C.: "I discovered (without having the least previous intimation or even suspicion of any thing of the kind) three persons of colour, who were born free, and had been forcibly seized in the time of night, bound and transported in the night, out of their native state (Delaware) and sold as slaves for life, to itinerant *Man-Dealers* in Maryland."[9] Information collected by Torrey resulted in these people being restored to freedom.

The 1839 book by Theodore Dwight Weld, *American Slavery as It Is: Testimony of a Thousand Witnesses*, detailed some instances of kidnapping and informed the public that: "It is a notorious fact, that large numbers of free colored persons are kidnapped every year in the free states, taken to the south, and sold as slaves."[10]

In 1853, Harriet Beecher Stowe published a follow-up work to her novel *Uncle Tom's Cabin*. This book, titled *A Key to Uncle Tom's Cabin*, documented the type of occurrences involving slavery that were portrayed in her fictional work. In a chapter about kidnapping (which related the cases of Solomon Northup and sisters Rachel and Elizabeth Parker), Stowe noted that the business of slave trading "has among its other horrible results, the temptation to the crime of kidnapping." She elaborated by writing that: "Around the trader are continually passing and repassing men and women who would be worth to him thousands of dollars in the way of trade—who belong to a class whose rights nobody respects, and who, if reduced to slavery, could not easily make their word good against him. The probability is that hundreds of free men and women and children are all the time being precipitated into slavery in this way."[11] In the same year, Solomon Northup's *Twelve Years a Slave* was published, and Northup also told his stories via lectures and plays.

POLITICIANS

A number of politicians opposed slavery, but two who targeted the kidnapping problem specifically were George Bradburn in Massachusetts and Victory Birdseye in New York. Both reported on the matter to the legislatures in their respective states.[12] The results were laws in both states that specified procedures for locating and rescuing residents who had been enslaved in other states.[13]

RESCUERS

Citizens could help see that kidnap victims were rescued in two fundamental ways: by taking seriously their claims to freedom and taking steps to help them regain their freedom (through court hearings or otherwise); and by undertaking journeys, armed with paperwork required for the liberation of victims.

Southerners

In the early 1800s, a magistrate (whose name was not revealed) listened to Ignatius Beck, who was held as a slave somewhere near the Virginia–North Carolina border, and decided to help him by contacting some of Beck's acquaintances in Philadelphia. Papers proving Beck's free status were forwarded to the magistrate, who also hid Beck at his home for a while and had his son escort him part of the way back to Pennsylvania.[14] Two mayors of cities in Virginia (Benjamin Clark, of Fredericksburg, and Joseph Mayo, of Richmond) wrote to northern officials concerning people in their cities whom they believed were kidnapped freemen.[15] Also, the mayor of St. Joseph, Missouri, contacted people in Illinois concerning Mary Boyd and others, as did a Missouri relative of one of the likely kidnappers.[16]

In Kentucky, a farmer named Thomas Vantreese was sympathetic to the story of Stephen Dickinson's victimization and steered him to an attorney, who began the process that ultimately freed him.[17] In New Orleans, a major slave-trading center, two transplanted men from Massachusetts, Jacob Barker and Rowland Gibson Hazard, earned the disdain of some local citizens due to their work helping enslaved freemen (who mostly had been put to work on chain gangs). Hazard—in order to meet with people held in jail—slept only five hours a night since his access to them was limited to early mornings and evenings. Barker and Hazard obtained the release of nearly 100 people.[18] When Judge Lorenzo Graves learned that the slave he had purchased in Kentucky was actually freeman John Hight, he personally went to a slave jail and released him from his cell. Graves also presented Hight with money, a present for his mother, and even accompanied Hight and his northern rescuer to the free soil of Ohio.[19]

A number of southern attorneys provided legal assistance on behalf of victims. In North Carolina, lawyer George C. Mendenhall began a legal process that resulted in Frank Jackson's liberation and return to his home in Pennsylvania.[20] Hester Jane Carr was assisted by Petersburg, Virginia, attorney William C. Parker, who oversaw a freedom suit on her behalf.[21] In Mississippi, Aaron Cooper was assisted by prosecutor William B. Shields.[22] In Solomon Northup's case, Louisiana attorney John P. Waddill provided critical assistance to Northup's rescuer from New York (Henry B. Northup), which led to Northup being located on the plantation of Edwin Epps, followed by his liberation.[23]

Northerners

Northern citizens who undertook rescue missions often had to make lengthy and arduous trips in order to accomplish their objectives. Sometimes they were compensated for the time and expenses, but other times they were not.

Dr. Jesse Torrey, an early chronicler of American slavery, stumbled onto several victims of kidnapping when he went to an attic in Washington, D.C., to see a woman who had attempted to kill herself rather than be sent south. Torrey interviewed these people and took steps to get them released. Numerous citizens provided assistance to him, and financial contributions paid for his trip to Delaware to obtain proof that the people were free and had been kidnapped. They were released after a court session in June 1816.[24]

Rescue missions often required significant trips that were inconvenient for those who undertook them. In a case with similarities to that of Solomon Northup years afterward, Eli Terry was a slave for years in Texas, until word of his whereabouts reached friends in Indiana. Three men undertook an arduous journey to rescue him, and their reception in Texas was not entirely positive.[25] Joshua Coffin, a northern opponent of slavery, traveled to Tennessee, where he was able to locate Isaac Wright, and spirited him away while Wright's master was off gambling.[26] Sheriff William Rhodes, from Illinois, went south with Elijah Morris in search of the children of the latter. They were able to locate and retrieve the children, with the cooperation of a plantation owner who wanted to see justice carried out.[27]

Joseph Cochrane, acting as an agent of New York State, made the long trip to Louisiana, where—with the cooperation of a plantation owner— he viewed all of the 200 slaves in residence, seeking a man who had (incorrectly, it turned out) been reported to have been kidnapped and taken there.[28]

Lessons for Today

Before the Civil War, kidnapping flourished. This happened as a result of a number of incentives—economic, legal, and political—that allowed criminals to obtain "filthy lucre" with minimal threat of punishment (punishment that, even when administered, was often light). For various reasons, laws against kidnapping tended to be disregarded, as were the rights of victims, who typically found that various impediments blocked their efforts to regain their freedom under the law. Not the least of these was that, in many cases, the law did not allow African Americans to testify in court proceedings (in particular, when defendants were white).

The rights of free blacks received short shrift—not just in slave states, but also in northern states. It was a period when ethnic minorities—people of African descent, Native Americans, and immigrants—were not seen as equals to the Caucasians, who—it was felt—were the original settlers of America. Complacency over legal measures intended to protect the rights of these groups of citizens made it that much easier for kidnappers to carry on their illicit and immoral business. Racial prejudice was, of course, a factor: even in the North, stereotypical views about blacks led some whites to subscribe to the belief that blacks were actually better off as slaves.

Governmental actions ended up aiding the work of criminals. The ban on the importation of slaves into the United States (though not entirely effective at ending the international slave trade) limited the supply of fresh slave labor—which was much in demand at the time. Buyers were willing to pay hefty prices for bondsmen, a result that does not seem to have been anticipated by the government, since little was done to prevent the kidnappings that somewhat predictably resulted. The fugitive slave laws of 1793 and 1850, intended to ensure the return of escaped slaves, had the side effect of adding to the difficulties encountered by kidnapped freemen trying to obtain their release. Though some people (especially those opposed to slavery) realized that the 1850 law would likely be a boon to kidnappers, governmental mechanisms failed to adequately counter that resulting development.

No doubt one of the reasons the American system of slavery engendered so much cruelty was a result of the near total control slaveholders were allowed over their chattels.[1] The Stanford Prison Experiment, conducted by psychologist Philip Zimbardo in 1971,[2] demonstrated that, even in a clearly simulated environment, ordinary people who were placed in a situation where there were no restrictions on their behavior toward people who were subjugated resulted in cruel and abusive conduct. In a real-life social and legal setting that clearly tolerated (perhaps even expected) such conduct, it is not surprising that slavery in the United States resulted in so much iniquity.

Slavery almost entirely involved racial prejudices that in part justified ill treatment of members of what many citizens believed to be an inferior race. (This possibly served as a defense mechanism for owners of slaves, who could therefore tell themselves that—regardless of how they treated their slaves—they were still better off than if allowed to conduct their own affairs as free individuals.) Mistreatment of members of one class of people, however, can naturally expand to other classes. Thus the ranks of the enslaved also included some whites (not all of whom met the rule of having a single drop of African blood, or who were the progeny of interracial pairings). There were some white people who were kidnapped and sold into slavery.[3] Among these were Patience Hicks, a poor white girl (who had probably been "dishonored" by a man) and Salome Muller, a young orphaned immigrant. Jurist and abolitionist William Jay, a son of John Jay, noted several examples of enslaved whites (and also the case of the orphaned Irish girl, Mary Gilmore, who was nearly cast into bondage as a fugitive slave), and stated that: "*Any* poor friendless unknown person, might ... be publicly seized and handcuffed, and sent into interminable bondage." In a letter to New York City mayor C. W. Lawrence in 1837, Jay wrote that: "Slavery is not confined to one complexion, and ... there is not a member of the Common Council of your city, who if kidnapped, would be unsaleable on account of the whiteness of his skin."[4]

What lesson can we, today, take from these stories of kidnappings that happened over 150 years ago? It is clear that kidnappers thrived as a result of racial prejudice and minimal concern for the rights of a particular group of citizens—free African Americans. Within the justice system, complacency relative to the prevention of kidnappings and the capture and punishment of abductors meant that the crime could be pursued profitably and without great risk to its perpetrators. Kidnappers prospered, and their base of victims was not limited strictly to African Americans—Native Americans and whites were also victimized, though to a lesser degree. It is certainly true that whatever can be done to one of us, can—in time—be done to *any* of us. We need to understand, today, that a lack of concern for the rights of others—in combination with a sense of complacency relative to legal measures for preventing crimes and punishing wrong-doers—can come home to roost.

8

Victims' Case Studies

This chapter contains case studies of numerous victims of kidnappings, arranged alphabetically by last name. Cases included here are ones that could be documented using various information sources. Sources used were historical newspapers and journals, local history books, personal narratives, legal publications, and genealogical databases. As much as possible, the outcomes and aftermath of these cases is presented, so as to show the impact of the kidnappings on victims and perpetrators.

There were more instances of kidnapping than are given here. Criteria applied for inclusion were: that the victims' names could be ascertained in newspaper accounts or other documents (nineteenth-century newspapers often included stories relating to victims whose names were not reported—making the incidents difficult to confirm); and that evidence could be located showing that victims were in fact freemen and not fugitive slaves (contemporary publications did not always make distinctions between the two categories).

JOHN ADAMS

On July 4, 1827, John Adams, an 18- or 19-year-old African American boy, came into the city of Washington, D.C., "from the country." He was accompanied by a black man, and they had brought produce to sell. At about 11:00 a.m., the man went away briefly, leaving John in charge of their cart, which was near Parker's store at Center Market, near 7th Street.[1] When he returned in a few minutes, the boy was gone, and could not be found. John was free, and had been brought up by a free family in Montgomery County, Maryland. He was an orphan but had been treated well by his adoptive family; therefore, it was unlikely that he had gone off on his own. "The painful suspicion is entertained that he has been kidnapped." It was requested that any information on his whereabouts be left at the newspaper office.[2]

GEORGE ANDERSON

George Anderson grew up in the Five Points area of Manhattan. His parents were Andrew and Jane Hudson,[3] or Anderson and Jane Hutcheson.[4] In 1840, he was a 13-year-old student at Colored Grammar School No. 1, on Mulberry Street, and lived on East Broadway. At that time, school records showed that his guardian was J. Smith.[5] At school he was taught by a black man named Peterson,[6] and he was a good enough student that he learned to read and write—although newspapers in the 1850s consistently described him as being almost an idiot.[7] Anderson had looked after a horse belonging to Dr. Graeme (or Graham).[8]

On January 14, 1858, Anderson encountered two men in New York, who offered him $8 a month if he would go to Pennsylvania with them and look after some circus horses. One of the men used the name Mason Thomas, the other was named Walton. Anderson accepted the offer, and was taken first to Jersey City, New Jersey, and then to Philadelphia. He and Thomas stayed there for a day or two, with Thomas keeping Anderson in the room with him. From Philadelphia, Anderson was taken to Richmond, Virginia, where Thomas put him up for sale at Pulliam's auction house. Thomas claimed that Anderson had been his slave in Missouri, who had run away from him, but whom he had located in New York.[9]

The sale of Anderson, therefore, was carried out with the understanding that he was a runaway, which would have influenced the purchase price (since buyers were leery of slaves who were in the habit of running off). He was sold for either $400 or $450, either to "Messieurs Ralland and Bossieux" or to a Mr. Raglan.[10] Whichever party purchased him became dissatisfied afterward and had obtained a refund. This, no doubt, was because Anderson would not stop insisting that he was a free man.

Anderson's protestations resulted in the arrest of Thomas by Capt. Wilkinson and Lt. Wheat,[11] and both he and Anderson were confined until the truth of the matter could be determined. Richmond mayor Joseph Mayo came to believe Anderson and to distrust Thomas. He sent a letter to New York mayor Daniel Tiemann, seeking confirmation of Anderson's free status. Mayo related Anderson's account of having been hired to take care of some horses, and noted that "though I have no legal proof here to sustain George's statement, it is so plausible that I have remanded Thomas till the 30th." Also raising suspicion was the fact that "Thomas does not give a satisfactory account of how he came to own George."[12]

Mayo asked that Tiemann respond as soon as possible, and he did so by sending a telegram to Mayo asking that he keep Thomas in custody.[13] Mayo, in turn, replied that he would keep Thomas incarcerated, but that "in order to place the matter beyond the possibility of a doubt it was necessary that the evidence of a white man should be procured, who was acquainted with Anderson in New York."[14]

This mayor of a southern city also had a point to make. "I have done nothing more than my duty in vindicating the laws of a sister State and thereby preventing a wrong to one of her citizens," Mayo told Tiemann. He did not, however, feel that sectional problems could be resolved "as long as any State of this Union retains on its statute book laws made in palpable contravention of the constitution of the United States"—an obvious reference to the failure of northern states to return fugitive slaves.[15]

Tiemann had located an African American who knew Anderson to be a freeman, and that man provided referrals to some white men who were also aware of his status. Tiemann was able to obtain an affidavit from a man named George T. Trimble, who had been a school trustee in 1840. Trimble's statement established that Anderson was free and had, indeed, attended school in New York at the time he claimed.[16]

Two New York policemen (Sergeant Croft and Officer McArthur) were dispatched to Richmond and were able to begin their return trip before Thomas's attorney could take any actions to delay the process.[17] Traveling by steamship, they arrived in New York, with both Thomas and Anderson, on February 15.[18]

Thomas (whose real name was Oscar Mason Thomas, though he sometimes used the aliases Mason Thomas and Mason Spaulding)[19] was arraigned in the Court of General Sessions shortly after reaching New York, and was described as "a genteely dressed individual." Bail was set at $10,000 and, unable to make it, he was put in jail.[20] Anderson was also taken into custody, since he was a material witness and could not make the $1,000 bond required to insure his appearance at Thomas's trial.[21]

The kidnapper was tried on April 8 and 9, before City Recorder George G. Barnard. Thomas seemed to know some influential people in New York. He was "very respectably connected, and a number of his friends have been in attendance during the trial."[22] He was represented for at least some of the proceedings by former attorney-general Levi S. Chatfield and former judge Sydney H. Stuart.[23]

The newspapers reported only the barest details of the evidence presented in court. It is not even clear whether the victim himself testified.[24] Local witnesses confirmed that Anderson was a free person, who had lived in New York for some time. Evidence was also provided by some residents of Virginia. Alice Wilson said Thomas had told her that Anderson was his slave who had been located in New York, and that he had "kept Anderson in his room most of the time while in Philadelphia." In a deposition, "Rufin Raglan" said he had purchased Anderson from Thomas, and a man named Davis verified this, having witnessed the transaction.[25]

Much of the reporting of the court session focused on Recorder Barnard's summation of the evidence, and his charge to the jury. Thomas had been indicted on three counts: for having kidnapped Anderson in New York State, for having "inveigled" him out of the state, and for having inveigled and kidnapped him with the intention of selling him as a slave.

Barnard instructed the jury that they must disregard the first count, the reason being that the evidence did not support Thomas having kidnapped Anderson in New York. Instead, because Anderson had agreed to leave the state, it was up to the jury to decide "whether the prisoner when he thus induced the boy Anderson to leave the State, did intend to sell him as a slave. If he formed the intention in any other State than this, yet he would be guilty." The defense objected to the latter point.

Pointing out that persons of color in New York were considered to be free unless they were proven to be slaves, Barnard further told the jury that they must determine that "if he consented to go out of this State, the consent was not extorted by threats or under duress." In the defendant's favor, the jury could take into account his good character, and that "any doubt" they had as to his guilt should result in an acquittal.

After receiving their charge, the jury retired, and reached a verdict within a half-hour, finding Thomas guilty. His counsel immediately raised objections, requested an arrest of judgment, and indicated his desire to appeal.[26] Barnard heard the arguments of the defense attorneys later in the month, and pledged to issue a ruling during the next term of the court.[27] He did so on May 22.

Noting the defense attorneys' objections to the three counts, Barnard decided that, since the second count, for inveigling, was enough to sustain Thomas's conviction, he would only concern himself with that count. Concerning it, he observed: "The idea that a man would voluntarily consent to be sold as a slave, is so preposterous, and an outrage on reason, such an insult to human feelings and passion, that the Legislature might well say such a case can never arise, or if it should, it can only occur in consequence of the consent being obtained by trick,

artifice, or compulsion, or by undue practices on a feeble intellect."
Apart from this reasoning: "In this case it was proved affirmatively,
that the person sold, strongly and decidedly dissented, and expressed
such dissent."[28]

The defense's objection to the inveigling count was merely that it had
not been specific enough, but this argument was dismissed by Barnard,
who said it had been detailed enough to be valid. Barnard then sentenced Thomas to 10 years in prison, at which point "the prisoner man-
ifested but little emotion when his sentence was pronounced."
Barnard's ruling had additional impact, because: "The decision of
the Recorder is all the more important, as it will govern other cases
of the same kind, which will very shortly be tried in the same Court."
(This comment was perhaps in anticipation of the case relating to the
March 1858 kidnapping of Sarah Taylor.)[29]

It does not seem that the case against Thomas went any further in
the courts. At any rate, he did go to prison.[30] Thomas was pardoned
on February 25, 1864, after having served more than half of his sentence. His rights as a New York citizen were restored the following
September.[31] He resided in upstate New York for a number of years,
before taking his own life in 1881.[32]

Research has not revealed any information on Anderson's activities
or place of residence after the 1858 trial.

GEORGE ARMSTRONG

In an article titled "Imitating Solomon Northrup," a District of
Columbia newspaper told of the "strange conduct of two white and a
colored man, who were lurking about in the country around the Chain
Bridge." The three were observed by a "J. Frizzell,"[33] who "suspected
them of tampering with slaves" (that is, he thought abolitionists were
helping a slave escape). Frizzell attempted to apprehend all of them,
but the principal, "Wm Benjamin," was able to escape. Frizzell took
the other two, Fred Axter and George Armstrong, into the city of
Washington. "The bearing of the two," the *Star* stated, "indicated their
northern training and education," and the black man, named George
Armstrong, was "certainly an educated darkey." Armstrong claimed
to have been born free, and was a native of Jefferson County, New
York,"[34] who had arrived via Baltimore, and "had allowed his two
companions to offer him for sale." The reason given for his willingness
to do so was that he had found it hard to earn a living in the North and
had decided to live in the South. (The suggestion that a free black had

conspired to sell himself was not unprecedented: it had been made about Solomon Northup at several different times.)[35]

Armstrong, from Watertown, New York, had been missing for several weeks, with no clue as to his whereabouts until July 5, when his sister received a letter from a Washington law firm, Carusi and Miller. The facts conveyed in that letter were presented to Governor Edwin D. Morgan, who "caused to be made out the necessary papers and credentials, to authorize and empower Mr. John A. Haddock, of Watertown, to proceed to Washington to procure the liberation of this free colored man, imprisoned for no other crime, it would appear, than that of being black."[36]

In Washington, the *Evening Star* reported on the court case involving Armstrong.[37] Armstrong was represented at the hearing by Carusi and Miller, who requested that he be discharged. Haddock, having traveled from Watertown, New York, identified Armstrong as a free man. Benjamin's escape was noted, along with the acknowledgment that he had "offered Armstrong for sale, knowing him to be a free negro."

In addition to verifying Armstrong's free status, "Mr. Haddock stated that he hoped that the authorities would have the man Benjamin indicted, as it was an offense that ought to be promptly and properly punished, and said that he thought the identical person could be obtained by requisition upon the Governor of New York without the least difficulty, as he had no doubt that he knew the individual and where he resides." (No further reports on the case were found in Washington newspapers, so it would appear that little if any effort was made to apprehend Benjamin.) The third man, whose name was given as Frederick Ackse in this report, was discharged, as he claimed only to have hooked up with Armstrong and Benjamin on the way to Washington. Given Haddock's testimony, the judge had Armstrong secured in the jail until his formal release could be arranged.

Armstrong's release took place soon afterward, since he and Haddock returned to Watertown on July 13.[38] According to a Syracuse newspaper, Armstrong said he had been "enticed from Watertown to New York by Benjamin, to see the city, and from there to the South to see the country. After starting the trip he was told by Benjamin that in order to travel he must represent himself as his slave, and after arriving in Washington he attempted to sell him."[39]

IGNATIUS BECK

Ignatius Beck was born a slave on the tobacco plantation of Joseph Beck,[40] which was located near the present city of Bowie, Maryland.

He was born around 1774 or 1775, but at the age of 16 was "legally guaranteed manumission at his 25th birthday," according to historian Terry Buckalew.[41] During the year 1798, Joseph Beck "hired out" the labor of his slave, Ignatius, who joined a workforce of 400 slaves who were put to work building the U.S. Capitol building in Washington.[42] At some point after having gained his freedom, Beck moved to Philadelphia, Pennsylvania.[43] There, he earned a living by manufacturing "blackball," a precursor to shoe polish, and he was active in the Mother Bethel African Methodist Episcopal Church.

Around 1810, Beck was hired by "a respectable-looking man" who was planning a trip south, and wanted Beck to be his "body servant," at good wages. He therefore left Philadelphia, riding a horse provided by his employer, and they went south. Somewhere near the Virginia–North Carolina border, the man told Beck, that because the next day was Sunday, they would not be traveling that day, and the man suggested that Beck might want to attend religious services, along with some slaves belonging to the keeper of the tavern where they were lodged. Beck was told that he was free to do this, so long as he returned Sunday evening. Beck was agreeable and went to a Baptist church, some seven miles away.

He dutifully returned to the inn, where he found to his surprise that his employer had left, taking the horses with him. Bemoaning the fact that he now had no means to go home, he was informed by the innkeeper that he was already home, and that "You are my property; I have bought you of your master."[44]

As recounted by Isaac T. Hopper, who conversed with Beck upon his return to Philadelphia, Beck now "saw the snare into which he had fallen." He explained to his new master that he was a free man, with a family in Philadelphia, "but this had no effect upon the monster who now claimed him as his slave." He was instructed not to bring the matter up again.

Beck decided to accept the situation without complaint, and eventually (perhaps as much as three years later)[45] inquired of white citizens if there was anyone in the area who might help him regain his liberty. These inquiries led him to a local magistrate, who, upon hearing Beck's story, was anxious to assist him. Having been told of Beck's friendship with Rev. Richard Allen in Philadelphia, the pastor was contacted, and he, in turn, enlisted the help of Hopper. Hopper was able to get authenticated copies of Beck's manumission from Samuel Brooks in Washington, D.C. This paperwork was forwarded to the magistrate in Virginia, along with a letter asking that he help Beck.

Upon receipt of this packet, the magistrate was completely convinced of Beck's free status and told him that instituting legal proceedings that would free him would be difficult and lengthy, and that he would advise Beck of the best way to proceed. A commotion arose as word of the matter leaked out, and the magistrate housed Beck in his cellar for several weeks for his safety, until things quieted down.

Instead of initiating a freedom suit, it was decided that the magistrate's son would escort Beck toward Philadelphia. After riding 100 miles on horseback, the son gave Beck instructions on how to proceed, and Beck pressed on to Philadelphia. Back home, Beck related the whole story to Hopper, who advised him that they should keep the matter between themselves, but for Beck to notify him if he should hear anything about the man who had lured him away. Some weeks later, Beck spotted the man and followed him to his residence on Lombard Street in Philadelphia. Hopper obtained an arrest warrant, and went to the house with an officer, but the man had left and there was no trace of him.

Beck continued his residency in Philadelphia where he was one of the 1,100 blacks who worked on the defenses of the city during the War of 1812.[46] He pursued various occupations (the invention of shoe polish having eliminated the demand for the "blackball" he had previously manufactured). He was an antislavery activist; in 1831, he was appointed chairman of the Free Produce Society of Philadelphia (an organization devoted to encouraging the consumption of products produced by free labor only),[47] and he contributed cash to the Vigilant Committee of Philadelphia in 1839.[48] He was a key witness in court proceedings involving William Stansbury, who had been claimed as a fugitive slave.[49]

Beck died in Philadelphia on October 14, 1849.[50] He was buried in the Bethel Burying Ground, connected with the church to which he belonged.[51]

MARY BOYD

Jeremiah "Jerry" Boyd, described as "a decent colored man of Galena,"[52] and his wife Mary lived in Galena, Illinois. Jerry had run away from his master in Kentucky, but his brother had bought him out of slavery, making him a freeman. Boyd moved to Galena, and was able to purchase his wife's freedom using money he had earned and which other people had given to him.[53]

In the fall of 1860, a man named Gooden (though he used the name "Wilder") came to Galena, seeking African Americans willing to relocate to Iowa and take jobs there. Several individuals agreed to go, including Boyd and his wife Mary. (They agreed to go despite warnings about Gooden that had been forwarded from Iowa.)

The Boyds left in Gooden's wagon on September 28 along with two other members of their household, a teenaged mulatto girl named Charlotte Alexander, and a white female infant. During the trip, the group encountered another man, by the name of Boulton, who asked if he could accompany them. Boyd became suspicious of his two escorts and made a point of loading his revolver in front of them one evening, when the party was not far from Iowa City. Boyd developed a plan that would allow the Boyd family to escape, but it went awry when one of the men confronted Boyd saying "Jerry, I am afraid of you," after which he shot him dead.[54]

Goodwin and Boulton took the remaining victims to Missouri, and began making arrangements to sell them as slaves. "There is no doubt," said a newspaper, "that the white men were kidnappers, and that the colored people, as well as the white girl, may be sold into Slavery."[55] Boulton left them with his father-in-law.

A number of communications received back in Galena told people there that some kind of trouble had transpired. Iowa authorities contacted them after Boyd's body was discovered, and papers found on his person indicated he was from Galena. In addition, Boulton's father-in-law wrote a letter about the people who had been entrusted to his care, and the mayor of the city of St. Joseph, Missouri, asked that some white people go there to help with the case against the suspected kidnappers. The men were in custody there, but under Missouri law, the word of the black women was not sufficient evidence. Also, Mary Boyd herself wrote a letter to the mother of the white girl, with information on what had transpired.

Citizens in Galena had raised $500 as a reward for the capture of the culprits.[56] Two men, Wellington Weigley, and Samuel Hughlet, left for Missouri. In St. Joseph, they received excellent cooperation from officials and took custody of Gooden (Boulton remained in jail, pending possible extradition to Iowa on a murder charge).Weigley and Hughlet, along with the victims, headed back to Illinois by rail. Along the way, Gooden, who had been able to loosen his handcuffs and manacle, jumped from the moving train and escaped.[57] Back in Missouri, Boulton was bailed out, and also avoided paying for his crime.[58]

DAVID CAESAR

David Caesar, identified in court papers as a "free boy of colour," and "a mulatto," "not more than eight years of age," was kidnapped in Henrico County, Virginia, by Alfred R. Davenport. This probably occurred around 1828. Davenport was indicted by the circuit court, and it was charged that he "did feloniously steal, take and carry away, one mulatto boy named *David Caesar*, who was a free boy and not a slave, the said *Davenport* at the time *knowing him to be free.*" Davenport was convicted under a statute that forbade "*stealing* or *selling any free person for a slave, knowing* the said person so sold to be free."[59]

The language of the statute under which he was charged was somewhat imprecise. For a perpetrator to be guilty, must he have known that the "stolen" person was, in fact, free? And was it illegal to simply *steal* a free person, or must the free person also have been *sold* as a slave? These issues had been raised by Davenport's attorneys at the trial (at which the Virginia attorney general presented the prosecution's case). After his conviction, the matters were brought up again in an appeal in November 1829. They were decided against Davenport. In a decision written by Judge William Brockenbrough,[60] it was noted that the statute, as worded, only required that a free person be stolen—knowledge of the person's free status was only necessary if the person were not only stolen, but also sold as a slave.

The statute's preamble said "whereas several evil disposed persons have seduced or stolen the children of black and mulatto free persons, *and* [emphasis added] have actually disposed of the person so seduced or stolen as slaves." But the statute itself had the word "or," indicating that stealing a free person was a crime, regardless of whether the person was also sold. (Of further interest is the preamble's indication that there had been a spate of kidnapping of free children of color.)

With the appeal decided against Davenport, his conviction, and sentence of two years' imprisonment, stood.

HESTER JANE CARR

Hester Jane Carr was born of free parents in Accomack County, Virginia, in about 1816.[61] Her mother, Anna, had been emancipated by a Mr. Carr, to whom she had belonged. Her father had moved to New York, and died there of smallpox when Hester Carr was quite young. In 1835, Carr took a schooner to New York, showing her free papers to the ship's captain, who may have mistakenly kept them.[62]

In New York City, Carr obtained employment as a servant in the home of Dr. James Cockcroft, who lived on Forsyth Street. In July 1836, Carr met a woman who wanted her to go with her to Columbus, Georgia, and be her maid. Carr agreed to the arrangement, and they headed south.[63] When they reached Baltimore, it was explained to Carr that, due to the laws in Virginia, she could be jailed and possibly sold as a slave (since she was a free person of color, apparently without free papers). It would be best if she pretended to be the slave of her future employer. Carr agreed to do so.

At Petersburg, Virginia, Carr was sold for $750 to a slave trader, Richard Beasley, who was in the business of buying slaves in Virginia and selling them in the Deep South at a profit.[64] The woman who had enticed Carr from New York was traveling with a "paramour"[65] and left Petersburg with the cash. Carr somehow obtained the assistance of Petersburg attorney William C. Parker, who instituted a freedom suit on her behalf.[66] Parker contacted some people in New York, including Dr. Cockcroft, who supplied affidavits to be presented in court.[67]

Carr's case of being abducted was brought up at a meeting in New York, held to find ways to combat kidnapping.[68] It was some months before Carr's suit was decided in court. Beasley, the court decided, had done nothing wrong in purchasing her, and she was indeed his slave. Lawyer Parker contested the ruling, and the case was reopened. Unfortunately, Carr died in May 1837, before the proceedings were resumed.[69]

DIMMOCK CHARLTON

The man who came to be known as Dimmock Charlton was aboard a Spanish slave ship when it was taken by a British ship early in the eighteenth century. He was transported to England and given a job as cabin boy on HMS *Peacock*, where he was called John Bull. He was on board the *Peacock* when she was sunk by the USS *Hornet* in 1813, during the War of 1812.[70]

Charlton and others were seized as prisoners of war and taken to New York. He was placed in the charge of a Lt. William Henry Harrison (he has been confused with the later president of the same name), who took him to Savannah, Georgia. Harrison left him there with Judge T. U. P. Charlton[71] until he could find out what the government wanted done with him.

Later, when Harrison asked for "John Bull," Judge Charlton informed him he had died of a fever. Right after this, Judge Charlton told servants in his household that the man was no longer to be called John Bull, but Dimmock Charlton, and he sold him (actually, he gave him to a tailor whom he owed for a suit of clothes). Charlton objected to this, saying he was not a slave. He was then taken to Augusta, Georgia, where, presumably, he could cause less fuss.

Charlton was sold various times over the next several years, ending up back in Savannah. Charlton claimed that several times he had raised money to buy his freedom but was double-crossed. He took a wife, and they had several children. Eventually he became the property of James Kerr,[72] whom he was able to convince to purchase his family members so they could be together. Charlton lived with Kerr for years, until Kerr sold all the family members to different owners. Charlton, upset, began telling how he had been wrongfully enslaved years earlier. He had kept quiet before, because he was fearful that he would be sold into the interior of Georgia, or perhaps further south. It was his belief that being near the seaport of Savannah provided his best chance to resolve his status.[73]

When Charlton's new owner learned his history, he quickly sold him, and this also happened with his next owner. Finally, Charlton was purchased by Benjamin Garman, who lived up to an agreement he and Charlton had made that Charlton would be allowed to purchase his freedom. After attaining freedom, Charlton took the steamer *Alabama* from Savannah to New York in the 1850s. There, he became aware that sisters of James Kerr had brought one of his granddaughters to New York, and, as part of an overall goal of obtaining the freedom of his family, he went to court and succeeded in getting her freed.[74]

Though some doubted his story (which surely is an incredible one), it was confirmed in several ways. At the court proceedings involving Charlton's granddaughter, Louisa T. Kerr testified: "I long since heard of his having been on board the Peacock when taken by the Hornet, and I believe that part of his story is true."[75]

Joseph S. Fay, who had known Charlton for 20 years or more, wrote a letter to the *New York Times*, in which he admitted to having heard about Charlton's claim to being a British subject "within [the last] two years." He tended to doubt it, because of the late date at which Charlton was relating it, but admitted that if some documents could be found, "there may be some claim for the probability of that part of his tale."[76]

Finally, with a letter of introduction from John Jay, Charlton went to England and there found a man who recalled the presence of a colored boy on the *Peacock*, and who, after talking with Charlton, was convinced that it had been him.[77] Charlton's story was also believed by Mary L. Cox and Susan H. Cox, of Philadelphia, who assembled a pamphlet about him;[78] by a *New York Times* reporter; and even by Frederick Douglass. The *Times* writer said "his integrity and reliability are so well vouched for that it would be found difficult to doubt or discredit his story."[79] Douglass found him to be "as honest and as deserving of respect and kindness as his tormentors have been dishonest and deserving of abhorrence and execration."[80]

Though the acting British consul at New York thought the case was too old to resolve, Lord Napier, British Minister at Washington, took some steps to investigate it.[81] Charlton took his grandchild to Canada, then to Boston, where he sought to obtain custody of her from a couple who had agreed to lodge and board her. Due to Charlton's uncertain finances, a judge decided the girl should remain with them.[82]

MILLY CHAVIS

In the 1780s, Milly Chavis lived with her mother Winny Chavis in Brunswick County, Virginia. They were part of a significant number of free blacks in Virginia.[83] Chavis was kidnapped when she was only about six or seven years old and sold as a slave. During her life, she was the property of a number of slaveholders, finally ending up as one of the slaves owned by James Arthur, of Pittsylvania County.[84]

In 1821, Chavis filed a petition to institute a freedom suit against Arthur. Her petition was granted and the matter came to trial on March 20, 1822, after several delays requested by the parties to the case.[85] At the court session, a woman named Polly M'Kinney testified that she recalled the kidnapping years earlier of a young girl who had a scar on her thigh, such as Chavis had. Arthur and his legal team seem to have been poorly prepared, and the jury decided in favor of Chavis, and she was presumably released.

Arthur made several efforts to get a new trial, arguing that new evidence had surfaced. Several of his requests were rejected, but finally he was given another chance to press his claim in court. In February 1828, Arthur presented the evidence he claimed he had not had time to gather six years earlier. His new evidence included a witness who said that Chavis had received the scar as an adult when she stepped into a potato hole; information that cast doubt on Polly M'Kinney's reliability as a witness; and some documents relating to the chain of custody of Chavis as a slave (among the latter was a bill of sale that had been located in Tennessee). Chavis, Arthur claimed, had been a slave in Goochland County, Virginia, and not the daughter of a free woman in Brunswick County.

It was argued, in Arthur's behalf, that his mind was weak, and he had been unable to properly prepare for the original trial. One judge noted, however, that he had many people who could have assisted him, and that in court, he surely was "more than a match for the pauper [Chavis], a woman of colour [*sic*], who had been held from her childhood in slavery; and who had to take the burthen of proof, and establish her claim to freedom."[86]

It was observed that the case was about more than "the poor remnant of this old woman's life," since it was questionable "if she was really of any value worth contending for." The case had potential impact on "suits for the freedom of some of those [Chavis's] children [that] were depending, when this cause was tried." Those cases, the judge said, had probably already been decided, however.[87] In the end, the court's ruling went against Chavis, and she again became Arthur's slave. She did not die a slave, however, because on January 16, 1829, Arthur released her and a daughter from slavery.[88]

JAMES CLARKSON, HARRISON HUBBARD, AND MARGARET DAVIS

In April 1849, James Clarkson, Harrison Hubbard, and Margaret Davis ("three free negro youths")[89] were hired to cut corn stalks for James T. Wooters in Caroline County, Maryland. They worked at this for one or two days, then "suddenly disappeared, and no one could learn aught of their whereabouts." One early report called it an "alleged" case of kidnapping that occurred in the first week of April; other sources termed it an outrage.[90]

Local citizens suspected that the three had been abducted, and several people went looking for them. After searching for several days, it was learned that they had been taken through Huntington Creek, Worcester County, and then to Norfolk, Virginia. Efforts were made to have the children released and returned to their parents. Implicated in their abduction, along with Wooters, were Smith W. Corkran (who was jailed) and several other men. A Kent County slave trader named Parker was suspected of having orchestrated the kidnapping.

AARON COOPER

Aaron Cooper belonged to a family of slaves that had been owned by Thomas Hanson in Kent County, Delaware. Hanson gradually released his slaves from bondage, but generally not until they were 25 years of age. Aaron was manumitted in 1792.[91] Before he acquired his freedom, Cooper was an apprentice miller. Afterward, he worked as a baker. He met a woman named Hetty in Philadelphia, married her there, and returned to Delaware, where they started a family.[92]

One night in May 1811, after the family had gone to bed, there was a knock at the door. When Cooper answered it, five white men rushed in. They were armed and, in front of the rest of the frightened family, grabbed Cooper and took him away. Carried into Maryland, Cooper was sold by them to slave trader Robert Martin. They had presented Martin with Cooper at 4:00 a.m., saying he was a slave who had run away before, and they wanted to make sure he did not escape again.[93]

Martin, waiting until later in the morning, questioned Cooper and was informed that he was anxious to be sold because his master was a very hard one. (Later, when Martin understood what had transpired, he said that the men had apparently "learnt him his lesson," because he had no inkling that Cooper was a free man.)[94]

When word of the crime got out, several local men, some of them friends of Cooper's, went in pursuit of the kidnappers and their victim. They crossed into Maryland, and came across witnesses who had seen the group, and missed finding them at Dixon's Tavern by just 24 hours.

The rescuers were able to get assistance from some Maryland judges, who issued arrest warrants, but got little cooperation from one sheriff, and they learned, before another warrant could be acted upon, that Cooper had been taken on board a ship that had already sailed. The men made an effort to intercept the ship at a nearby port, but it was already on its way to Norfolk, Virginia. At that point, they gave up the search for Cooper.

Within a few months, Cooper was in Natchez, Mississippi, where Martin, the slave trader, had sold him to Parmenas Briscoe, who ran a cotton plantation. With the assistance of William B. Shields, attorney general for the Mississippi Territory, Cooper filed a petition seeking his freedom.

Late that summer, Briscoe wrote to some men in Delaware, inquiring about Cooper's status. He asked them for a quick response, because, if Cooper were indeed free, he wanted to confront Martin, and get justice for both himself and Cooper. The response from Delaware was that yes, Cooper was indeed free but had recently been kidnapped, with Martin having an involvement in it.

While Cooper's freedom suit inched its way through the judicial system, he toiled away as Briscoe's slave. The case came before two different judges, and finally, in April 1814, a jury determined that he was a free man, and not a slave. He was awarded compensation (though the amount was not mentioned in the court papers), and returned to Delaware where he rejoined his family.[95]

JIM CORN

Jim Corn was a free black man living in Stokes County, North Carolina. Sometime in the spring of 1848, he accompanied Abram Weaver and

John Brown, who were making a business trip together. Weaver supplied a wagon, which was pulled by Brown's horse. They were not very successful at their trading.

They had hoped to sell a supply of fish that Brown had taken in the wagon, and some guns brought by Weaver. When they encountered a man named Robertson, the question arose as to whether Weaver planned to take Corn "over the mountains" into Virginia. Weaver said that though this had been spoken of, it was not his intent, but that if Corn wanted to go, he would not be allowed to sleep in the wagon. Brown reluctantly agreed that Corn could accompany them, after Weaver agreed to pay any additional expenses it might require.[96] They traveled through Surry County, and then into Virginia, where Brown knocked Corn to the ground following a spat. Weaver advised Brown not to abuse Corn, as he "intended to put him into his pocket before he got back."[97]

Brown afterward testified that at that time, as on another occasion, it was his belief that Weaver was merely joking about selling Corn. But upon reaching Burke's Garden in Tazewell County, Virginia, Weaver had some discussions with a man named Lowder, and Brown came to the conclusion that Weaver *did* plan to sell Corn. Brown then unjoined his horse from the wagon and returned to North Carolina. There, he told the story to Levi Stafford. Brown had not seen Corn since leaving Virginia.

In court, in addition to Brown's testimony, other evidence was presented that Weaver had admitted to having sold Corn, and that he had taken him to Virginia from Stokes County, where Corn resided. Corn apparently was sold again, and ended up in Louisville, Kentucky, where he sued for his freedom and was released, according to newspaper reports (which do not specify precisely when this occurred).[98]

Weaver's trial was held in the fall of 1852, in Surry County. He was found guilty and sentenced to be hung on the first Friday in October. His counsel entered objections to certain decisions made by the trial judge and appealed to the Supreme Court, which heard the case at its December term.

In the Supreme Court's decision, reference was made to the defense's objections to rulings by the trial judge. Separate statutes dealt with kidnapping free negroes and with stealing slaves. The statute relating to free negroes stipulated that they must be taken by force, with the perpetrator intending to sell them outside the state. But when it came to slaves, the law said that they could be taken by "violence, seduction or any other means." The trial judge had erred in charging the jury, telling them that "any means equivalent to actual violence, as deception, seduction and persuasion" would constitute guilt. The Supreme Court ruled against this interpretation, saying "how a free negro, who is an intelligent being and a free agent, can be taken and conveyed out of the State unless force is used in taking him, cannot well be conceived."[99]

In addition, it was noted that the trial judge had told the jury that, if the victim had consented to leave the state and to be sold as a slave ("where the free negro was privy to the intent, and consented to go and be sold as a slave, under the expectation of sharing the spoils"), that they should find Weaver not guilty. This concept, said the Supreme Court, was not present in the statute. Weaver was granted a new trial, but it seems unlikely that one ever took place, as there appear to be no press reports about it.

Weaver, whom newspapers called a "notorious individual," had had other run-ins with the law. In 1851, he had been charged, along with some others, of having sold a slave belonging to another man. The slave had also been sold to Lowder, in Burke's Garden, Virginia.[100] In 1853, Weaver was found guilty of having received stolen goods and sentenced to a public whipping, which was carried out. According to the press report of this case, he had been in prison for two years previous to this.[101]

MARGARET DAVIS

See James Clarkson, Harrison Hubbard, and Margaret Davis.

STEPHEN DICKINSON, ROBERT GARRISON, AND ISAAC WRIGHT

In November 1837, Stephen Dickinson,[102] Robert Garrison, and Isaac Wright signed up as crewmen on the steamer *Newcastle*. The three men lived in the New York City area.[103] Dickinson had previously worked on a Long Island farm,[104] and Wright had grown up in Philadelphia.[105] Nothing is known of Garrison's prior background.

The steamboat was bound for the South, providing packet service between Florida and New Orleans. It usually transported a few slaves along with its other cargo.[106] Dickinson, Garrison, and Wright had known each other in New York, and became even closer companions while on the boat.[107]

In mid-February 1838, while the boat was docked at New Orleans, a man named George A. Botts came on board and spoke for a time with the captain, Jonathan Dayton Wilson. The captain went into the city several times, and not long afterward, the ship's mate, Thomas Lewis, ordered the three men to go ashore with him so they could pick up a load of hemp. In the city, Lewis took them to Harper's Jail, where they were confined.

Botts made an appearance, asking the men whether they were free, if they were from New York, and where they had lived there. After getting their responses, he had them taken outside where they were each given 35 lashes with a bull whip. Botts cautioned them that any further mention of having been on the steamboat, Captain Wilson, or being from New York would result in an even more severe beating.

Several weeks later, they were transported to Vicksburg, Mississippi, along with several others from the jail (including another man who was also free). It was perhaps on their trip up the river that Wright encountered an Englishman, to whom he explained his predicament. When he returned to the North, around March 1838, the man passed on the information to some antislavery people.[108]

At Vicksburg, Mississippi, a slave trader named Rudisill, to whom they had been transferred, had difficulty selling them. Finally, a deal was struck, but the buyer backed out after having misgivings. He came back afterward, when Rudisill was not there, and questioned the men about their status. They naturally were reluctant to be forthcoming, but a slave told him that the three were from New York and were free. The man became convinced, saying he would try to write to their friends on their behalf. He also told Rudisill, who contacted Botts, and "Botts, in reply, directed him to get rid of us as soon as he could and as well as he could." They were sold, to separate individuals, not long afterward.[109]

At this point, the stories of the three friends diverge. Dickinson ended up in Kentucky and was a slave to Richard Percival for several years. Eventually, he met a farmer named Thomas Vantreese, a kindly man whom Dickinson trusted with his real story. Vantreese was not surprised, telling him "that he thought from my appearance that I had not been brought up a slave." A lawyer named Cradock was enlisted who wrote to New York and received confirmation of what Dickinson had said. The sheriff was notified, but Percival took Dickinson to Vicksburg before he could be seized. A complaint was made to Rudisill, who blamed Botts. Percival then took Dickinson to New Orleans so he could confront Botts. While staying at the Planters Hotel, Dickinson told the proprietor there what was going on, and an attorney named Elwyn took up the case.[110]

A sheriff took Dickinson into safekeeping, and soon afterward, Elwyn obtained free papers for him. These, unfortunately, were given to Percival since he had paid the fees for them. Botts was forced to refund $600 of Percival's money, and Percival suggested that Dickinson return to New York by way of Kentucky, saying he would help fund the cost of his trip. But once away from New Orleans, Percival made the newly freed man give him a note for $200, to make up for the incomplete refund he had gotten from Botts. It was agreed that Dickinson would work on a steamboat until the money was paid. Despite working for months on several different boats, Dickinson got shorted on his pay for various reasons. Finally, he went north aboard the *Natchez*, reaching New York after an absence of close to three years. He proceeded directly to his father's house, and "upon meeting our rejoicing was mutual."[111]

In Vicksburg, Wright and Garrison had been sold to a Mr. McMahan, who took them to Tennessee. Upon finding out that they were probably free men, he wrote to James Hill in Philadelphia to say that, if proof of their status were sent to him, he would release them, without requiring any compensation. Papers were sent, but McMahan died not long afterward—but not before he had reneged on his promise, having sold Wright to Hinson Gift. Garrison was sold also, but according to Dickinson, "who he was sold to, or where he was taken, I never learned.[112]

Gift also wrote to Philadelphia about Wright, making the same offer to release him that McMahan had made. As a result of Gift's letter, Joshua Coffin traveled to Memphis, Tennessee, in December 1838. Soon after his arrival, he walked to Raleigh, where Gift lived. Asking for directions to the house, an old slave explained that Gift was away on a gambling spree. Coffin also learned that Gift had given Wright to Jonathan Simpson in settlement of a gambling debt. Simpson was also away, but he had left Wright behind to care for his house.

Coffin had the slave take him to meet Wright, and a plan was hatched for his departure with Coffin. Wright was to wait at a steamboat landing, then go on board while Coffin made an arrangement with the captain to carry them. This worked out, and when the boat was over 200 miles away from Memphis, Coffin penned a letter saying "I took him away from Memphis without the consent or knowledge of any human being in Memphis or Raleigh." Boastfully, he wrote "I have in fact kidnapped him into freedom."[113] Wright's absence was noticed by Simpson, who placed an ad for the "runaway" slave named Isaac at the end of December.[114]

Garrison, as suggested by Dickinson in 1840, probably remained a slave.[115]

In the months following the trio's disappearance, their case had been looked into by people in New York, particularly David Ruggles, of the local vigilance committee.[116] Information and witnesses were sought and located;[117] Captain Wilson was arrested,[118] and funds were solicited to pay for expenses connected with a mission to rescue the men.[119] Thomas Lewis, who had taken the men to the jail in New Orleans, had been apprehended in New Bedford, Massachusetts (thanks to Ruggles).[120] Ultimately, neither Wilson nor Lewis suffered any significant repercussions from their roles in the matter.

HENRY DIXON

Henry Dixon spent time in the cities of Auburn and Rochester in New York State in the mid-nineteenth century. He was described as "a fine-looking, genteel and intelligent mulatto."[121] Neither Dixon nor his parents had ever been slaves. His father had kept a blacksmith shop in Rochester, and both men had attended a Sunday school there. When he lived in Auburn, the younger Dixon had worked as a barber at a hotel.[122]

Other details of Dixon's early life are somewhat sketchy. He was said to have been born in Canada, Michigan, or possibly England.[123] Most of his early years were spent in Canada, but he then went to New York, and worked on canal boats near Rochester. After a few years there, he went to Ohio, and then, around 1849 to 1850, he was in England for a short time.[124]

Sometime in the mid-1850s, he went to the District of Columbia and worked as a hack driver. With all his travels, his friends and family lost track of his whereabouts, until some letters were received from him. One letter was addressed to James S. Seymour, a clerk at an Auburn bank.[125] Information in the letters prompted Dixon's sister, residing in Buffalo, to contact Rochester's Ashley Sampson, an attorney and former judge.[126]

In the letters, Dixon explained that he had begun to head back to New York, but that, during an overnight stay somewhere between Washington and Baltimore, he had been "seized by some unknown ruffians" while sleeping, and had been confined for some time before being taken to Macon, Georgia. There, he was enslaved.[127] At the time he wrote the letters, he was a slave to James Dean,[128] and he asked that his friends in New York assist him in regaining his freedom.[129] (Some accounts say that Dixon, rather than being abducted, was arrested and found guilty of some unstated crime in Maryland, and was sold as a slave to pay off the expense of keeping him in jail.)[130]

Once Dixon's whereabouts and status became known, his friends in New York began working to liberate him. His letters, and other paperwork, were sent to New York governor Myron H. Clark, who appointed Stephen S. Austin as an agent to recover Dixon.[131]

(This was according to the provisions of the 1840 law that had been used to rescue Solomon Northup in 1853.)

Austin went to Macon and located Dean, who would only say that he had sold Dixon "to some person and to some part of the country unknown."[132] Additional inquiries by Austin, and consultations with a Macon law firm, Poe & Grier, proved fruitless, and Dixon could not be located.[133] Poe & Grier recommended that Austin return to New York, and promised to pursue the matter further in Georgia. Austin went home, the trip having cost $400.[134]

Sometime after Austin's unsuccessful mission, Sampson received a communication from Poe & Grier, who had word from Dean that: "If he ever owned the negro in question," he was willing "to surrender him to his friends for seven hundred dollars."[135] Dean, Sampson reported, "is represented to be a heartless, unprincipled man" who refused to tell where Dixon was, but "offers ... to re-purchase Henry, and deliver him to his friends." According to the Georgia attorneys, this was the only way to obtain Dixon's release, and they suggested that "early action is necessary to prevent his being sold into irretrievable slavery."[136]

In New York, some consideration was given to having the governor make a formal demand for the return of Dixon, but such an effort apparently did not get very far.[137] Instead, money was collected, and an adequate sum (which Dean claimed was below market value) was forwarded to Georgia. Dean took Dixon to the attorneys' office, and when advised by Grier that his liberty had been arranged and that he could return to New York, Dixon "looked blank, disappointed and dumbfounded. He resolutely refused to be free." He was worried that his New York friends would neglect him once he had been freed, and that "he should have a harder time in getting along there than in Georgia." Dean, he said, was "a friend and protector who would not permit him to suffer." Cautioned by Grier that, should Dean die, he could end up in the hands of another master, Dixon said "he would rather risk it than to go to New York." Dixon stuck with his decision, even when interviewed privately by Grier.[138]

Informed of Dixon's response, Sampson and others in New York were disbelieving. Possibly, they thought, the Georgians had found a man to impersonate Dixon. As a consequence, another man was dispatched to Georgia in the summer of 1857.[139] Samuel D. Porter[140] was acquainted with Dixon, and when he was able to meet the enslaved man, he was convinced that he was indeed Henry Dixon.[141]

Porter observed that Dixon was "a complete wreck of his 'former self,'" who worked separately from the other slaves on the plantation, tending chickens and doing light work. He could not be hired out to work on the roads or railroads. Dixon told Porter that "he was the bearer of despatches [*sic*] from Queen Victoria to the Islands of Jamaica, and that he could at any time command a government vessel in the execution of his mission." After hearing this, Porter concluded that the man was suffering from a "mental aberration."[142] Porter was unable to convince Dixon to return to New York, so he went home, and the money that had been raised was returned to the contributors.

News of Dixon's preferring the life of a slave to one of a freeman was carried in southern newspapers, of course.[143] But at least one northern paper supported his choice. "We think he decided well," said a Providence, Rhode Island, paper. "The colored men of the South, we are satisfied, are far happier than the colored men of the North."[144]

There was another turn of events, however. In the spring of 1858, Porter received an update on Dixon (Sampson had passed away the previous November). The letter was from Edmund Molyneux, British consul at Savannah.[145] Dixon was now in Savannah, having been hired out by Dean, and was now "very anxious to secure his liberty," being fearful that he otherwise would go back to Dean's plantation, or be sold south. The asking price was now only $350, which may have been an indication that he was not "of sound mind." With the money raised earlier having been given back to the contributors, the death of Sampson, and the financial stress experienced by a man of means with an interest in the case, it was unclear whether funds could be again be collected.[146]

The newspapers mostly seem to have lost interest in the story. However, apparently an adequate sum was raised, because by April 1859, Dixon had gone back to New York, visited acquaintances in Auburn and Rochester, and then traveled to California to visit his sister. A letter from him informed the newspaper of his desire to go to India.[147]

JONATHAN AND SAMPSON DREDDEN

Stephen Dredden was a free black who lived with his family at Broad Creek Hundred in Sussex County, Delaware, not far from the Maryland border.[148] In June 1817, Dredden was requested to appear in court in Laurel, Delaware. Two men, slave traders William Riggen and William Banning, had made a claim against him (possibly accusing him of being a runaway). Prior to the day of the proceeding, a neighbor, Sarah Moore, strongly advised that Dredden's wife accompany him, in case the men should try to seize Dredden. Moore offered to watch the couple's children while they were away. In the end, Mrs. Dredden did go with her husband on the morning of June 20, leaving her young ones in Moore's care.[149]

The court session, which involved what Dredden called "pretended claims," dragged on due to delaying tactics by Riggen and Banning. The men were seen in Laurel talking to George Moore, another slave trader. Consequently, it was almost sunset when the Dreddens started for home, arriving just about dark.

Dismay greeted them, since only three of their five children were present. Their 9-year-old daughter explained what had transpired: Moore, after going into the woods, had come back in and asked that this daughter turn her baby sister over to her 5-year-old sister, so that she and her two brothers, Sampson (age 11) and Jonathan (age 7) could go into the woods and help Moore collect firewood. The daughter refused this request, so Moore left with only the two boys, telling the daughter later that they had not come back yet because they were still outside looking for bird's nests.

Moore displayed nonchalance after the parents returned, telling them: "don't grieve about your children, it is not worth while, for you will never see them any more." But the parents did grieve, and their wailing attracted some of the other neighbors, who also shed tears. As Dredden said: "They were parents and had children, and they saw that we, though black, were parents too, and felt as such."

Riggen, Banning, and some other men had been seen near the Dredden home (prior to their arrival in Laurel), and were seen at 10:00 that night, leading the two boys toward Maryland. On July 18, Dredden swore out an affidavit before Wattson Pepper, a Sussex County justice of the peace, and the information was printed by various newspapers, in hopes that someone would come forward and help locate the boys and the kidnappers. Dredden promised to anyone that could help that "he will remember them in his prayers to *Almighty God*, so long as he lives." The newspaper items generally began with Dredden's mournful plea: "PARENTS! FATHERS! MOTHERS! You know how to feel for those who have children. Arrest the monsters in the shape of men; they have broken down my spirit with grief. Stop the Kidnappers! for although I am black, I have a heart like you, and they have pierced it through with sorrow—they have stolen my children!"[150]

Regrettably, Dredden found out nothing more about Sampson and Jonathan.[151]

EMILY, GEORGE, LOUISA, AND WILLIAM FAUVER

In the 1840s, Benjamin W. Fauver lived with his wife, Easter (or Hester), in Pond Settlement, Gallatin County, Illinois. The family had apparently moved to Illinois from Alabama sometime between 1836 and 1841.[152]

On April 5, 1849, the Fauver home was invaded by four men. The father was tied up, and four of his children were taken away: Emily (age 16), George W. (9), Louisa (18), and William Q. (4).[153] The incident was reported in a letter from S. D. Marshall, a Shawnee Town attorney, who made the observation that kidnapping was "a regular trade in this part of the State," and that such criminals were organized and numerous. "We know who the men are," said Marshall, referring to the perpetrators, "but cannot punish them in consequence of the disqualification of negroes as witnesses." As a result of prejudice against African Americans: "The great difficulty is in proving the *forcible taking*—in fact a *taking at all*." Marshall offered some suggestions for changes to state laws in regard to these types of crimes.[154]

The heartbroken father put up money for use as a reward, and Marshall said that neighbors contributed to it as well. Using language similar to that used in ads for runaway slaves, the amount of $25 was offered for recovery of each of the children found within the state, or $50, if found elsewhere. For "apprehension and conviction of the thieves (four in number)," $100 was offered. Fauver asked for "the aid of all good people" in regaining his children and punishing the criminals.

Two of the suspected culprits, John C. Hanna and Cabel Carr, were caught several months later, in Shreveport, Louisiana, and a newspaper remarked that: "We are glad to learn that the kidnappers are likely to be punished."[155] In January 1850, proceedings in Illinois were commenced against Hanna and Carr, and also William McGehee and John Clark. These four men were charged with kidnapping, but they were granted a continuance two days later.[156] They possibly were never brought to justice. One of lawyer Marshall's suggestions had been to place limits on the number of continuances granted in such cases, since he said that kidnappers commonly used them to delay proceedings and avoid being punished.[157]

The Fauver children were rescued, though the details of how this happened are not apparent. Their names and approximate ages are listed in a household headed by their mother (the father was not among the members of the household) in 1850.[158]

SIDNEY O. FRANCIS

On September 12, 1839, two men came to the home of Mrs. Diana Francis in Worcester, Massachusetts. When she opened the door and saw the men, she realized theirs had been the voices she had heard talking with her eight-year-old son, Sidney Orison Francis. Outside the door, the two men, Dickinson Shearer, and his nephew, Elias M. Turner, had approached the young African American boy, and Shearer had asked if he would like to go away and live with him. "Yes, I guessed so," was Sidney's answer.[159]

Inside, conversing with Sidney's mother, the two men—who gave their names as Purlin Shearer and John Dickinson—explained their purpose. Shearer had a store in the town of Palmer, about 30 miles from Worcester. In his household he had a colored boy, who did chores in the store and in his home, but the boy's family would be moving away soon, and he was looking for someone to take his place. Would she allow Sidney to go away with them? He would be tasked only with light work, including looking after a horse, and Shearer would also send him to school part time. (Shearer had asked if he had been to school, and the mother said he had not.)

Shearer asked if Sidney had been away from home before, getting the answer that he never had been, which he said made him like him that much better. When someone else in the neighborhood suggested another boy that might be able to go, Shearer, after getting a positive response to his query about whether "he had been about much?" said that *that* boy "would not answer their purpose."[160] (Probably it was important to Shearer to get a child who would not recognize that he was leaving Massachusetts.)

Diana was amenable to such an arrangement, but needed to know the opinion of her husband, John Foster Francis. She told the men to take Sidney to the rail depot, where his father was working, and get his permission. After talking to the men, Mr. Francis reluctantly agreed to the arrangement, sending them back with instructions for his wife to, as she later recalled, "fix him up the best way I could and let him go." She packed up the boy's clothes while Turner (who had accompanied him back to his home, while Shearer went to fetch his horse and wagon) explained that he was a clerk in Shearer's store and had been living with him for two years, and thought him a nice man. Just before Turner led the boy away from his home, Mr. Francis showed up. He requested the names and place of residence of the men, and he wrote down what turned out to be false names in his account book.

Turner and Sidney Francis left on foot. At the Central Hotel, they met Shearer, who took custody of Francis, telling Turner to fetch the horse and wagon and to pick them up along the way. Shearer walked with the young boy to Nobility Hill on Worcester's Main Street, where Turner caught up with them, and they all rode to Palmer. There, they had dinner at the home of Shearer's brother, Dr. Marcus M. Shearer. They then went to the house of Turner's parents, Col. Elias Turner and Hannah Turner.

The next morning, after eating a breakfast prepared by Mrs. Turner, Shearer took Francis down to the stage depot and boarded a coach bound for Hartford, Connecticut. At Hartford, they switched to a steamboat, and then continued south. After traveling via a combination of steamboats, trains, and stages, they arrived at Fredericksburg, Virginia, on September 15, where they lodged for several days at the Farmer's Hotel. It was at this hotel that Fredericksburg resident Thomas H. Lipscomb saw Francis, and, at some point, noticed that the boy was able to read handbills posted at the barber shop. This struck him as odd, since few black children in Virginia—whether free or enslaved—were able to read.

Lipscomb took it upon himself to look into the case, suspecting that Francis may have been kidnapped from the North. His motives are not obvious, since he was a slave trader himself.[161] Perhaps he was concerned about the injustice of a free person being enslaved, or perhaps he felt that incidents of kidnapping reflected badly on the business he was engaged in. Or, maybe he was looking to put out of business a competitor who was able to obtain slaves for little expense via kidnapping.

Whatever his motivation, Lipscomb went into action. He had Shearer arrested and went off in search of Francis, who had been sold to Francis L. Wilkinson (who had been involved in the kidnapping, a few weeks earlier, of Nahum G. Hazard, also from Massachusetts).[162] Wilkinson had taken a circuitous route out of Richmond to bring Francis to his home in Cartersville, Virginia (which, Lipscomb suggested, was to avoid being associated with the earlier kidnapping, since Wilkinson had put Hazard up for sale in Richmond).

Lipscomb undertook a quest to find Francis, traveling with some assistants to Richmond, then proceeding to Cartersville. In that town, at Wilkinson's home, he and some "officers of justice" got Wilkinson out of bed and confronted him. Wilkinson at first denied that the Francis boy was there, but Lipscomb "firmly assured him that denial was vain, inasmuch as he had traced him step by step from Fredericksburg, and had in his possession ample proofs of his guilt." Francis, housed in the cellar along with other children, was called by Wilkinson, and Lipscomb removed him and took both him and Wilkinson back to Fredericksburg.

Meanwhile, Fredericksburg mayor Benjamin Clark had composed a letter. It was addressed to the mayor of Worcester, because Shearer "did not know their [Sidney's parents'] names, had never seen them but once, and then for an hour only." Upon being questioned, Shearer had admitted that the boy was free but claimed that his parents had "permitted this boy to come with him." Shearer's story, Clark wrote, "is so absurd to create a strong impression that he is a kidnapper."[163]

Clark also wrote that Dickinson Shearer (apparently Shearer used his real name in Virginia) had shown up in Fredericksburg with a black youth whom he called Franklin, saying he was his slave. Suspicions had been raised, an investigation had been undertaken, and Shearer was under arrest. Clark requested that authorities in Worcester look into the matter, and that they send evidence "to prove the boy's freedom and to identify him," pointing out that the identification must be made by "some white person." The case provided Worcester abolitionists an "opportunity of displaying their human feelings."[164]

Clark asked that Shearer's background be checked, saying he understood he was from "Pelham, Massachusetts" (he should have said Palmer) and that a Dr. Shearer there was his brother. Efforts were underway in Fredericksburg to find the boy, and "all that humanity requires will be done here" to retrieve him. Though Shearer was in custody, he "cannot be long detained without evidence," and Clark asked that sworn statements be sent and someone dispatched immediately to identify the victim.

On September 23, the same day that the letter was received in Worcester, Diana Francis completed an affidavit relating the basic facts of how her son had come to leave home. (No time was wasted, it seems, in answering the letter from Fredericksburg.) Diana probably did the paperwork because her husband was away. (About two days after Sidney Francis had left the house, his father went to Palmer in search of him, and was there told by relatives of Shearer that the boy was further west, in Washington, Massachusetts, and he had headed to that place to find him.)[165] Waiting for the father's return would have caused delay in responding to the request from Virginia.

Also on the 23rd, an indictment was returned charging that Shearer and Turner "unlawfully, fraudulently, and wickedly ... did take, obtain and inveigle" Francis out of the state, with the intent to "sell and transfer" him as a slave.[166]

Authorities in Massachusetts began a series of steps toward the goals of having Francis returned home and of ensuring that his kidnappers were brought to justice. Two men, brothers George M. Rice and Benjamin P. Rice, were sent to Fredericksburg to rescue Francis (as per Clark's instructions, presumably one or both of them knew the boy personally and could verify that he was indeed a free person). The Rice brothers received good cooperation from citizens in Virginia.[167] Sidney Francis soon was on his way back to Worcester.[168]

Ivers Phillips, a deputy sheriff of Worcester County,[169] was sent to Virginia by Massachusetts governor Edward Everett to take custody of the suspects and take them back to face justice in Massachusetts.[170] Shearer and Wilkinson both sought to be released on bail, but their requests were denied.[171] Though a Fredericksburg paper said it was expected that the suspects would be turned over to Massachusetts authorities, there may have been some contention between the two jurisdictions: "The officers who were sent out to Virginia by Gov. Everett ... to demand Wilkinson and Shearer for trial, have returned without them; they must first have some trial in Virginia, where Wilkinson will probably have his full trial, and Shearer will be sent back to Massachusetts."[172] It was also reported that a decision had been reached that *both* men would be sent to Massachusetts for their encounter with justice.[173] As the process of bringing Shearer to Massachusetts progressed, Turner, still living in the Bay State, was arrested on September 27. Shearer, in custody of Phillips, returned to Worcester on November 28.[174] Wilkinson was not brought to Massachusetts, and Shearer was "certain that W. will not be brought to Mass. for trial."[175]

On January 23, 1840, the two who had been apprehended were put on trial in Worcester before the Court of Common Pleas for Criminal Cases. Over 30 people testified, some called by the prosecution and some by the defense attorneys. District Attorney Col. Pliny Merrick presented the government's case, and defendants Shearer and Turner were represented by Isaac C. Bates, Ira M. Barton, and Reuben A. Chapman (the latter from Springfield).[176]

Some of the most convincing evidence was provided by the Francis family themselves. Sidney's mother and father testified as to their conversations with Shearer and Turner (Shearer had done most of the talking), and young Sidney himself told of his going away with the two men, being fed at the Palmer home of Shearer's brother, Dr. Marcus M. Shearer, and staying overnight with Turner's parents. The following morning, Shearer had taken him onto the stage bound for Hartford, Connecticut, and Francis related the journey—via steamboat, railroads, and stagecoaches—that finally landed him in Fredericksburg, Virginia, where "A man then came and bought me."[177]

Other testimony was given by two people who had been present when the kidnappers had spoken with Sidney's parents, as well as several whom Shearer had queried about the availability of young black boys who could go live with him in Palmer. Joshua B. Fowle, who had been in charge of the poor house in Shirley, Massachusetts, told how Turner, accompanied by William Little (a cousin of Turner's mother), had asked him the previous fall about taking away some black children.

Surely one of the most compelling witnesses—and one who received the approbation of the Massachusetts press—was Thomas H. Lipscomb. He was sometimes referred to as J. P. Lipscomb, and with "Esq." following his name. He may have been a justice of the peace in Fredericksburg, which could help explain the actions he took in seeing that Shearer and Wilkinson were arrested, and to find the kidnapped boy. The jury must have been impressed by this "voluntary witness" who had traveled so far and who had his arm in a sling due to a broken arm.[178]

A review of the testimony shows that the district attorney presented a very solid case, so strong a case, in fact, that Bates, representing Shearer, told the jury that he probably should be convicted for "inveigling away the boy under false pretences [*sic*]."[179]

The defense's case made use of relatives of Shearer and Turner, supporting the idea that they were merely following up on a request by Turner's mother that he find her a young black girl to help her or, failing that, an older black boy. Some doubt was cast on whether Shearer had intended to sell Francis into slavery or had simply taken him to Virginia to be his servant. (Evidence was presented that he had previously lived in Massachusetts but had relocated, first to Canada, then to Virginia. He had returned to Massachusetts in 1839 to try to collect on an inheritance—and had been unsuccessful.) In his closing statement, Bates pointed out that Shearer's intent to make Francis a slave—required by the second count of the indictment—had in no way been proven. Chapman, addressing the jury on behalf of Turner, noted that it had never been shown how he was to have benefited from the crime, nor that he understood Shearer's real purpose. Evidence showed that he was merely seeking a servant for his parents.[180]

Merrick, summing up for the prosecution, spent little time discussing Shearer, as the proof of his guilt seemed very clear. He carefully reviewed the evidence showing "that Turner was an active participant in the crime and must have known Shearer's object." Why, he argued, would he think that Shearer would take a free child to Virginia, when it was against the law to bring free persons of color there? The contention that Turner sought a helper for his parents was "a mere pretence [*sic*], as an after thought." If this were his objective, why did he stop pursuing it once Francis had been obtained? And why, when Francis stayed overnight at the Turner home, did his mother not express any interest in his remaining there as her servant?[181]

At last the case was turned over to the jurors, who deliberated for less than an hour. Both men were found guilty, though it was recommended that mercy be extended toward Turner. His attorney having entered objections, the judge postponed Turner's sentencing. Shearer's punishment was announced at once: two days of solitary confinement, followed by seven years at hard labor in state prison. Later on, Turner was sentenced to 18 months in prison. The maximum sentence each could have received, as spelled out in Section 20 of Chapter 125 of the Revised Statutes of Massachusetts, was 10 years in state prison, or a fine of up to $1,000 plus up to two years' confinement in a county jail.[182]

In the aftermath of the trial, Sidney Francis presumably led a typical, though short, life. He worked as a carpenter, dying in Worcester on March 2, 1850.[183]

As for his abductors: Turner is probably the E. M. Turner who later operated a hotel in Southbridge, Massachusetts. He died in 1886 and is buried with family members at Palmer.[184] Shearer, after completing his prison sentence, lived in Massachusetts until 1850. He then left the state, apparently never to return. Nonetheless, he was sued in 1856 by Turner's father, who sought compensation for his expenses connected with the kidnapping trial (which he had paid, since Shearer had no wherewithal at the time). This suit was decided in Turner's favor, with Shearer ordered to pay Col. Turner $271.[185]

ROBERT GARRISON

See Stephen Dickinson, Robert Garrison, and Isaac Wright.

ABBY GUY

Abby Guy[186] was a woman with a white complexion, who lived in Arkansas in the 1840s and 1850s. She had married a white man with the surname Guy. Prior to being brought to Arkansas in 1844, she had been a slave in Alabama, but in Arkansas, she had lived the life of a free person.

Following the death of her husband, her previous master, William Daniel, claimed that Guy and her children were his slaves. She went to court, explaining at various times that either she or her mother had been kidnapped and sold into slavery.

It took a series of court trials and appeals to resolve the matter. Instead of investigating the kidnapping claims, in order to determine her legal status, Guy's physical appearance and behavior were the main factors in the proceedings. It was ultimately decided in court that she and her children were free persons, and not slaves.

WILSON GEORGE HAYS AND CHARLES SMITH

Wilson George Hays was from Ohio,[187] and Charles Smith had been a resident of Brownsville, Pennsylvania.[188] Both had been born free and had gone to Lawrence, Kansas, where they worked as cooks at the

Eldridge House.[189] In 1858, free blacks in Lawrence became concerned following a spate of kidnappings in that area, and they sought assistance from some of the white residents. A process was begun to help black citizens to relocate to areas were they would enjoy greater safety.

Several trips were made, with white men (including John Brown) escorting blacks as they traveled. Hays and Smith were on one such journey, led by Dr. John Doy. Doy was accompanied by his son, Charles, and a white man name Clough. Before starting out, Charles Doy had the people being escorted show him their free papers. Out of the 13 men, women, and children being escorted to Holton, Kansas (which was on the way to Iowa, their ultimate destination), only Hays and Smith did not have documentation of their status,[190] but since it was known that they had been freeborn, they were allowed on the trip. Traveling in several wagons, the party was ambushed not far from Lawrence by a group of men (mostly from Missouri, but including some Lawrence men whom Dr. Doy recognized). Though the black men were armed, the attackers had the drop on them, and they did not use their weapons.

Doy, confronting the attackers, asked "if they had any papers to show that any of the colored people were claimed as slaves, or if their professed owners were present." The group's response was to call him a "nigger thief."[191]

Taken across the Missouri River, most of the blacks were parceled out to Missourians from whom they supposedly had run away. These were: Ransom Winston, "says he belongs to the estate of Jos. Winston, of St. Clair County, Mo."; Dan Bright, "belongs to widow Bright in McGee's addition to Kansas City, Mo."; Abe Rosbey, his wife, and two children (one age 5 and the other 18 months), "says he belongs to Rosbey of West port, Mo."; Ben Logan, "belongs to Geo. Kirk in McGee's Addition to Kansas City, Mo."; a 22-year-old girl named Malinda, "belongs to Mrs. S. M. Wilson, Clay county, Mo."; Catharine West, "belongs to T. H. West, Kansas City, Mo."; Mary Russell, "belongs to W. H. Russell, Leavenworth City"; and Dick, "belongs to W. A. Newman, Weston, Mo." These people, it may be presumed, became slaves to the associated "owners."[192]

Hays and Smith were uncooperative and could not be forced to say from which masters they had supposedly run away.[193] Dr. Doy, held along with his son at the jail in Platte City, Missouri (pending their trial as "negro thieves"), saw Hays and Smith when those two were brought to that jail from an attic in Weston, Missouri, where they had at first been kept with the other people of color. The others "had been taken away forcibly or prevailed on to choose masters."[194]

There, Jake Hurd and George Robbins told Hays, Smith, and William Riley, another black from Lawrence, that "they had better choose masters as the others had done, and not get into any more trouble."[195] The three men responded that they would rather stay in the jail, and wait until friends showed up with proof of their freedom. They were left at the jail, and upon Doy's advice, they asked the jailer to have a magistrate come see them, but that never happened.[196]

On February 3, Doy witnessed an ugly scene when Hurd returned, intent on taking Hays and Smith away. They refused to leave with him, again saying they preferred to wait until papers showing they were free had arrived. This elicited, from Hurd: "I'm your master now, you d—d niggers, and by G-d I'll make you mind me." He then "whipped them most unmercifully to make them confess they were slaves."[197] Despite the inflicted brutality, Hays and Smith still would not deny they were free men, and Hurd apparently decided that it was not all that important anyway, and left with both men, cuffing one in the face when he waved goodbye to Doy.

Doy called out to the jailer, to prevent the two men being taken away, but he would not help. "What was to be the fate of these poor men I could not doubt," wrote Doy. "I afterwards learned that he [Hurd] sold them in Independence, Missouri, for one thousand dollars apiece."[198]

After suffering many indignities, Doy was put on trial and found guilty. He received a five-year sentence, but before he could be transferred to the state prison, he was rescued by some daring men from Kansas. The following year, Doy published a narrative that related, along with the details of his ambush, incarceration, and rescue, several other stories of kidnapped blacks that he was aware of.

In his book, published in 1860, Doy noted that he had heard that Smith had been able to regain his freedom and had returned to Pennsylvania, though he admitted he had not been able to confirm that.[199]

NAHUM G. HAZARD

Nahum Gardner Hazard[200] was a young boy who lived with his family in an area of Lunenburg, Massachusetts, known as Flat Hill. On September 2, 1839, a neighbor, William Little, came to his home with two other men. Little had been informed by a man named Geeger that Mrs. Hazard was looking for a position for her son. Little gave her the impression that he knew the other men, who wanted a boy to go live with them and work at a tavern they operated in Washington in Berkshire County.[201]

It seemed like a good opportunity for the boy, since the men said he would be well cared for and that they would even see that he got an education when he was older. They assured her that her son would be brought home at any time, if she so desired. She decided to allow the two men, James Shearer[202] and Francis L. Wilkinson, to take Hazard with them.

Young Hazard was transported, not to Berkshire County, but to Richmond, Virginia, where he was left at a slave jail operated by Bacon Tait.[203] According to some accounts, Hazard played marbles with other children in the jail, but became bored and asked for a book to read.[204] Since it was not typical for African American children in Virginia to be literate, there was some question about where he had come from, and inquiries were sent to people in Massachusetts by William Jonathan Clark, who was connected with a vigilance committee in Richmond. Clark wrote letters on September 21 and September 23, addressed to George Whittemore, Amos Stearns, and George Brown,[205] who passed the letters on to George Bradburn, who was attending an antislavery meeting in Boston.[206]

Bradburn went to Lunenburg and found Mrs. Hazard in a meadow where she was picking cranberries. After speaking to her, he was certain that it was indeed her son Nahum who was held at Richmond. She told what had transpired on September 2, and admitted that she had been concerned and had had some friends write letters to check on Hazard's well-being.

Bradburn immediately had Little arrested as an accomplice, and he spoke to Governor Edward Everett about appointing someone to go to Virginia and bring Hazard home. Everett at first thought he had no authority to do so, but Bradburn pointed out that the legislature had adopted some resolves (instigated by Bradburn) that allowed the governor to act in such cases.[207] Everett then appointed Major William Brown,[208] whom Bradburn had learned was acquainted with Hazard. Brown went to Richmond at once, and Hazard soon rejoined his mother.

An indictment against Little, Shearer, and Wilkinson was returned on September 23, and Everett also sent paperwork to the governor of Virginia, seeking extradition of Shearer, Wilkinson, and other suspects in a different kidnapping.[209] Though Wilkinson was in jail in Fredericksburg, Virginia, efforts by Massachusetts to gain custody of him were fraught with difficulties. Wilkinson, perhaps through the efforts of friends, had been sued for an unpaid debt and, under Virginia law, could not be sent out of the state until that case was resolved.[210]

Worcester deputy sheriff Ivers Phillips, who had been sent to Virginia, reported to Governor Everett that the civil case would not be decided until May 1840 or later. Worse, Phillips found that the jail there was quite insecure, and was even told by Fredericksburg mayor Benjamin Clark that he was afraid that friends of Wilkinson would try to spring him. Phillips took the precaution of hiring a guard to watch the jail. Before he left for Massachusetts (with Dickinson Shearer, accused of having kidnapped Sidney O. Francis,[211] in custody), Phillips paid off and discharged the guard. Governor Everett wrote to his Virginia counterpart about his concerns, who had the warning forwarded to the jailer "to put him upon his guard."[212]

On February 3, 1840, Little was tried in Fitchburg for having aided and abetted the kidnappers, and was found innocent. Bradburn (who attended the trial) said that the evidence was inconclusive, and the newspapers noted that Little's deafness was a factor, that he had been misled by Shearer and Wilkinson, and that his role in the affair was merely telling them that Mrs. Hazard was interested in finding a position for her son, which was true.[213]

Efforts to bring Shearer and Wilkinson to justice failed, and they never paid for their crime.[214]

It seems likely that Wilkinson escaped from custody in Virginia, given the concerns expressed by various officials about that possibility. Dickinson Shearer, while in the custody of Ivers Phillips, told him "the friends of Wilkinson are determined to rescue him, and that he is certain that W. will not be brought to Mass. for trial."[215]

Hazard lived in Townsend, Massachusetts, eventually relocating to Leominster, where he resided for many years. He served as a soldier in the Civil War.[216]

PATIENCE HICKS

Patience Hicks was a young white woman who lived with her mother in Columbus, Georgia. In March 1859, James C. Wilson stayed at their home, where he was sick for part of the time. Wilson apparently became infatuated with Hicks and tried to get her to marry him, but her mother, Cassey Ann Hicks, would not allow it. Wilson took Patience to the house of Rev. John Guilford in Henry County, Alabama, to whom he sold her as a slave. Because she had been in the sun a great deal, her complexion was "rather dark." A newspaper at the time said that "we think that we have seen a great many people who are recognized as white persons, who are of a darker complexion than this girl, even in her present condition."[217]

In August, Patience's mother initiated a lawsuit against Guilford. She could do this because she, her daughter, and her granddaughter were white. In a previous case in Alabama (*Field v. Walker*), it had been determined "that persons of color could not try their right to freedom on *habeas corpus*."[218] The suit sought the release of Patience and her infant daughter, who "are not slaves, but free white persons."[219]

In court, four witnesses "proved beyond the possibility of a doubt that the said Patience L. and her daughter, Cassey Ann, are free white persons." Contrary to the story related by a newspaper that Wilson was a spurned suitor, evidence showed that Hicks was "decoyed from her house, under promise of marriage, by said James C. Wilson."[220] One account said that the daughter of Hicks was born after Wilson had sold her to Guilford, and inferred that Wilson was the father, and "not the first kidnapper who has sold poor dishonored white girls into slavery."[221]

Guilford offered testimony that Hicks was a black person and a slave, whom Wilson had bought from someone named Jones in Florida.[222] But it was also said that Guilford, despite knowing Hicks was free, "did everything in his power to retain her as his slave."[223]

Hicks and her daughter were "discharged from the service of said John Guilford" by Judge G. W. Williams. Guilford appealed the case, not in order to re-enslave the females, but to avoid paying the court costs as he had been ordered to do.[224] On appeal, it was ruled that, because Hicks and her daughter were white "they could not, under our law, be slaves" since "no person can have property in a white person."[225]

The case of Hicks attained some notoriety because she was white and poor. The *National Era* asked: "How many of the hundred thousand illiterate poor whites of Virginia have been thus disposed of in the Southern markets[?]" The number of "such poor whites there [who] are now writhing under the lash of the slavedriver, God only knows." Hicks had been released because: "witnesses happened to be at hand who could prove the freedom of the poor girl; but if she had been kidnapped in Virginia or North Carolina, instead of a neighboring county in Georgia, her doom as a slave for life would have been sealed forever!"[226]

JOHN HIGHT AND DANIEL PRUE

John Hight and Daniel Prue were free men of color who lived and worked in the Geneva area in central New York State.[227] Daniel Prue, age 18 in 1855, lived with his parents and his five younger siblings.[228]

In November 1857, a young man with the impressive name of Napoleon Bonaparte Van Tuyl worked as a store clerk in Geneva,

New York.[229] In 1855, Van Tuyl lived with his parents in Penn Yan, where his father was a bookkeeper.[230] Apparently not content with what he earned at the store, he developed a scheme to make some fast money. He approached Hight and Prue, offering them a chance for a good-paying job at a hotel in Columbus, Ohio.[231] They accepted this offer.

The three men departed by train, headed for Ohio. During the trip, Van Tuyl struck up a conversation with some strangers on the train, and told them he had found two runaways and was taking them back to Tennessee. Prue apparently overheard part of this conversation.[232] He became very nervous and got off the train at a town called Carlisle. Van Tuyl called on his new acquaintances for assistance. One, Jenkins, tried to help Van Tuyl get Prue back onto the train, but they could not. Van Tuyl then asked the other two men to take charge of Hight and take him to Kentucky, while he and Jenkins went back after Prue.

Getting off the train at the next opportunity, they then traveled back to Carlisle, and they located Prue in Franklin, Ohio. Though they tried to retake him, onlookers prevented it, and Van Tuyl and Jenkins were arrested for kidnapping. People told Prue to leave the area, so he "made his way to Columbus, Ohio on foot, sleeping in barns and getting along the best he could."[233]

With Prue's departure, there was no witness against Van Tuyl and Jenkins, so they were released.[234] A letter was sent to Prue's father in Geneva that began with "Dan Prue is in trouble," and explained what had transpired.[235]

While Van Tuyl and Jenkins were thus occupied, the two other Kentucky men took Hight to Covington, Kentucky, and put him in a jail there. Van Tuyl and Jenkins arrived there a few days later, and Van Tuyl made a deal to sell Hight to Jenkins. Though he made out a bill of sale showing a purchase price of $750, he actually only took $500 from Jenkins, giving him a bargain for the trouble he had endured.[236]

Jenkins sold Hight to someone else right away, for the full $750. The buyer was Judge Lorenzo Graves, who took Hight to Warsaw, Kentucky, and then sent him to a slave pen in Louisville, "with instructions to have him sold at a certain price, the first opportunity."[237] Somewhere along the way, while being transported, Hight "informed a passenger of the facts in the case, and where he was from, and the information was communicated to his friends at Geneva."[238]

After the letters written by or for Hight and Prue reached Geneva, citizens there were exceedingly upset, and a request was made to Governor John A. King, who appointed attorney Calvin Walker as an agent to locate and rescue the two men, and to apprehend the kidnapper.[239]

Walker, along with Robert Lay, who knew both Prue and Hight (who had been a servant of his), left New York State and soon located Prue in Columbus, where he had gotten a job in a stable. Walker and Lay next went to Kentucky and were able to locate Graves, who agreed that Hight was a free man after reviewing the papers Walker had in his possession.[240] Graves sent word to the slave pen in Louisville that Hight should not be sold as he was a free man, and he went there with Walker and personally released Hight from the cell.

To ameliorate the situation, Graves gave Hight money and a present to take to his mother, and he accompanied the three New York men back to Cincinnati, having vowed that he would see Hight returned to a free state. Walker, Lay, and Hight then returned to Geneva.

Authorities there figured out where Van Tuyl was, after they intercepted a package that had been sent to his fiancée. Officer Ambrose Bedell therefore went to Niagara Falls, and located Van Tuyl—who had been spending freely—and placed him under arrest and took him back to Geneva.[241] Van Tuyl's return to the state caused some agitation. At Cortland, his life was threatened, and one woman tried to hit him with an iron bar. On his arrival in Geneva, "he was met at the rail road station by an immense crowd of intensely excited and indignant citizens, most of whom were black," and the officials had a hard time keeping him from being injured on his way to jail.[242]

Bail was set at $1,500, paid by his father and a Penn Yan lawyer,[243] but Van Tuyl skipped out.[244] He was located in New Orleans, taken back to Kentucky, and then brought back to New York to stand trial for inveigling.[245] Bail was set at $5,000 this time, but Van Tuyl left town once more, attempting to make it look as though he had been murdered.[246] He was located, in New Jersey this time, and brought back to face justice again.[247]

The jury was unable to reach a decision,[248] however, and a second trial was held.[249] This time a conviction—for inveigling—was obtained, and Van Tuyl was sentenced to two years at Auburn State Prison. (The maximum sentence for his crime was 10 years.) On the same day, a man who had been convicted of stealing two horses was sentenced to four years.[250]

Van Tuyl was committed to prison on April 16, 1859.[251] He served his two years, and died about a year after his release.[252]

Little seems to be known of Hight's activities afterward,[253] but Prue lived in Geneva for quite some time, served in the 8th Regiment of Colored Troops during the Civil War, and became unbalanced after receiving a wound at the Battle of Olustee in Florida. He died at the home of a relative in Canandaigua, New York, in 1893.[254]

WILLIAM HOUSTON

William Houston was born in Gibraltar around 1810. His father
was from San Domingo, and his mother was from London, England.
The family relocated to Liverpool, England, where his mother ran a
boarding house for sailors. Houston moved to London and lived there
for a while, but around 1840, he went to Liverpool and got a position
as a steward on a ship, *Broad Oak*, and went to New Orleans. After a
few days in New Orleans, he encountered the ship's captain[255] with
another man, whom the captain told of Houston's desire to return to
England. The man, Espana de Blanc, told Houston he could arrange
passage back there by traveling to New York first, so Houston boarded
a steamboat with de Blanc and headed upriver. When they reached
St. Martinville,[256] de Blanc took him off the boat, "forcibly took from
him his papers, so that he is deprived of important evidence of his
freedom,"[257] and put him to work as his cook. Houston was treated
as a slave for five years. Finally, he had an opportunity to talk to a lawyer, but when de Blanc learned this, he put Houston in chains and sent
him to New Orleans, where a cousin sold him to a man who kept
a bar.[258]

He was with this man for a short time, then was sold to a man
named Lynch, who ran a store. During the two years he was with
Lynch, he was hired out to work. This included him working for Captain William T. Willis, who had passed through New Orleans with a
group of soldiers on their way to fight in the war with Mexico.[259]
Houston, as a drummer, was at the battles of Monterey and Buena
Vista and received wounds during each, which necessitated several
months of recuperation in Tampico. When he was better, he returned
to New Orleans, where he became the property of a Mr. Richardson.[260]
Richardson learned that Houston might be a British subject and
refused to pay Lynch the purchase price. Houston ended up in jail,
sequestered until the dispute could be resolved. Months later, he was
sold by the sheriff, and his new owner was J. F. Lapice.[261]

Houston was then able to contact the British consul, William
Mure,[262] who helped him obtain some legal support, and he instigated
a lawsuit against Lapice, seeking his freedom. Houston was sequestered by Sheriff Lewis,[263] pending the settlement of the litigation.
In jail, he worked as a cook and a white-washer. After over a year, he
believed he had been forgotten and wrote to Consul Mure, who came
to the jail and asked if he was prepared to sail to England that night.
Houston was, and was soon on board the *Ann Doherty*, which reached
Liverpool on January 1, 1852.[264]

Several months after his return to England, Houston sought redress in the courts there. He made a complaint with a magistrate, against the ship captain from his voyage, years ago, to the United States, but the magistrate told him he could do nothing, as the captain was not within his jurisdiction.[265]

Reports of the experiences of this forlorn British subject were carried in many newspapers at the time, including the *Times-Picayune* in New Orleans, which mocked it as being a fabrication. Apparently, the story of an enslaved man suing to be freed, reported in another New Orleans paper just two years earlier,[266] as well as the recent decision of a local judge that his story was valid and that he indeed was free, was overlooked by the *Picayune*. It related his tale, taken from the *London Times* of March 23, but called it a "Munchausen [sic] story." Noting some inaccurate place-names mentioned by Houston, the paper concluded that: "The story is simply impossible." It added, defensively: "Nothing like this series of adventures could happen in Louisiana, under its laws or among its people." They printed the tale merely "as a specimen of Abolition falsehood and English credulity."[267]

A few weeks later, in a follow-up that described Houston as "an arrant impostor" who had been "swindling the English people out of their money," the *Picayune* provided a postscript. In England, a magistrate had come forward after hearing about Houston, and advised that the *Broad Oak*, the ship Houston said he had taken to New Orleans years before, had never sailed from Liverpool to New Orleans. As a result, monetary contributions that had been made to assist Houston were held back from him until the wishes of the subscribers could be determined.[268]

HARRISON HUBBARD

See James Clarkson, Harrison Hubbard, and Margaret Davis.

FRANK JACKSON

Frank Jackson was born of free parents in Mercer County, Pennsylvania, in about 1828. He was brought up by John Young, who was, by all reports, an ardent abolitionist.[269] Jackson lived in the New Castle area for some time.

Sometime around 1851, when Jackson was living in West Greenville, Pennsylvania, he had a chance to work for Charles May, a drover, and helped him take some horses to Virginia, where they were sold. Before leaving Virginia, however, May conducted some additional business, selling Jackson as a slave to Samuel Scott of Campbell County. This was the beginning of years of bondage for Jackson, during which he was owned by 10 to 12 different owners in the states of Virginia, South Carolina, and North Carolina.[270] In an attempt at "self-rescue," Jackson ran away from his master in Virginia, but was captured and then sold to a man by the name of Deshhazen.[271]

Jackson's absence had been noted by friends back in Pennsylvania, and in June 1851, they were notified that he was in jail in Campbell County and that he would be released if someone went there with his free papers. George C. Morgan, a tailor who was acquainted with Jackson, made the trip, only to find that Jackson was no longer there. He was told that he had been sold again, and was somewhere further south, so Morgan went back to Pennsylvania emptyhanded.[272]

Years later, a letter inquiring about Jackson was received in New Castle, Pennsylvania, from George Cameron Mendenhall, a North Carolina attorney.[273] Mendenhall was a Quaker who had fallen into disfavor for marrying outside the faith. He became a slaveowner, because of slaves who belonged to his wife.[274] Mendenhall had spoken to the Pennsylvania freeman, who was then a slave to Frederick W. Swann[275] in Moore County, North Carolina. He had run away from Swann and had been locked up in the jail there, which is where Mendenhall met him. Mendenhall felt Jackson's story was true and got from him names of friends in Pennsylvania, to whom he addressed letters.

Mendenhall had initiated legal proceedings on Jackson's behalf, and the process would require evidence from people in Pennsylvania to succeed. Depositions from some of Jackson's old friends were forwarded to North Carolina, and at the urging of Philadelphia's Passmore Williamson, Morgan went on a second mission to rescue Jackson, financed by contributions from Pennsylvania residents. (Morgan, feeling that having a military title would be beneficial during his time in the South, led people to believe that he was a colonel.) Official paperwork was sent to the governor of North Carolina, to make the process of freeing Jackson as smooth as possible.[276] Mendenhall had posted bonds so that Jackson could get out of jail, bought him some clothes, and took him to his residence, but Swann found out and came and retrieved his property.[277]

"Colonel" Morgan arrived just in time for the trial, which began on August 23, 1858. Mendenhall sought damages for Jackson, in the amount of $1,500. Jackson at first did not recognize Morgan, but when addressed by him, was elated. (He blew Morgan's cover, by referring to him as a tailor, so it was clear to those present that he was not a military man.)

At the trial, before Judge R. M. Saunders, the depositions from Pennsylvania were presented, and Morgan identified Jackson as a free person. The jury's decision was quick: Jackson was free and could leave immediately.

Jackson and Morgan began the trip back to Pennsylvania. Morgan had experienced good treatment from southerners during his mission, but he found that traveling with a free black presented challenges. In several cities, he had to put up bond so that Jackson could board trains, and at Baltimore, he had to call upon a preacher there, a former acquaintance from the Keystone State, to vouch for him before Jackson was allowed on the cars.

Jackson and Morgan passed through Philadelphia, and Jackson rejoined his parents in New Castle on September 6, 1858.[278] He remained in the area for a number of years, and, in 1863, went to New Brighton, Pennsylvania, and enlisted in the 41st Regiment of Colored Troops. Military records show he was a hospital assistant and a drummer while in the army.[279] After the war, he did odd jobs in order to support his family, all of whom had died by 1897.[280]

PETER JOHN LEE

Though Peter John Lee was usually described as a fugitive slave who escaped from Virginia with a number of others in 1833, his wife said that he had actually been a freeman there but decided to move to the North after being badly harassed.[281] His northern neighbors believed he was free, also.[282] In 1833, a number of men stole a boat in Northampton, Virginia, and traveled to New York. Afterward, the governor of Virginia requested that New York governor William L. Marcy locate 17 men involved in the incident and turn them over to Edward R. Waddy for transportation back to Virginia. There, they would be tried for theft of the vessel. It is significant that the men were requisitioned as fugitives from justice, and not as escaped slaves. (If Lee was indeed free, as his wife claimed, he may have taken the lead in the escape, deciding to liberate some slaves as well as remove himself from a place where he had been persecuted.)[283]

Marcy's warrant was remarkably imprecise.[284] Many of the alleged participants in the theft of the boat were identified only by first name. The warrant required any law enforcement officials throughout the state to look for the men and to turn them over to Waddy. One man, who was returned to Virginia not long after the incident, was tried and sentenced to be hung. Instead, he was pardoned and sent away as a slave—suggesting that the motive was the return of slaves, rather than the apprehension and punishment of felons.[285]

For several years after his arrival in New York, Lee lived as a free man. He gained employment with Seth Lyon, a Connecticut justice of the peace, and lived in Byram, Connecticut, at the state line with New York.[286] Lee had a wife and the couple had two children and reportedly were happy.

On November 20, 1836, he received word that an acquaintance of his wanted to see him in Rye, New York, a place he sometimes visited.[287] Once in New York State, Lee was grabbed by a group of men, perhaps as many as 12.[288] Among them were Tobias Boudinot and Daniel D. Nash, both New York City officials: Boudinot was a constable, and Nash was a police marshal.[289] Both men had developed reputations for catching runaway slaves and also for abducting free citizens on the pretext that they were fugitive slaves.[290]

Lee was gagged, tied up, and quickly taken away in a wagon. The party stopped at a Mamaroneck tavern on the way to New York, where Lee was treated to some liquor.[291] The next day, without any sort of official proceeding,[292] the captured man was put on board a ship bound for Virginia. There, he was put on trial and sentenced to hanging, but was instead turned over to a slaveholder, said to be his master.[293]

Due to the fact that Lee was arrested as an escaped felon rather than as a fugitive slave,[294] that the crime he was accused of had occurred over three years previously, and the suddenness of his arrest and removal from New York, there would seem to be serious question that he was actually a runaway. Those who apprehended him provided no evidence of his identity and did not follow the normal procedure for extraditions.[295]

Happily, Lee made another escape attempt some years later and again became free, possibly reaching Canada.[296]

WILLIAM AND PEGGY LUCAS

William and Peggy Lucas were two of the children born to Harry and Lucinda Lucas. Harry had been one of numerous slaves owned by Captain William Helm, a Virginia plantation owner. Helm decided to relocate to New York State and, around 1800, sold his plantation in Prince

William County, and with his family and belongings—including dozens of slaves—made a three-week journey to upstate New York.[297]

Helm settled for a while at Sodus Point on Lake Ontario, but in a few years relocated to Bath in Steuben County. One of Helm's slaves was a man named Austin Steward, and, thanks to Steward's autobiography, we have firsthand information on Helm's lifestyle. He was not careful with his money, and he loved to gamble. He purchased two farms in Bath, which were worked by his slaves. He also had a grist mill, where Steward was hired out to work.[298]

Not long after his wife died, Helm married the widow of one of his fellow Virginians. Over time, they grew apart and divorced, and the consequent alimony payments added to Helm's financial problems. He began selling off some of his slaves. Due to his financial problems, some of them were also sold at public auction, to settle his debts.[299] Helm eventually became discontented with his monetary situation and developed some plans to improve it.

Not only had a number of his slaves been sold, but many had also run away from him or become free due to provisions of state laws.[300] Helm decided to gather up some of his former chattels, take them to a slave state, and sell them. Steward explains that his first attempt involved staging a large party to which many of his former slaves were invited. He intended to abduct a number of them, but his motive became known, and a large fight broke out at the party. He therefore was not able to reclaim any of them.[301]

Following this failure, Helm obtained a covered wagon and, in 1818 or 1820,[302] gathered up a number of blacks from the vicinity of Bath,[303] tossing them into the wagon. He was assisted by a driver, along with a man with a whip who followed the wagon to guard against escapes.[304] On the way to Olean Point (from which river travel to Kentucky could be accomplished), many victims did manage to get away. After a delay at Olean, needed for construction of a boat, Helm began loading his "cargo," but this was met by resistance by some victims, including Harry and Lucinda Lucas.[305]

In the end, Helm was successful at abducting only two people: William and Peggy Lucas. These children were taken to Kentucky and sold. Friends and family in New York heard nothing of them after that.[306] Helms was tried for kidnapping in the Court of Oyer and Terminer at Bath in 1820 or 1821. He was found guilty, sentenced to six months in the county jail, and fined $100.[307] He was pardoned by the governor after serving about one month of his sentence[308] and died a pauper in 1826, reportedly having been taken care of in his final years by his one remaining slave.[309]

ISAAC MOORE

In 1858, 14-year-old Isaac Moore was a black teenager living with his mother at 231 Second Street in Manhattan.[310] He was described as an intelligent boy who could read and write well. On the morning of August 4, he was walking along Houston Street, not far from his home, when a tall, well-dressed man accosted him. The man at first tried to persuade Moore to go on board a ship docked in the East River at the foot of Third Street. When Moore refused, the man forcibly carried him to the schooner *Ann Ellis*,[311] where Moore was shut up in the hold for four days.

On Sunday, August 8, Moore was released from the hold, and was allowed to "go on deck and make himself useful."[312] He was given a tumbler and told to go fetch a glass of water for the captain, who was in his cabin. Up on deck, seeing that there was no one around, he threw the tumbler into the river and made his escape. Newspapers gave differing accounts of his getaway: he either jumped onto another ship docked next to the *Ann Ellis*, then jumped onto the dock; jumped onto another ship, then onto a passing canal boat, which took him to shore; or jumped directly into the water and was picked up by a canal boat.[313]

Once he was back on solid ground, he returned home, and, not long after, went to the 11th Precinct and told Police Captain Squires what had happened. Squires immediately dispatched one or more officers, but when they arrived at the pier, it was found that the *Ann Ellis* had already shoved off and was on its way out to sea. The ship was registered in Virginia, and it was assumed it was heading for that state.[314]

Though Moore was certainly abducted and confined, his sale as a slave was aborted. In all likelihood, the perpetrator's intent was to take him south—on a schooner perhaps filled with other victims—and sell him for financial profit. "The police seem to believe that there has been a deliberate attempt to kidnap this boy for the purpose of carrying him off South and selling him into slavery."[315]

CATHARINE, DAVID, JAMES AND MARTHA MORRIS

Elijah Morris came to Golconda, Illinois, sometime in the early 1840s. As required by law, he presented his free papers to a judge, which showed that a court in Davidson County, Tennessee, had determined him to be free.[316] The family lived in peace until the night of October 1, 1842, when a number of men stormed into their home, taking away with them about $600 worth of gold and silver and four children: Catharine (aged 11), Martha (9), David (6), and James (5).

Before the sun had risen, Morris alerted his neighbors, and an immediate attempt was made to track the kidnappers and the stolen children, but with no success. Some notices were printed in newspapers seeking information on the crime,[317] but there was still no progress in identifying the criminals, even though a reward was offered. "It was evident that there could be but one object in view by the kidnappers, and this limited the search to the slave-holding states."[318]

The local sheriff, William Rhodes, eventually received information that the Morris children were slaves at a plantation in Mississippi (or in Mississippi County, Arkansas).[319] He and Elijah Morris traveled to the plantation and asked the owner if he had purchased any slaves matching the descriptions of the missing children. He replied that he had. When he was informed that they might have been kidnapped, he agreed that if that were proven to him, he would give up any claim to them and let them go home. Rhodes suggested a plan to decide the matter: all three men would walk out to the field where the children were at work hoeing cotton and see if they recognized him (which he felt they would) and also their father, of course.

While the three men were still some distance from the children, one called out "La! yonder comes Mr. Rhodes, yes and papa, too!" Satisfied, the slaveowner said the young ones should leave with their father. He also presented Rhodes with a bill of sale, showing that he had bought them from a man by the name of William H. Vaughn. This man was known to the sheriff: there were suspicions that he had previously been a pirate, and it was known that he was heavily armed.[320]

Upon returning to Illinois, legal action was taken, and Vaughn was summoned before a Pope County grand jury.[321] It was believed not only that he knew who the kidnappers were, but also "that he actually knew the children, that it was he who planned not only this outrage but others of a like nature."[322] Vaughn at first would not say who had delivered the children to him, but finally was prevailed upon to do so. He named six men—Joshua Handly, Peyton Gordon, Caleb Slankard and John Simpkins, all of Pope County, and Joe Lynn and Hiram Campbell, who were residents of Massac County.

The local men were arrested and jailed without delay, and Lynn and Campbell surrendered themselves not long afterward and were able to make bail. Ten days later, Vaughn died suddenly of apoplexy, which local people believed "came on immediately after taking a drink of whiskey given him by one of the parties who had been indicted."[323] Since Vaughn had been the only person who could testify concerning the identity of the men who had abducted the children, the suspects were released for lack of evidence.[324]

ALEXINA MORRISON

Alexina Morrison, who appeared to be a young white woman, claimed that she was the child of white parents who had been kidnapped in Little Rock, Arkansas, in 1857 and then sold as a slave in New Orleans.[325] She ran away from the man who had purchased her, James White, a slave trader. White sought to reclaim his property, but Morrison sued for her freedom. Morrison's case was tried several times. One trial in Jefferson Parish, Louisiana, ended in a hung jury. The case was tried again, with the venue changed to New Orleans.

Despite her story of having been abducted, her lawyers presented no evidence of her having been kidnapped (though unsuccessful attempts were made to obtain testimony from some friends of Morrison, which might have supported her story).[326] Instead, her counsel argued that she was wrongly enslaved because she was white—physicians and other witnesses testified that her appearance showed no evidence of African descent.

White's attorneys presented proof in support of her previous, legal bondage as a slave named Jane Morrison. Their evidence countered the tale of kidnapping, but it was rejected by the judge due to various flaws. This time, the jury was able to reach a decision: Morrison was white and free.

White appealed the case, and the Louisiana Supreme Court took it up. They determined that the evidence bearing on Morrison's status as a slave, and of her mother's having been a slave, should have been allowed, and remanded the case for yet another trial that would include the previously rejected evidence. Morrison could not rely on "the presumption of freedom, arising from her color."[327]

Though evidence was presented regarding her history (which, the Supreme Court said, showed that the "plaintiff was born a slave, the offspring of a mulatto woman slave" who had been conveyed from her original owner [and owner of her mother] to White), it was noted that, concerning her story of kidnapping: "It is remarkable that she has not made the faintest approach toward establishing these allegations ... by proof."[328] A jury again decided that she was not a slave. The jury was not unanimous in its decision, but Morrison agreed to accept a verdict reached by the majority.[329]

Regrettably, details of Morrison's abduction were never presented in a court of law. But, since the proof she submitted in support of her claim to freedom was limited to the color of her skin, revealing the story of her having been kidnapped would seem to have been of little benefit to her—unless it had actually occurred.

SALOME MULLER

Salome Muller and her family were among several hundred German immigrants who arrived at New Orleans in 1818. As a result of an arrangement with the captain of one of the ships that brought them from Europe, her family and some of the other Germans were made indentured servants. Muller's father and surviving brother (her baby brother and her mother had passed away before reaching America) died as they were being transported north from New Orleans. Somehow Muller (and perhaps her sister Dorothea as well) was made into a slave for life, even though she was white. She was the property of New Orleans businessman John F. Miller for years. Miller sold her in 1838 to Louis Belmonti, also of New Orleans.

Though years before, some of the other Germans had tried to locate the two missing sisters, they had had no luck. In 1843, a woman named Kari Rouff (known as Madame Kari) saw Muller while in Belmonti's shop and recognized her despite the passage of so many years. She took Muller to see Eva Schuber, another one of the Germans who had arrived in New Orleans in 1818, and Schuber also recognized her, saying: "here is the long lost Salome Muller!"[330]

Muller initiated a freedom suit, which she could do in Louisiana.[331] She also sued Miller for damages. Miller published a statement intended to "prevent the forming a hasty and erroneous opinion upon the subject." He claimed that the woman was a slave who had been left with him by Anthony Williams, who had been unable to sell her in Alabama. Williams "left the girls with me to be sold" and Miller paid him a $100 advance. In February 1823, Miller found a buyer—his mother—and she had been in their possession up until the time he sold her to Belmonti. Obviously concerned about his reputation, Miller pointed out that "no person who has ever known me can believe that I could be capable, knowingly, of attempting to convert a white apprentice into a slave for life."[332] (Was he leaving himself a little wiggle room by including the word "knowingly"?)

In a trial in New Orleans against Belmonti and Miller, evidence was presented by both sides. In the end, the judge decided that the slaveholders' case was more convincing and ruled that Muller *was* a slave. Muller's attorneys appealed to the Louisiana Supreme Court. New evidence was presented before them, and this time, the decision was that Muller was a free white woman, who had been held in bondage contrary to law. One of Muller's attorneys said that: "with tears in their eyes, the Judges of this court have boldly proclaimed the righteousness of her prayer, and commanded her shackles to fall!"[333]

There was a high level of interest in the case at the time. A pamphlet was published about it,[334] and it was widely covered by newspapers around the nation during various stages of the litigation.[335]

Further proceedings included an unsuccessful action against Muller by Miller, claiming fraud on her part,[336] and an effort by Muller to obtain the release of her children held by Miller.[337] (Results of her attempt to obtain custody of her children are not evident.)

Years later, in 1855, details of the story circulated again, when a book—perhaps inspired by the Muller case—was published about a fictitious Ida May, a white girl made into a slave.[338] Muller's story continues to fascinate Americans, with several articles and books in recent years.[339]

SOLOMON NORTHUP

Solomon Northup's narrative has been widely used through the years as a source of information on slavery in the South.[340] But its firsthand account of a kidnapping also reveals a great deal about how crimes of this nature were carried out.

The two men who "inveigled" Northup did not live far away from him—they were from an adjoining county. They therefore would have been familiar with the seasonal nature of business in Saratoga Springs, New York, a popular resort. In the warm months, the hotels and other establishments there did banner business, and employment was plentiful. African Americans held many of these jobs.[341] During the winters, work was not as easy to find. Northup recorded that he would make what income he could by manual labor, including working on railroad construction and laboring on Champlain Canal repair projects.

The men who lured Northup away from home approached him late in March 1841, before Saratoga's busy season. They told Northup their names were Merrill Brown and Abram Hamilton, but they were actually Alexander Merrill and Joseph Russell (both from nearby Fulton County). They undoubtedly understood that there would be workers in Saratoga who would be low on funds at that time of year. They spent several days in Saratoga before they selected Northup as a potential victim and approached him.[342]

Appealing to his sense of pride in his musical talent, they said they had heard of his skill with the fiddle, and that they had been finding it difficult to obtain musicians for a circus with which they were connected. They then made him an offer: if he would go away with them for a short while, they would reward him with excellent pay. Northup agreed to go to New York City with them. During the trip there, the men showed Northup much kindness and consideration. They no doubt wanted him to feel that they could be trusted, especially since they planned—once they reached New York—to request that he accompany them out of the state and go to Washington, D.C.

Before they left New York, the men suggested going to an office where free papers could be obtained for Northup. Doing so likely served several purposes: first, it put Northup further at ease; and second, it would make it easier for them to travel with a person of color. An undocumented African American could be challenged, even when in the company of a white person.[343] The men cautioned Northup about going out on the streets of Washington alone. Had he done so, with no free papers, he could have been taken for a slave, and put in a slave jail from which they would probably have had difficulty regaining custody of him—after all, they had no bill of sale or other paperwork saying he was their slave.

In Washington, Northup found that his "employers" were especially generous to him, giving him more cash than was actually due him (which they well knew they would soon get back). Ultimate con artists, they wanted him to think of them solely as friends, and to have no suspicion of their real motives.

On the day of President William Henry Harrison's funeral procession, the men walked throughout the city with Northup, giving him a chance to take in the sights. Little business was carried out on that day in the city, so they took the opportunity to treat him as a friend—stopping at various drinking establishments, and sharing liquor with him. Northup, rather than being treated to beverages, was probably being displayed to potential purchasers; slave dealers often conducted business in taverns.

Northup became quite ill overnight, and woke up in Williams' Slave Pen. Beatings served to silence his claims to freedom. Thus began his extended period as a slave, related in detail in his autobiography, *Twelve Years a Slave*.

After his rescue years later, Northup's return home to New York State was delayed by a stopover in Washington, D.C., during which he and his rescuer, attorney Henry B. Northup, brought charges against James H. Birch, the slave trader who had sent him to Louisiana years earlier. The effort was unsuccessful, partly because Northup, being black, could not legally testify in court. The following year, after the publication of his book, a reader came forward who was able to identify the men who had tricked Northup into going away. Though an indictment was handed down and criminal proceedings took place, the kidnappers were never convicted. The case against them was dropped in 1857.[344]

At various times, stories were published alleging that Northup had colluded with his kidnappers, expecting to share in the proceeds from his own sale.[345] Northup (who strongly denied allegations of collusion)[346] was not the only kidnap victim to be accused of plotting to sell himself. It was also said of Eli Terry, and to a lesser extent, George Armstrong.[347]

DANIEL PRUE

See John Hight and Daniel Prue.

CHARLES SMITH

See Wilson George Hays and Charles Smith.

GEORGE WASHINGTON TALBOT

George Washington Talbot was a free black living in Cecil County, Maryland. In 1857, he was confined in the jail at Elkton for having disturbed a religious event at Principio. While Talbot was in jail, another person of color escaped, and Sheriff John Poole recruited Talbot to help him apprehend the escapee. Perhaps they pursued the man, or perhaps it was a ruse, because Poole ended up taking Talbot to Richmond, Virginia, where he met a man named Beatty. Talbot was offered for sale to slave dealers.[348]

The dealers, Pulliam and Company, were reluctant to conclude a deal because Poole did not have any paperwork showing he owned Talbot, who resolutely claimed to be free and even gave some information about his place of residence. Poole insisted the man was a slave, and went back to Maryland so that he could get documents to satisfy the traders. Back in Elkton, he forged a bill of sale and apparently got H. H. Mitchell, the clerk of the Cecil County Circuit Court, to prepare an affidavit confirming his familiarity[349] with the parties involved. An official seal was even used to give greater authenticity to the documents.

Poole went back to Richmond with the materials and presented them to the traders. He received a cash payment of $150, and a check for the balance of the agreed-upon price of $1,050. The bank having closed for the day, Poole could not cash it, and he and Beatty, his partner in crime, then went to Baltimore. Beatty tried to cash the check at a bank there, but being unknown to the bank's staff, he was told he needed proof of his identity. He left the bank in order to obtain this, leaving the check with the bankers.

The bankers became suspicious, and the local authorities put Beatty in jail and also arranged for Poole to be incarcerated at Elkton, where he had gone. Deputy Marshal Stephen H. Manly, a Baltimore policeman,[350] went to Richmond to find Talbot and to procure what evidence he could. He located Talbot, and asked that the Pulliam firm turn over the paperwork they had received from Poole. They would not do so, unless he paid them the $150 they had already paid out. Pulliam and Company also offered to sell the papers to a Maryland attorney representing the kidnappers, who had shown up. He agreed to purchase the papers but had to return to Maryland in order to get the funds to do so.

Manly renewed his request for the evidence and, after being denied again, started a legal proceeding to have both Talbot and the documents turned over to him. After a hearing, Judge Meredith ordered that his request be honored, and Manly went back to Maryland with Talbot (who was returned to the jail, since there was still a charge pending against him) and the documents, which in fact were proven to have been forged.[351]

Because Poole, as sheriff, was in control of the jail at Elkton, he was instead confined in another building, for a time at least. He was then taken to Towsontown and, in December 1857, he was transferred from there to the jail in Elkton.[352] On the day after Christmas in 1857, he was released when some friends put up bail, in the amount of $4,000. He was jailed again when these men withdrew their security, however. He escaped from custody, probably with assistance, in June 1858, and a reward of $200 was offered for his recapture. He probably remained at large.[353]

SARAH TAYLOR

Sarah Taylor (who was also known by the name Sarah Harrison) lived with her family in New York City. In March 1858, a man named James P. Finley (also known by the alias Harry A. Howard), a Canadian whose manners were "very affable and gentlemanly," along with a woman of questionable character named Ann Brainard (or Ann Howard), convinced the mother of the 14-year-old girl to allow them to take her to Newark, New Jersey, where it was planned that she would work as a servant.[354]

They left New York by train on March 8, but did not get off at Newark. They instead went to Washington, D.C., and lodged at Willard's Hotel. The couple began trying to sell Taylor to a slave trader (even though slave trading had been banned in the city in 1850, as part of the Compromise of 1850). Taylor figured out that her companions were attempting to sell her (they were asking for $600), and she "made so much trouble about it" that the couple "thought it best to decamp to Maryland."[355]

The hotel's proprietor, a Mr. Willard, became aware of the incident and sent a telegram to New York City mayor Daniel F. Tiemann, who looked into the matter. Taylor's mother was located in New York, and she provided an affidavit detailing what had taken place. Tiemann asked Willard to keep Taylor at the hotel pending the arrival of some police officers in Washington.

Two policemen, Barry and Lusk, interviewed a New York City man, Dr. F. C. Clay, who knew Finley and had been with him on the train when it had left New York. The officers then went south. With the help of Willard, they determined that the couple had headed toward Baltimore, and eventually found out that Finley was staying in Ellicott's Mills in Howard County, Maryland. Barry went undercover as a postal clerk, waited for Finley to come to collect his mail, then followed him to a hotel where he also found the woman. The culprits were taken back to New York. Taylor was also taken home, and she rejoined her mother.[356]

Finley and his supposed wife were taken before the mayor on March 25, who then sent the case to the City Recorder.[357] They were indicted, and the Recorder set bail at $5,000 for each defendant. Present at the proceeding were antislavery activists Lewis Tappan and Dr. James McCune Smith, who paid the bond required to guarantee Taylor's appearance as a witness.[358]

In an appearance before Recorder George G. Barnard, Finley and his companion both pleaded not guilty. The case was put off until the court's next term, due to some of the witnesses being in Canada. Finley was tried in June, found guilty, and sentenced to two years in prison. He was pardoned by Governor Edwin D. Morgan the following January, with the stipulation that he return to Canada.[359] The resolution of the charges against the woman involved do not appear to have been reported.

ELI TERRY

Eli Terry lived with his father at Broad Ripple, near Indianapolis, Indiana. His father had been a free person of color in North Carolina,[360] who had relocated to Indiana. In October 1842, James Carter, who resided near the Terrys, hired the younger Terry to help him take some horses to Missouri, where he planned to sell them. Terry would also work for him there for one year.

Terry went, and the two men, along with Carter's son, reached Missouri without any problems. Per the arrangement, Terry remained with Carter for a year,[361] at the end of which Carter gave him a horse, bridle, and saddle as payment for his services. Plans to return to Indiana were indefinite, but one evening Carter told Terry to be ready to leave the following day.

As they began their trek, Terry noticed that they did not seem to be heading toward Indiana. He pointed this out to Carter, who informed him that he knew they were going in the wrong direction, but that he wanted to stop to see his brother, who lived near the Arkansas River. Following that, they would sell their horses and take a steamboat home.

Upon reaching the place where the brother resided, they found he was not there. Carter told Terry that he had found out that his brother had removed to Texas, and that they would be going there. As they approached Texas, Carter informed Terry that due to the laws there, Terry should pretend to be his slave rather than hold himself out to be a freeman. Terry followed Carter's advice.

A few miles from Clarksville, in Red River County, Carter left Terry and went into town with his son. When they returned, they took all the horses, leaving Terry behind. Not long afterward, a man came and collected Terry, because he had just bought him from Carter as a slave. Terry now recognized Carter's perfidy.

Carter, using the name William Brewer, had sold Terry to Edward West[362] on October 4, 1843, for $600.[363] Terry's "asserting that he was free availed nothing."[364] With his claim to freedom ignored,[365] Terry (now called "Jack") apparently tried to liberate himself, because he ran away several times.[366]

Back in Indiana, Terry's absence had been noticed, but nothing could be learned of his whereabouts. Finally, years later, John Ryman, a lawyer in Lawrenceburgh,[367] was given some information. Ryman had gone to New Orleans on business, and while there, he encountered a man from Clarksville, Texas, who told him of the sad story of the man from Indiana who was a slave, though claiming to be free. Ryman passed on this knowledge to members of the Society of Friends in Indiana, who raised funds to hire Ryman to go to Texas to seek Terry's release.[368]

Money was also raised to defray the expenses of the trip, which would also include two men who would be witnesses as to Terry's free status. These were Thomas W. Council,[369] who had known Terry's father in North Carolina, and Paris Harrison, from Hamilton County.[370] Armed with various documents that proved Terry was free, these three men set out on the arduous journey. Not knowing what sort of reaction they would get in Texas, they considered arming themselves with Bowie knives and pistols but decided against it, since Council believed it would make matters worse for them should they encounter a mob.[371]

They left Indiana in the first part of December 1849 and, after traveling almost a month, arrived in Clarksville. They were fortunate in that they soon found some people friendly to their cause, who informed them that "Jack" (as Terry was known there) now belonged to a man named Chatfield. A *habeas corpus* proceeding was initiated at once. (As luck would have it, the trio had arrived just before Chatfield planned to take his slave to New Orleans, where he intended to sell him.) Terry was at once sequestered by the local sheriff, a step that ensured he would not be removed from the area until the matter was resolved in a court of law. As word of what was going on got out (Council wrote that "the news spread like fire on a prairie, before a strong wind"),[372] citizens took quite an interest. Terry was taken to the office of an attorney named Morrill,[373] and a large crowd assembled there even before the sheriff arrived with Terry. Though there were some people in town who supported the rescuers, most did not. "If the law prevailed we were safe, if the mob triumphed, we were gone," Council observed.[374]

At the hearing, Judge Mills[375] asked that Terry look around the room and see if there was anyone there he recognized from Indiana. The man was probably somewhat puzzled, but soon spotted an old friend and cried out, "there is Mr. Harrison, and he knows I am free." Judge Mills questioned Terry at length. Chatfield, who owned Terry at that point in time, seemed not to be concerned about losing him and did not resist. West, a party to the whole business, was out of town, but his interest was represented by a man who argued against Terry's being released. Because of the absence of West, the judge postponed the proceedings until his return, but he did openly declare his satisfaction that Terry was a free man, that "he believed the negro was as free as he was."[376]

The judge's words helped relieve some of the tension among the crowd, some of whom had pointed out to the rescuers a tree branch upon which six people had previously been hanged. (Though the Clarksville newspaper indicated that "Jack" had been given up without resistance,[377] Council's account notes significant opposition.)

With West not due back in town for over a week, the Indiana men had no choice but to wait it out in Clarksville, but they were not molested. By the time the case was resumed, feelings seemed to have died down quite a bit. West's lawyer made a long speech, but Judge Mills did not find it persuasive, and he made his ruling that Terry was discharged from bondage and was free to leave at any time.

In opposition to the judge's declaration, an appeal to a higher court was mentioned by West's attorney, but Council pointed out that, in the event the appeal was unsuccessful, he would seek monetary damages for the years of service Terry had supplied, as well as for the pain and suffering he may have sustained as a result of beatings. To seal the deal, he offered to have Terry sign a document waiving his claims to any such remuneration. The intention to appeal was given up.

Despite the official conclusion, the Clarksville newspaper chose to lay some of the blame for the entire incident on the victim himself. Terry "for years had borne the character of a slave, and was brought here and sold as a slave, without asserting his freedom." The whole thing may have been "an intentional fraud in which the negro was a party colluding." If not an intentional fraud, "it was a passive fraud on his part," because he had not announced that he was a free man.[378]

The following year—after the release of another wrongfully enslaved person—Terry's case was again discussed: "there was no doubt that he had colluded with the man who sold him, to deceive the purchaser, and had afterwards made repeated attempts to escape."[379] It was pointedly noted that, despite resistance encountered by southerners trying to retrieve fugitive slaves in the northern states, Terry had been readily given up, in spite of doubts about his innocence in the matter.

Council and his companions, which now included Terry,[380] left Clarksville without being molested at all and began their long trip north. The final task, on returning to Indianapolis, was to restore Terry to "the embraces of a doting father."[381] Information on Terry's life after reaching home is spotty. He is probably the black man by that name who married Sarah Hamilton in 1854.[382] Someone named Eli Terry was connected with the Indianapolis Coffin Company, but there is not conclusive evidence that it was the same person.[383] Curiously, a black man named Less Terry, whose father was an Indiana man named Eli Terry, resided in Clarksville in the early twentieth century, and his death certificate shows he was born in Indiana in 1867.[384]

JOEL HENRY THOMPSON

Joel Henry Thompson was the infant son of William Thompson and his wife, Catharine. Both had previously lived in Elkton, Maryland, where William was a free person (known as Peregrine "Perry" Berry), and Catharine had been a slave named Betsey Galloway.[385] Around 1845, they left Maryland together, claimed to have gotten married in Wilmington, Delaware, and moved to Chester, New Jersey, to start a new life.[386] Here, in a free state, two children were born to them, of which Joel was the youngest.[387]

One day in August 1850, John Frisby Price, a man of color,[388] paid them a visit. He was well known to them and invited Mrs. Thompson to stop at his house in Philadelphia, the next time she went to do her marketing. He emphasized that she should bring Joel, a baby less than two years old, because his wife was quite anxious to see him. The following week, mother and child did make the trip to Philadelphia, and went to Price's home. Witnesses later reported having seen them there, and also that Price had led them away, down an alley, toward the home of George F. Alberti.

At Alberti's residence, the woman found out that she was being apprehended as a fugitive slave. A city alderman was present, who prepared some paperwork intended to legitimize her arrest as a fugitive. Another man who was there told her she should go along quietly to make things easier for herself. Someone there, apparently an attorney, advised Alberti that the boy, having been born in a free state to a slave who had gone there prior to becoming pregnant, was free. Alberti tried to convince Mrs. Thompson to leave her son with him, and that he would make sure he was returned to his father, but she was distrustful and would not turn over the baby. It was later claimed that Alberti decided not to separate mother and child, out of humanity (it was said he had "as tender a heart as ever animated a human bosom").[389] However, Price (who received $75 for his part in the affair)[390] had pointedly told Catharine to be sure to bring the baby with her, and Alberti received a half-share of the purchase price of both, when they were sold in Maryland.

At some point, Alberti struck the woman with a club, bruising her face, to "quiet" her.[391] Alberti had hired a driver, Thomas Richardson, an ex-convict who had been pardoned, and he drove away with Alberti, mother, and child, having been told that she had been accused of stealing. After crossing the state line into Delaware, Mrs. Thompson pleaded with him to let her and her son go, and it was only then that he found out she had been apprehended as a runaway slave. He made some objection to Alberti, but was told to drive on.

After making several stops, the party arrived in Elkton, Maryland, where Alberti left them, returning with James S. Mitchell. Upon seeing the woman, Mitchell exclaimed: "We have got you, you black bitch, at last."[392] Catharine, who reportedly had made no denial of being a fugitive, begged him to release her son. Mitchell refused, saying he would keep the boy and send her to the slave market in Georgia.[393]

Meanwhile, in New Jersey, Joel's father had become concerned when his wife failed to return and had gone to Philadelphia, discovered what had happened, and began legal proceedings. Warrants were issued for Alberti and Price, and they were eventually indicted, along with Mitchell, for having kidnapped Joel.[394] Because Mitchell was in Maryland, Pennsylvania had to requisition (extradite) him, but Maryland governor Enoch Louis Lowe decided that under Maryland law, the baby was a slave belonging to Mitchell, and he refused to deliver him to the Pennsylvania authorities.[395]

A trial took place in Philadelphia on February 28, 1851, before Judge A. V. Parsons. The prosecution's main witness was Richardson, who had driven the carriage to Maryland. Though the defense made efforts to attack his credibility, his testimony was convincing. Judge Parsons, when charging the jury, made it clear that personal feelings relating to slavery should not enter into their decision, and explained the law to them. After a quick session deliberating, the jury found both men guilty.[396]

Parsons had both incarcerated pending sentencing, which took place on March 24,[397] when he fined Alberti $1,000 and gave him 10 years at hard labor. Price was fined $700 (more than negating the $75 he had earned by luring the victims into Alberti's clutches) and received eight years in the penitentiary.

Many citizens were upset at this outcome, both in Pennsylvania and Maryland. It was a factor in the gubernatorial election in Pennsylvania, and in 1852, a newly elected Democratic governor, William Bigler, pardoned both prisoners. The state of Maryland provided Alberti and Price with compensation for their prison time.[398]

At the time of the trial, William Thompson testified that he had not seen his wife and son since they had left home in August 1850, and research has yielded no evidence of their fates. Alberti died in 1869, his demise noted in a vitriolic obituary in the *Philadelphia Telegraph*, which observed that his life had been marked by "a long course of unfavorable conduct."[399]

DAVID TREADWELL

David Treadwell was one of a number of people of color[400] whom James H. Thompson planned to take from New York for the purpose of selling them as slaves in the South. (Though Treadwell had been a slave, it was determined that, because he had been kidnapped

previously, he was a free person according to state law.) Thompson, a
resident of Georgia, was known to authorities in New York City as
an "old offender"[401] who had had dealings during the winter of
1816–1817 with a Captain Storer, who had taken kidnapped blacks
from New York City and Philadelphia to Baltimore to be sold.
Thompson had been arrested in North Carolina while conveying some
of those victims to Georgia.[402]

Thompson came back to New York in the spring of 1817 and, with a
man named Crabtree, devised a plan to obtain people of color and
carry them to the South where they would be sold for a large profit.
Thompson purchased a schooner, the *Creole of New York*, hired William
Stillwell as its master,[403] and enlisted helpers Royal A. Bowen and
Moses Nichols. Nichols ran a brothel and/or gambling house.[404]

Traveling to Albany and Poughkeepsie, the men (mainly Nichols)
bought slaves, telling sellers they were meant for their own use (it was
against New York law at that time to export slaves to other states). The
victims were told several stories: "At one time they were told they would
be employed as gentlemen's servants; at others they were to be hos-
tlers."[405] Treadwell was told he was to be taken north, up the river.[406]

One woman, taken away from Poughkeepsie, "during the whole
passage was observed to read frequently in the bible [*sic*], and at other
times to weep and refuse all other sustenance offered her." When the
captain asked why, she said she feared she would be taken out of the
country.[407]

The various victims—two of whom were from Albany, six from
Poughkeepsie, and one from New York City—were gathered at
Nichols' house on Love Lane, until they were taken by carriage one
rainy night to the schooner. "This [number of victims] being a tolerable
cargo, and delays dangerous, they were preparing to depart with their
booty."[408]

On the morning of June 27, while the schooner was in the Hudson
River, a boat rowed out to it. In the boat were brothers Samuel and
Joseph Willets, members of the Vigilance Committee, which had been
tipped off by a Poughkeepsie man named Kelly that some scheme
was afoot. Hailing the schooner, the Willets boarded it and inquired
who was on board besides those who were on deck. Thompson said
there were only two crew members. The question was posed again,
and a person peeked through a crack in the door of a cabin, and a voice
was heard to say that there were other people on board. Two women
emerged from the cabin. The hold was then opened, and more people
came up on deck.

Thompson explained that two of them were his slaves, and the
others had been put on board by Nichols and Bowen. He was, he said,

bound for Poughkeepsie and Albany to take on a load of cheese he intended to carry to Baltimore. Joseph Willets left to notify the police, and Thompson tried to leave in the boat, but Samuel Willets told him to stay on the schooner until his brother returned. Police officers soon came and took Thompson and his cohorts into custody, and the schooner was seized by the Customs House.

At the trials of Thompson and Bowen,[409] prosecutors (one of whom was Peter A. Jay, son of founding father John Jay) argued that several of the blacks were actually free, and that the offenders were guilty of kidnapping. Defense counsel insisted all the blacks were slaves, and that the defendants were only guilty of transporting slaves out of the state.

One of the points argued during the trial involved a change that had been made to state law on March 31, 1817. Whereas the statute previously had defined the crime of kidnapping as applying to persons of color "not being a slave," the latter wording had been deleted, so that the kidnapping statute applied to any person of color.

The jury found both defendants guilty, but more court sessions took place the following term, after the defense appealed. Some of the victims now testified, including Treadwell. He was at first objected to as a witness by the defense, who said he was a slave who belonged to Nichols (and therefore not eligible to testify in the case), but the prosecution argued that because Thompson had been previously convicted of trying to send Treadwell out of the state, Treadwell had gained his freedom, per state law.[410]

In his charge to the jury, the mayor (Jacob Radcliff)[411] told them: "On this trial, some of these people of color taken on board this vessel appear to be slaves; the others free." Both defendants were again found guilty. Bowen, as a mere accomplice, was fined $25.00. Thompson was sentenced to three years in prison, though he reportedly escaped not long after being sent to the penitentiary.[412]

MARY UNDERHILL

Mary Underhill worked as a servant at a private home on Franklin Street in New York City. In November 1819, a man named Joseph Pulford told her he could set her up in a position that paid $100 a year, if she were willing to relocate. Underhill expressed an interest, and Pulford told her she should "keep dark and say nothing."[413] He asked her to meet him the following Sunday evening, ready to leave with her packed things. He would take care of the arrangements for her departure.

Pulford had conversed with Captain Glasshune, master of the brig *Sarah Ann* (which was about to sail for Havana),[414] offering to sell the captain some black people. Though Glasshune feigned interest, he actually alerted a man named Henry J. Hassey, who brought John C. Gillen, a constable, into the picture.[415] Pulford and Underhill met as planned, and he led her to the ship that was docked at the foot of Rector Street. Pulford told her to wait there while he conferred with the captain, giving her instructions, that should any passersby notice her, to tell them that she was waiting for her husband. Pulford came back after a short delay and told her he had not been able to find the captain. Leading her into an alley, he explained that he was going to pretend to sell her to the captain, and that he would give her half of the money he would receive. She then was to wait for a moment when the captain was not looking, jump from the ship, and run off.

The captain then made an appearance, along with Gillen. The constable pretended that he was a merchant named Johnson from Havana. "Johnson" was looking to buy some blacks—he had 40 on board the ship already, and would like to have two more. Pulford told him he had a woman waiting nearby, one of 30 he had taken recently, and that he would sell her for $50. Johnson (that is, Gillen) wanted to see her, telling Pulford that he did not want to buy "a pig in the poke." Pulford did not want to bring her out until he had received the money. The two engaged in an argument that led to Pulford being warned not to speak so loudly "as it was dangerous business."[416]

Pulford, who said he could even get two more people that very evening, finally led the supposed buyer to the alley, where Underhill was still waiting. As the money was about to change hands, Pulford balked at writing out a receipt, at which point Gillen told him, "You must go along with me!" The disbelieving kidnapper responded, "Oh! You're joking." But he, along with Underhill, was taken by Gillen to the police station.

Pulford was put on trial in December 1819, at a session of the Court of Sessions, which was presided over by New York City mayor Cadwallader D. Colden, a man with established antislavery leanings.[417] Underhill gave testimony and apparently was a credible witness, since Colden pointed out to the jury that she was "unimpeachable," except for her "extreme simplicity and ignorance," which might have been why "the prisoner selected her as a fit object by which he might accomplish his nefarious design."[418] Her narrative was backed up by witnesses Hassey and Gillen.

Pulford's defense was that he had not forcibly seized her, nor had he taken her against her will. It would seem to be a weak argument, given that the statute under which he had been indicted clearly included "inveigling" as one form of the offense—tricking people into going away was as much a crime as physically seizing them. Colden therefore ruled that: "To constitute kidnapping or inveigling, no force is necessary."[419] Though he made some negative comments about slavery, he also advised the jury that they must not allow their decision to be guided by emotion, but to deliberate calmly on the matter. Their consideration was brief: they found the defendant guilty immediately.

Then, Colden also acted immediately, sentencing Pulford to the maximum sentence allowed: 14 years at hard labor in state prison. The defendant fully deserved this, he said, because he was a "habitual kidnapper," by his own admission. Colden announced his regret that the law did not allow execution as punishment for the crime, but did tell Pulford to expect "no release from imprisonment."[420] Upon hearing the sentence, one person in the courtroom—Pulford's sister—"shrieked fearfully and fainted."[421] Whether Pulford served out (or survived) his full sentence is not known. Neither is it known what Mary Underhill did after the trial.

PETER WHITE

In 1844, Peter White was a 10-year-old child in Equality, Illinois. He and three younger children were abducted and taken to Arkansas, where they were sold as slaves for $800. They were rescued by Equality resident Walter White and brought home.[422] The kidnapper was not identified, but over the years, suspicious have been raised that it was John Crenshaw, who ran a salt works in the area.[423]

After his rescue, White resided for many years in Equality.[424] In the early 1900s, Professor George Washington Smith interviewed him and mentioned him in his book about the history of southern Illinois, which includes discussion of kidnappings that took place in that region.[425]

FANNY, MARYANN, ELIZA, JOSIAH, AND INFANT WIGGLESWORTH

Vincent Wigglesworth was a farmer in Clermont County, Ohio. The family "had lived peaceably in the county for sixteen years," when, during the night of October 30, 1842, their home was invaded by six armed men. The men, who were apparently from Kentucky, had come after Wigglesworth's wife, Fanny (whom they probably believed to be a runaway slave), and "her children, though born out of bondage, must share her lot."[426]

There may have been some question about Fanny's status as a free person. There is paperwork showing she had been given to a woman as a "life estate," and upon that woman's death, ownership would have reverted to her original owner. Two of the suspected kidnappers may have had some ownership rights to her.[427] However, in the 1840 census, the Wigglesworths were listed as free persons of color.[428] Also, concerned citizens at the time of the kidnapping expressed their belief that Fanny *and* her children were "free and entitled to the protection of our laws" and that they had been taken "without the least demand for them [as fugitives] or right to them under our law."[429] The children, Maryann (age 15), Eliza (10), Josiah (5), and a 16-day-old infant had all been born in Ohio, and were therefore free under Ohio law, regardless of the status of their mother.[430]

The Wigglesworth victims never returned home, in spite of the significant efforts and expenditures made by Vincent Wigglesworth and Robert E. Fee, the intervention of government officials, and the concerns expressed by members of the public.[431] Fee tracked the kidnappers through Kansas and found the victims in Independence, Missouri, but was unable to obtain their release.[432] It was reported, nearly a century after their abduction, that: "The mother and children were sold to different owners and widely separated."[433]

ISAAC WRIGHT

See Stephen Dickinson, Robert Garrison, and Isaac Wright.

This depiction of the slave trade from the 1830s shows the U.S. Capitol in the background. Many slave traders carried on business in the District of Columbia prior to 1850. (Library of Congress)

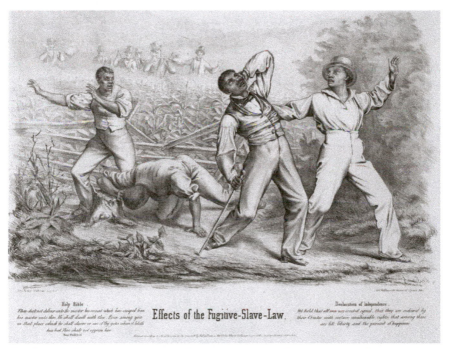

This broadside combines a graphic portrayal of enslaved men with quotes from the Bible and the Declaration of Independence to protest the 1850 Fugitive Slave Law. (Library of Congress)

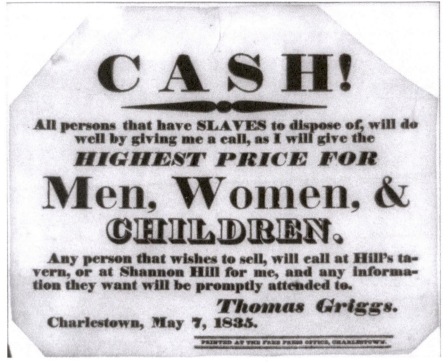

An advertisement by Virginia slave trader Thomas Griggs, seeking to purchase slaves. The buying and selling of slaves was often conducted in taverns. (Library of Congress)

In 1816, Jesse Torrey discovered several victims of kidnapping when he went to see a woman who had jumped from a building to avoid being sold south. Torrey wrote down details relating to the kidnap victims, and was able to obtain their release. (Jesse Torrey, *American Slave Trade* [London: J. M. Corbett, 1822], 73)

$300 REWARD!
ARREST THE VILLAINS.

Four free negro children were kidnapped and taken from the residence of the undersigned, in the "Pond Settlement," Gallatin County, Illinois, on the evening of the 5th inst., as follows :

LOUISA, aged 18 years, past; mulatto, black hair and eyes, spare made, about 5 feet high, and weighs probably a hundred pounds, had on a striped homespun dress; has weak eyes, a lump on each lid, and a little scar on the left side of the neck. caused by a burn.

EMILY, not quite 17 years old, mulatto, black hair and eyes, spare made, neither so tall or heavy as LOUISA, had on a striped homespun dress.

GEORGE W., a mulatto boy, about nine years old, heavy set, has a scar on the back of his left hand, made by an axe.

WILLIAM Q., five years old next June, mulatto, heavy set.

I will give $25 for the recovery of each of the children, if found in the State, $50 for each, if found out of the State, and one hundred dollars for the apprehension and conviction of the thieves (four in number,) or either of them. For the restoration of the children and punishment of the kidnappers, I implore the aid of all good people.

BENJAMIN W. FAUVER.

Shawneetown, April 6 1849.

This notice, offering a reward for the return of the kidnapped children of Benjamin W. Fauver, and for the capture of their abductors, appeared in the *Illinois State Journal* (April 23, 1849).

THE KIDNAPPING CASE.

Narrative of the Seizure and Recovery of Solomon Northrup.

INTERESTING DISCLOSURES.

We have obtained from Washington the subjoined statement of the circumstances attending the seizure and recovery of the negro man SOLOMON NORTHROP, whose case has excited so high a degree of interest. The material facts in the history of the transaction have already been given, but this narrative will be found a more complete and authentic record than has yet appeared :

SOLOMON NORTHROP, the subject of the following narrative, is a free colored citizen of the United States ; was born in Essex County, New-York, about the year 1808 ; became early a resident of Washington County, and married there in 1829. His father and mother resided in the County of Washington about fifty years, till their decease, and were both free. With his wife and children he resided at Saratoga Springs in the Winter of 1841, and while there was employed by two gentlemen to drive a team South, at the rate of a dollar a day. In fulfilment of his employ.

Public awareness of the kidnapping problem was increased by newspaper coverage, such as this article that appeared in the *New York Times* on January 20, 1853.

SCENE IN THE SLAVE PEN AT WASHINGTON.

In a Washington, D.C., slave pen, Solomon Northup was subjected to beatings until he refrained from asserting his status as a freeman. (Solomon Northup, *Twelve Years a Slave: Narrative of Solomon Northup* [Auburn, NY: Derby and Miller, 1853])

IN HIS PLANTATION SUIT.

Portrait of Solomon Northup from his 1853 book, *Twelve Years a Slave*. Though Northup is the most well-known kidnapping victim, his experience was by no means unique. (Solomon Northup, *Twelve Years a Slave: Narrative of Solomon Northup* [Auburn, NY: Derby and Miller, 1853])

As a child, Peter White was kidnapped in 1844 in Equality, Illinois, along with others. They were sold as slaves in Arkansas, but were rescued and brought home by Walter White. (George Washington Smith, *A History of Southern Illinois*, Vol. 1 [New York: Lewis Publishing Company, 1912], 473)

Joshua Coffin traveled to Memphis, Tennessee, in 1838, where he located Isaac Wright, a sailor who had been sold as a slave at New Orleans. Wright's master was absent, so Coffin took Wright away on his own initiative, writing a friend that "I have in fact kidnapped him into freedom." (Samuel T. Pickard, *Life and Letters of John Greenleaf Whittier*, Vol. 2 [Boston: Houghton, Mifflin, 1894], 478)

George Cameron Mendenhall, a North Carolina attorney, was instrumental in obtaining the release of Frank Jackson, a freeman from Pennsylvania who was kidnapped sometime around 1851. (Courtesy of Friends Historical Collection, Guilford College, Greensboro, NC)

Appendix

List of Victims Covered in Carol Wilson's *Freedom at Risk*

The following victims of kidnapping are discussed in Carol Wilson, *Freedom at Risk: The Kidnapping of Free Blacks in America, 1780–1865* (Lexington: University Press of Kentucky, 1994).

(Names with asterisks are also covered as case studies in Chapter 8 of this book.)

Richard Allen
Charles Amos
*George Armstrong[1]
William Bachelor
John Barnwell
Benjamin Baxter
James Bayard
Lavinia Bell
Bob
John Brown
Rosanna Brown
William Chase
Benjamin Chelsom
Constant
Clement Cox
John Davis
*Stephen Dickinson[2]

Henry Edwards
Henry Elkison
Marguerite Fayman
Charity Fisher
Adam Gibson
John Glasgow
Sarah Hagerman
*Sarah Harrison (Taylor)[3]
Henrietta
Henry
Peter Hook
Gilbert Horton
John Jacobs
Joe Johnson
Joe the Sweep
Philip Johnston
C. W. Jones

John Jones
Richard Keen
Lunsford Lane
Ephraim Lawrence
John Lewis
Little Jack
Little John
Lucinda
Abraham Luomony
Alexander Manlove
William Miller
Moses
Sarah Nicholson[4]
*Solomon Northup[5]
John Parker
Thomas Parsons
Richard Phillips
Leah Roche

Isaiah Sadler
Samuel Scomp
Polly Seiper
James Sweard
Jacob Simon
Cornelius Sinclair
Lydia Smith
Staten
Stephen
Levin Still
Peter Still
*Joel Henry Thompson[6]
Enos Tilman
Milton Trusty
James Valentine
Henry Williams
John Williams
Wynne

Notes

INTRODUCTION

1. Carol Wilson, *Freedom at Risk: The Kidnapping of Free Blacks in America, 1780–1865* (Lexington: University Press of Kentucky, 1994).

2. New York State Assembly, Select Committee on the Petition of Various Citizens to Prevent Kidnapping, Report No. 341, May 1, 1840, 4, available in Cornell University's Samuel J. May Anti-Slavery Collection, http://dlxs.library.cornell.edu/cgi/t/text/pageviewer-idx?c=mayantislavery;idno=27892510;view=image;seq=1 (accessed April 28, 2014).

3. "Exclusion of Free Blacks," Slavery in the North web site, http://slavenorth.com/exclusion.htm (accessed July 15, 2015).

4. Wilson, *Freedom at Risk*, 3–5.

5. See, for example, Anne Farrow, Joel Lang, and Jenifer Frank, *Complicity: How the North Promoted, Prolonged, and Profited from Slavery* (New York: Ballantine Books, 2005).

6. Wilson, *Freedom at Risk*, 7.

CHAPTER 1

1. "Fugitive Slave Acts," History.com, A+E Networks, 2009. http://www.history.com/topics/black-history/fugitive-slave-acts (accessed May 16, 2014).

2. Paul Finkelman, "The Kidnapping of John Davis and the Adoption of the Fugitive Slave Law of 1793," *Journal of Southern History*, Vol. 56, No. 3 (August 1990): 397.

3. Ibid., 407.

4. The evolution of the law is described in detail in Finkelman, "The Kidnapping of John Davis and the Adoption of the Fugitive Slave Law of 1793."

5. Finkelman, "The Kidnapping of John Davis and the Adoption of the Fugitive Slave Law of 1793," 400.

6. Ibid., 419–20.

7. Ibid., 422.

8. Joe Smydo, "Status of Slaves a 70-Year Conflict: Washington County Case of John Davis Inspired Nation's First Law Dealing with Slaves in Free States," *Pittsburgh Post-Gazette* (February 9, 2014); and "Fugitive Slave Acts," History.com.

9. "James H. Thompson and Royal A. Bowen's Cases," *New-York City-Hall Recorder* (August 1817): 128.

10. Ibid.

11. James B. Stewart says that some 50,000 slaves were brought in between 1808 and 1861. Stewart, "The Critical Role of African Americans in the Development of the Pre–Civil War U.S. Economy," in Cecilia Conrad, *African Americans in the U.S. Economy* (Lanham, MD: Rowman & Littlefield, 2005), 22.

12. Stanley Harrold, *Border War: Fighting over Slavery before the Civil War* (Chapel Hill: University of North Carolina Press, 2010), 10.

13. "The demand for enslaved blacks to produce cotton increased dramatically," and this, in turn, resulted in "the large-scale relocation of blacks." Stewart, "The Critical Role of African Americans," 22.

14. Stewart, "The Critical Role of African Americans," 22.

15. Ibid., 22–23.

16. "The incidence of kidnapping increased . . . during the late 1820s as demand for labor in the cotton-growing states mounted." Harrold, *Border War*, 30.

17. Edgar J. McManus and Tara Helfman, *Liberty and Union: A Constitutional History of the United States*, Vol. 1 (New York: Routledge, 2014), 249.

18. Its title was "An Act to give effect to the provision of the Constitution of the United States, relative to fugitives from labor, for the protection of free people of color, and to prevent kidnapping," and it had been enacted in 1826 in response to a Maryland commission that met with legislators, seeking a better system for returning runaways to Maryland. Edward Raymond Turner, *The Negro in Pennsylvania—Slavery—Servitude—Freedom, 1639–1861* (Baltimore: The Lord Baltimore Press, 1912), 231–32, 232n.

19. McManus and Helfman, *Liberty and Union*, Vol. 1, 250; and Finkelman, "The Kidnapping of John Davis," 410.

20. Per the *Prigg* ruling: "The recovery of runaways could be made virtually impossible simply by not providing local police assistance." McManus and Helfman, *Liberty and Union*, Vol. 1, 251.

21. Douglas, a U.S. senator from Illinois, helped achieve passage of the Compromise of 1850 (which included the Fugitive Slave Act) as an effort to deal with the differences between the North and the South over slavery. His comments on the Fugitive Slave Act appeared in: "Speech of Hon. S. A. Douglas, of Illinois" (Washington, DC) *Daily Union* (November 6, 1850).

22. "The Utica Convention," (New York) *Evening Post* (October 18, 1850); and "Michigan State Anti-Slavery Convention," *National Era* (July 1, 1852).

23. "Washington, D. C., Speech of Mr. Townshend, of Ohio," *National Era* (July 1, 1852).

24. James Oliver Horton and Lois E. Horton, "A Federal Assault: African Americans and the Impact of the Fugitive Slave Law of 1850," in Paul Finkelman (ed.), *Slavery and the Law* (Lanham, MD: Rowman & Littlefield, 2002), 143–60 (quotes from pages 151–52).

25. "Black Reaction to the Fugitive Slave Law of 1850: Terror in the Black Community." In *History of Black Americans: From the Compromise of 1850 to the End of the Civil War* (Westport, CT: Greenwood Press, 1983), The African American Experience, Greenwood Publishing Group, http://testaae.green wood.com/doc.aspx?fileID=GR7967&chapterID=GR7967-88&path=books/greenwood (accessed January 15, 2015).

26. James Freeman Clarke, *Anti-Slavery Days: Sketch of the Struggle which Ended in the Abolition of Slavery in the United States* (New York: John W. Lovell Company, 1883), 168. The testimony before the commissioner showed that significant evidence in Gibson's favor was ignored. "Kidnapping in Philadelphia. Human Liberty under the Fugitive Slave Law," *New York Daily Tribune* (December 25, 1850).

27. "Speech of Hon. S. A. Douglas, of Illinois." Some considered such an expectation to be "illusory": *Remonstrance: To the Honorable Senate and House of Representatives of the Commonwealth of Massachusetts, the Memorial and Remonstrance of the Undersigned, Citizens of Massachusetts . . .*, House, No. 121, Commonwealth of Massachusetts, March 1861, 4, available in Samuel J. May Anti-Slavery Collection, http://ebooks.library.cornell.edu/cgi/t/text/pageviewer-idx?c=mayantislavery;cc=mayantislavery;q1=solomon%20northrop;rgn=full%20text;idno=15853626;didno=15853626;view=image;seq=1;page=root;size=100 (accessed May 10, 2015).

28. "The Tribune on Law," (New York) *Evening Express* (November 23, 1860).

29. See discussion of the impact on the trial of Northup's kidnappers in David Fiske, Clifford W. Brown, and Rachel Seligman, *Solomon Northup: The Complete Story of the Author of* Twelve Years a Slave (Santa Barbara, CA: Praeger, 2013), 137.

30. "The Taney Hunt against Colored Americans," *Liberator* (August 28, 1857).

31. Don E. Fehrenbacher, *Slavery, Law, and Politics: The Dred Scott Case in Historical Perspective* (Oxford: Oxford University Press, 1981), 193.

CHAPTER 2

1. See case studies of Solomon Northup and Eli Terry. (All case studies cited in this chapter are found in Chapter 8.)

2. *Chicago Tribune* (June 7, 1865).

3. L. E. Chittenden (comp.), *Abraham Lincoln's Speeches* (New York: Dodd, Mead and Company, 1896), 46, 49.

4. Earning estimates based on tables in Stanley Lebergott, "Wage Trends, 1800–1900," in *Trends in the American Economy in the Nineteenth Century* (Princeton, NJ: Princeton University Press, 1960), http://www.nber.org/chapters/c2486 (accessed May 3, 2015).

5. Many whites thought blacks were "shiftless, lazy, unintelligent, and immoral." See Stanley Harrold, *Border War: Fighting over Slavery before the Civil War* (Chapel Hill: University of North Carolina Press, 2010), 7. A Rhode Island newspaper declared that: "The colored men of the South, we are satisfied, are far happier than the colored men of the North." "Refuses to Be Freed," *Providence Daily Post* (June 25, 1857).

6. Ulrich Bonnell Phillips, *American Negro Slavery* (New York: D. Appleton and Company, 1929), 445.

7. See Harrold, *Border War*, 26–27.

8. See James Oliver Horton and Lois E. Horton, "A Federal Assault: African Americans and the Impact of the Fugitive Slave Law of 1850," in Paul Finkelman (ed.), *Slavery and the Law* (Lanham, MD: Rowman & Littlefield, 2002), pp. 143–60 (quotes from pages 151–52).

9. "Advantages of a Free Country," *Voice of Freedom* (January 4, 1844).

10. See case study of Wilson George Hays and Charles Smith.

11. See case studies of Aaron Case; Catharine, David, James, and Martha Morris; and Fanny, Maryann, Eliza, Josiah, and infant Wigglesworth.

12. See case study of Isaac Moore.

13. *Provincial Freeman* (April 21, 1851), reproduced in Adrienne Shadd, *The Underground Railroad: Next Stop, Toronto!* (Toronto: Dundurn, 2005), iv.

14. *Provincial Freeman* (March 24, 1855).

15. See case study of Solomon Northup.

16. See case study of Sidney O. Francis.

17. See case studies of John Adams and Isaac Moore.

18. See case studies of Jonathan and Sampson Dredden and Joel Henry Thompson.

19. Letter from Elisha Tyson to U.S. Representative Alexander McKim, December 5, 1811, in "Kidnapping of Free People of Color," The National Archives Education Updates, http://education.blogs.archives.gov/2013/11/12/kidnapping-of-free-people-of-color/ (accessed January 4, 2015).

20. See case studies of Sidney O. Francis and Nahum G. Hazard.

21. Carol Wilson, *Freedom at Risk: The Kidnapping of Free Blacks in America, 1780–1865* (Lexington: University Press of Kentucky, 1994), 20ff.

22. See case study of Peter John Lee.

23. The New York Manumission Society reported that kidnappers were using this method in 1803. Thomas D. Morris, *Free Men All: The Personal Liberty Laws of the North, 1780–1861* (Union, NJ: Lawbook Exchange, Ltd., 2001), 26.

24. "The Case of Mary Gilmore," *Baltimore Gazette and Daily Advertiser* (July 3, 1835). A more detailed account appeared in "Case of Mary Gilmore," *Liberator* (August 1, 1835). Mary's mother had died in poverty years before the attempt to take her daughter as a fugitive slave. *Philadelphia Inquirer* (July 17, 1835).

25. "Hatred of the Poor," (Cincinnati) *Philanthropist* (March 24, 1841).

26. "The Minister Hunting his Slave," (Syracuse) *Evening Chronicle* (July 22, 1853). O. H. Smith, *Early Indiana Trials and Sketches* (Cincinnati, OH: Moore, Wilstach, Keys & Co., 1858), 278–79.

27. Jesse Torrey, *A Portraiture of Domestic Slavery in the United States*, 2nd ed. (Ballston Spa, NY: The Author, 1818), 97.

28. John Doy, *The Narrative of John Doy, of Lawrence, Kansas* (New York: Thomas Holman, 1860), 61.

29. See case study of George Anderson.

30. See case study of John Hight and Daniel Prue.

31. British and Foreign Anti-Slavery Society. *Slavery and the Internal Slave Trade in the United States of North America* (London: Thomas Ward and Co., 1841), 272.

32. Ibid.

33. Lee was usually described as a runaway slave, but he was not apprehended as such, and there is evidence that he had in fact been a free person of color in Virginia who relocated to New York. See case study of Peter John Lee.

34. "Letters of Negroes, Largely Personal and Private [Part 6]," *Journal of Negro History* (January 1926), 192.

35. "Something Like Kidnapping," *Daily Pittsburgh Gazette* (May 28, 1838).

CHAPTER 3

1. Robert H. Gudmestad, *A Troublesome Commerce: The Transformation of the Interstate Slave Trade* (Baton Rouge: Louisiana State University Press, 2003), 73.

2. Ibid.

3. *Daily National Intelligencer* (January 2, 1838).

4. British and Foreign Anti-Slavery Society, *Slavery and the Internal Slave Trade in the United States of North America* (London: Thomas Ward and Co., 1841), 207–8.

5. (New Orleans) *Daily Crescent* (February 13, 1851).

6. (Richmond, VA) *Daily Dispatch* (August 3, 1858).

7. Maurie Dee McInnis, *Slaves Waiting for Sale: Abolitionist Art and the American Slave Trade* (Chicago: University of Chicago Press, 2011), 92, 93.

8. Some felt that: "Kidnapping promoted lawlessness and encouraged disrespect for authority." Gudmestad, *A Troublesome Commerce*, 74.

9. Gudmestad, *A Troublesome Commerce*, 74.

10. L. E. Chittenden (comp.), *Abraham Lincoln's Speeches* (New York: Dodd, Mead and Company, 1896), 46.

11. Harriet Beecher Stowe, *A Key to Uncle Tom's Cabin* (Boston: John P. Jewett and Co., 1853), 173.

12. McInnis, *Slaves Waiting for Sale*, 92, 93; and Steven Deyle, *Carry Me Back: The Domestic Slave Trade in American Life* (New York: Oxford University Press, 2005), 239.

13. Gudmestad, *A Troublesome Commerce*, 167–68.

14. Ibid., 168.

15. Ulrich Bonnell Phillips, *American Negro Slavery* (New York: D. Appleton and Company, 1929), 195.

16. See case study of Sidney O. Francis.

17. Deyle, *Carry Me Back*, 238.

18. Ibid., 239.

19. Jesse Torrey, *American Slave Trade* (London: J. M. Cobbett, 1822), 66.

20. Ibid., 55–56.

21. Ibid., 74n.

22. See case study of Stephen Dickinson, Robert Garrison, and Isaac Wright.

23. Solomon Northup, *Twelve Years a Slave* (Baton Rouge: Louisiana State University Press, 1968), 23–26.

24. See case study of George Washington Talbot.

25. Slave trading often took place in taverns in Richmond, Virginia. Jack Trammell, *The Richmond Slave Trade: The Economic Backbone of the Old Dominion* (Charleston, SC: History Press, 2012). Taverns are also discussed in David Fiske, Clifford W. Brown, and Rachel Seligman, *Solomon Northup: The Complete Story of the Author of* Twelve Years a Slave (Santa Barbara, CA: Praeger, 2013), 49.

26. Northup, *Twelve Years a Slave*, 17.

27. In the District of Columbia, victims of kidnapping were "hurried away before they can be rescued." "Slavery in the District of Columbia," (Jamestown, NY) *Journal* (March 25, 1835).

28. See the discussion of "serial selling" in Chapter 5.

29. See case study of Aaron Cooper.

CHAPTER 4

1. *Constitution of a Society for Abolishing the Slave-Trade, with Several Acts of the States of Massachusetts, Connecticut and Rhode-Island, for that Purpose* (Providence, RI: John Carter, 1789), 14.

2. Thomas D. Morris, *Free Men All: The Personal Liberty Laws of the North, 1780–1861* (Union, NJ: Lawbook Exchange, Ltd, 2001), 24.

3. *Constitution of a Society for Abolishing the Slave-Trade*, 16.

4. Ibid., 14.

5. W. E. B. Du Bois, *The Philadelphia Negro: A Social Study* (New York: Schocken Books, 1967), 22.

6. Statutes cited in *New-York City-Hall Recorder*, Vol. 2, No. 8 (August 1817): 120.

7. Guion Griffis Johnson, *Ante-Bellum North Carolina: A Social History* (Chapel Hill: University of North Carolina Press, 1937), 597, electronic ed., http://docsouth.unc.edu/nc/johnson/ (accessed May 2, 2015).

8. William Brockenbrough, *Virginia Cases, or Decisions of the General Court of Virginia, Chiefly on the Criminal Law of the Commonwealth, Commencing June Term, 1815, and Ending June Term, 1826* (Richmond, VA: Peter Cottom, 1826), 147.

9. Johnson, *Ante-Bellum North Carolina*, 599.

10. James M. Wright, *The Free Negro in Maryland, 1634–1860* (New York: Octagon Books, 1971; reprint of 1921 edition), 109.

11. W. C. Smedes and T. A. Marshall, *Reports of Cases Argued and Determined in the High Court of Errors and Appeals for the State of Mississippi* (Boston: Charles C. Little and James Brown, 1847), 574.

12. Ira Berlin, *Slaves without Masters: The Free Negro in the Antebellum South* (New York: Pantheon Books, 1975), 99–100.

13. Morris, *Free Men All*, 24–25. A report by a New York Assembly committee said: "A person held as a slave, and claiming to be free, can only recover his freedom by law, through a difficult and expensive course of legal proceeding. . . . A suit for his freedom can only be brought by some white man, who shall sue as his guardian or next friend." New York State Assembly, Select Committee on the Petition of Various Citizens to Prevent Kidnapping, Report No. 341, May 1, 1840, p. 4, available in Cornell University's Samuel J. May Anti-Slavery Collection, http://dlxs.library.cornell.edu/cgi/t/text/pageviewer-idx?c=mayantislavery;idno=27892510;view=image;seq=1 (accessed April 28, 2014).

14. "An Act to Give Effect to the Provisions of the Constitution of the United States, Relative to Fugitives from Labour, for the Protection of Free People of Colour, and to Prevent Kidnapping," in James Dunlop (comp.), *The General Laws of Pennsylvania, from the Year 1700 to April 22, 1846* (Philadelphia: T. & J. W. Johnson, 1847), 383ff.

15. Edward Raymond Turner, *The Negro in Pennsylvania: Slavery—Servitude—Freedom, 1639–1861* (Washington, DC: American Historical Association, 1911), 238.

16. "New England for Freedom," *Cleveland* [OH] *Leader* (July 11, 1854).

17. *Albany Evening Journal* (July 7, 1854).

18. In regard to a fugitive slave taken without benefit of a hearing before a commissioner, and the kidnapping of the family of Jeremiah Boyd (and Boyd's subsequent murder), the *New-York Daily Tribune* said, "we are prepared to judge whether Personal Liberty acts in Free States are or are not necessary." *New-York Daily Tribune* (November 23, 1860).

19. Late in 1860, the U.S. House of Representatives approved a resolution declaring the Personal Liberty laws unconstitutional. "Washington, Dec. 17, 1860," *New York Herald* (December 18, 1860). Responding to the possibility of the Personal Liberty Law being repealed in Massachusetts, some citizens expressed their opposition to its repeal: *Remonstrance: To the Honorable Senate and House of Representatives of the Commonwealth of Massachusetts, the Memorial and Remonstrance of the Undersigned, Citizens of Massachusetts . . .*, House, No. 121, Commonwealth of Massachusetts, March 1861, 1, available in Samuel J. May Anti-Slavery Collection, http://ebooks.library.cornell.edu/cgi/t/text/pageviewer-idx?c=mayantislavery;cc=mayantislavery;q1=solomon%20northrop;rgn=full%20text;idno=15853626;didno=15853626;view=image;seq=1;page=root;size=100 (accessed May 10, 2015).

20. *Eighth Annual Report of the Board of Managers of the Mass. Anti-Slavery Society Presented January 22, 1840* (Boston: Dow & Jackson, 1840), xxvi; and

Frances H. Bradburn, *A Memorial of George Bradburn* (Boston: Cupples, Upham and Company, 1883), 140.

21. "The Worcester Kidnappers," *Emancipator* (October 10, 1839).

22. The text of this law was printed in an appendix to Solomon Northup's *Twelve Years a Slave*.

23. See case studies of George Armstrong and Henry Dixon.

24. *Laws of the State of Illinois Passed by the Nineteenth General Assembly, Convened January 1, 1855* (Springfield, IL: Lanphier & Walker, 1855), 186.

25. "Child-Stealing at the North," (Brattleboro) *Vermont Phoenix* (May 18, 1849).

26. See case study of David Treadwell.

27. Dorothy B. Porter, "David Ruggles, an Apostle of Human Rights," *Journal of Negro History* (January 1943): 23–50.

28. *The First Annual Report of the New York Committee of Vigilance for the Year 1837, Together with Important Facts Relative to their Proceedings* (New York: Piercy & Reed, 1837). The Ruggles quote comes from Porter, "David Ruggles, an Apostle of Human Rights," 34.

29. See case study of Stephen Dickinson, Robert Garrison, and Isaac Wright.

30. See case study of Nahum G. Hazard.

31. See case study of Frank Jackson.

32. Jesse Torrey, *A Portraiture of Domestic Slavery, in the United States* (Philadelphia: The Author, 1817); Torrey, *A Portraiture of Domestic Slavery in the United States*, 2nd edition. (Ballston Spa, NY: The Author, 1818); and Torrey, *American Slave Trade* (London: J. M. Cobbett, 1822).

33. For example, *The First Annual Report of the New York Committee of Vigilance for the Year 1837.*

34. These reports included Theodore Dwight Weld, *American Slavery as It Is: Testimony of a Thousand Witnesses* (New York: American Anti-Slavery Society, 1839), 140ff.; *The Thirteenth Annual Report of the American & Foreign Anti-Slavery Society* (New York: American & Foreign Anti-Slavery Society, 1853); *Annual Report of the American Anti-Slavery Society, by the Executive Committee for the Year Ending May 1, 1859* (New York: American Anti-Slavery Society, 1860), 69ff.; and *Twenty-Eighth Annual Report of the American Anti-Slavery Society, by the Executive Committee for the Year Ending May 1, 1861* (New York: American Anti-Slavery Society, 1861), 142ff.

35. *Slavery and the Internal Slave Trade of the United States of North America* (London: Thomas Ward and Co., 1841).

36. Harriet Beecher Stowe, *A Key to Uncle Tom's Cabin* (London: Sampson Low, Son, & Co., 1853), chap. 8; Mary Langdon, *Ida May: A Story of Things Actual and Possible* (Boston: Phillips, Sampson and Co., 1855).

37. Solomon Northup, *Twelve Years a Slave* (Baton Rouge: Louisiana State University Press, 1968; originally published in 1853).

38. Kate E. R. Pickard, *The Kidnapped and the Ransomed* (Syracuse, NY: William T. Hamilton, 1856).

39. William Still, *The Underground Rail Road* (Philadelphia: Porter & Coates, 1872), 37.

40. Weld, *American Slavery as It Is*, 141.

41. Ibid., 142.

42. Bradburn, *A Memorial of George Bradburn*, 5.

43. Ibid., 4–5.

44. See case study of Nahum G. Hazard.

45. The report was prepared in response to a petition by citizens who said that "they believe that evidence may be furnished of such cases [of kidnapping] by persons in the city of New-York." New York State Assembly, Select Committee on the Petition of Various Citizens to Prevent Kidnapping, Report No. 341, p. 1.

46. "Laws of the State of New York," *New-York American* (May 21, 1840); and "Address of the Whig Members of the Legislature," *Geneva* (NY) *Courier* (May 26, 1840). The text of the statute was printed as an appendix in Solomon Northup's *Twelve Years a Slave*.

47. Birdseye was pleased on hearing of Northup's rescue: "Never did his benevolent countenance beam with a higher joy—never did words escape his lips that partook so much of self-gratulation, as when . . . he learnt that, in virtue of that law, Mr. Solomon Northrup [*sic*], of Washington County, had been brought back to freedom and his family, from a cruel bondage of twelve years continuance, in the State of Louisiana." "Hon. Victory Birdseye," (Syracuse, NY) *Evening Chronicle* (September 24, 1853).

48. These articles have been republished in Daniel Meaders (ed.), *Kidnappers in Philadelphia: Isaac Hopper's Tales of Oppression, 1780–1843* (New York: Garland, 1994); and Meaders (ed.), *Kidnappers in Philadelphia: Isaac Hopper's Tales of Oppression, 1780–1843*, 2nd ed. (Cherry Hill, NJ: Africana Homestead Legacy Publishers, 2009).

49. For example, details of the 1825 abduction of a number of Philadelphians was reported in the *African Observer* (Fifth Month, 1827): 37ff.

50. See case studies of Emily, George, Louisa, and William Fauver; Jonathan and Sampson Dredden; and Catharine, David, James, and Martha Morris.

51. *The First Annual Report of the New York Committee of Vigilance for the Year 1837*, 16–17.

52. See David Fiske, Clifford W. Brown, and Rachel Seligman, *Solomon Northup: The Complete Story of the Author of* Twelve Years a Slave (Santa Barbara, CA: Praeger, 2013), chap. 7.

53. Henry B. Northup spoke at Albany, New York (*Frederick Douglass' Paper* [February 18, 1853]); Port Byron, New York (*Frederick Douglass' Paper* [July 29, 1853]); and the Essex County Fair in Ticonderoga, New York (Frederick G. Bascom, *Letters of a Ticonderoga Farmer* [Ithaca, NY: Fall Creek Books, 2009], 36).

CHAPTER 5

1. New York State Assembly, Select Committee on the Petition of Various Citizens to Prevent Kidnapping, Report No. 341, May 1, 1840, 3, available in

Cornell University's Samuel J. May Anti-Slavery Collection, http://dlxs
.library.cornell.edu/cgi/t/text/pageviewer-idx?c=mayantislavery;idno=278925
10;view=image;seq=1 (accessed April 28, 2014).

2. See case studies of Solomon Northup and Stephen Dickinson, Robert
Garrison, and Isaac Wright.

3. See case study of Wilson George Hays and Charles Smith.

4. See case studies of George Armstrong, Hester Jane Carr, and Eli Terry.

5. "Uncle Tom's Cabin—No. 2," *Salem* (NY) *Press* (July 26, 1853).

6. "Manifest of Slaves Intended to Be Transported on the Brig Orleans ...,"
dated April 27, 1841, National Archives and Records Administration,
Washington, DC, Slave Manifests of Coastwise Vessels Filed at New Orleans,
Louisiana, 1807–1860, Microfilm Serial: M1895, Microfilm Roll: 8.

7. See case study of Eli Terry.

8. See case study of Sidney O. Francis.

9. See case study of George Anderson.

10. See case study of John Hight and Daniel Prue.

11. For example, there is the runaway slave ad published after Isaac
Wright's rescue, which warned that he "no doubt will attempt to pass himself
as free." See case study of Stephen Dickinson, Robert Garrison, and Isaac
Wright.

12. "The Kidnapped Negro Restored to Freedom," *Cleveland Plain Dealer*
(December 19, 1857). See also the case study of John Hight and Daniel Prue.

13. See case study of Dimmock Charlton.

14. See case study of Stephen Dickinson, Robert Garrison, and Isaac
Wright.

15. See case study of Frank Jackson.

16. Abner Doubleday, *Reminiscences of Forts Sumter and Moultrie in 1860–61*
(Scituate, MA: Digital Scanning, Inc., 2001; reprint of 1876 edition), 34–35.

17. Jesse Torrey, *American Slave Trade* (London: J. M. Corbett, 1822), 80n.

18. Ibid., 82n.

19. Quoted in "The War at the South," *Emancipator* (August 5, 1841).

20. *North-Carolina Star* (September 8, 1841): 3.

21. Jacob Barker, *Incidents in the Life of Jacob Barker of New Orleans, Louisiana*
(Washington, DC: The Author (?), 1855), 221.

22. Ibid., 222. Barker's account of the release of a Native American from
Massachusetts appears in "Mass. Legislature. Report on the Deliverance
of Citizens Liable to Be Sold as Slaves," *Liberator* (March 29, 1839); and in
Massachusetts, General Court, Joint Special Committee on Deliverance of Citizens Liable to Be Sold as Slaves, *Report on the Deliverance of Citizens, Liable to Be
Sold as Slaves*, 14ff., available in: Samuel J. May Anti-Slavery Collection (Cornell
University), http://ebooks.library.cornell.edu/cgi/t/text/pageviewer-idx?c
=mayantislavery&cc=mayantislavery&idno=08839218&q1=jacob+barker&view
=image&seq=1&size=100 (accessed October 31, 2014).

23. Barker, *Incidents in the Life of Jacob Barker of New Orleans, Louisiana*, 222.

24. "Mass. Legislature. Report on the Deliverance of Citizens Liable to Be
Sold as Slaves"; and Massachusetts, General Court, Joint Special Committee

on Deliverance of Citizens Liable to Be Sold as Slaves, *Report on the Deliverance of Citizens,* 14ff.

25. Barker, *Incidents in the Life of Jacob Barker of New Orleans, Louisiana,* 222.

26. See case study of George Anderson.

27. See case study of Dimmock Charlton.

28. Solomon Northup, *Twelve Years a Slave* (Baton Rouge: Louisiana State University Press, 1968), 23.

29. Ibid., 239.

30. "Uncle Tom's Cabin—No. 2."

31. *Remonstrance: To the Honorable Senate and House of Representatives of the Commonwealth of Massachusetts, the Memorial and Remonstrance of the Undersigned, Citizens of Massachusetts . . .,* House, (Report) No. 121, Commonwealth of Massachusetts, March 1861, 4, available in Samuel J. May Anti-Slavery Collection, Cornell University, http://ebooks.library.cornell.edu/cgi/t/text/pageviewer-idx?c=mayantislavery;cc=mayantislavery;q1=solomon%20north rop;rgn=full%20text;idno=15853626;didno=15853626;view=image;seq=1; page=root;size=100 (accessed October 31, 2014).

32. Jesse Torrey, *A Portraiture of Domestic Slavery in the United States,* 2nd ed. (Ballston Spa, NY: The Author, 1818), 88.

33. (Savannah, GA) *Daily Morning News* (January 22, 1853).

34. See case study of William Houston.

35. Wendell Phillips Garrison and Frances Jackson Garrison, *William Lloyd Garrison, 1805–1879: The Story of His Life Told by His Children,* Vol. 3, 1841–1860. (Boston: Houghton, Mifflin and Co., 1894), 130.

36. Henry Wilson, *History of the Rise and Fall of the Slave Power in America,* Vol. 1 (Boston: James R. Osgood and Co., 1878), 582–83.

37. Ibid., 583.

38. Garrison and Garrison, *William Lloyd Garrison, 1805–1879,* 131n.

39. See case study of Eli Terry.

40. "Petitions for Freedom," (Boston) *Emancipator and Republican* (October 7, 1846). Payne's story is related in: David G. Smith, *On the Edge of Freedom: The Fugitive Slave Issue in South Central Pennsylvania, 1820–1870* (New York: Fordham University Press, 2014), 98ff.; Debra Sandoe McCauslin, *Reconstructing the Past: Puzzle of a Lost Community* (Gettysburg, PA: For the Cause Productions, 2005); and Mary G. Gandy, *Guide My Feet, Hold My Hand* (Canton, MO: M. G. Gandy, 1987). (The author was unable to consult the latter two works.)

41. See case study of Solomon Northup.

42. See case study of Eli Terry.

43. Case of *Abner W. Mercer, alias William Wilson, v. The Commonwealth,* in William Brockenbrough, *Virginia Cases, or Decisions of the General Court of Virginia, Chiefly on the Criminal Law of the Commonwealth, Commencing June Term, 1815, and Ending June Term, 1826* (Richmond, VA: Peter Cottom, 1826), 144ff. Quote appears on page 147.

44. "Kidnapping," *New-York Tribune* (August 12, 1847); "Kidnappers Caught," *National Police Gazette* (August 14, 1847); and "From Baltimore," *Philadelphia Inquirer* (August 18, 1847).

CHAPTER 6

1. John Thomas Sharf, *History of Maryland from the Earliest Period to the Present Day*, Vol. 3 (Baltimore: John B. Piet, 1879), 306; *Life of Elisha Tyson, the Philanthropist* (Baltimore: B. Lundy, 1825), 57–58.

2. Carol Wilson, *Freedom at Risk: The Kidnapping of Free Blacks in America, 1780–1865* (Lexington: University Press of Kentucky, 1994), 70.

3. A report that led to passage of the law mentioned that further information on kidnappings could be obtained from "persons in the city of New-York." New York State Assembly, Select Committee on the Petition of Various Citizens to Prevent Kidnapping. Report No. 341, May 1, 1840, 1, available in Cornell University's Samuel J. May Anti-Slavery Collection, http://dlxs.library.cornell.edu/cgi/t/text/pageviewer-idx?c=mayantislavery;idno=27892510;view=image;seq=1 (accessed April 28, 2014).

4. See case study of Stephen Dickinson, Robert Garrison, and Isaac Wright.

5. See "The Pennsylvania Abolition Society" issue of *Pennsylvania Legacies*, Vol. 5, No. 2 (November 2005). In particular, see Emma J. Lapsansky-Werner, "Teamed Up with the PAS: Images of Black Philadelphia," *Pennsylvania Legacies*, Vol. 5, No. 2 (November 2005): 11–15.

6. Collected in Daniel E. Meaders (comp.), *Kidnappers in Philadelphia: Isaac Hopper's Tales of Oppression, 1780–1843* (New York: Garland Pub., 1994).

7. See case study of Ignatius Beck.

8. Jesse Torrey, *A Portraiture of Domestic Slavery in the United States*, 2nd ed. (Ballston Spa, NY: The Author, 1818); also published as Jesse Torrey, *American Slave Trade* (London: J. M. Corbett, 1822).

9. Ibid., 80–81.

10. Theodore Dwight Weld, *American Slavery as It Is: Testimony of a Thousand Witnesses* (New York: American Anti-Slavery Society, 1839). Quote is from page 140, kidnapping incidents are on pages 89, 140–42, and 162.

11. Harriet Beecher Stowe, *A Key to Uncle Tom's Cabin* (London: Sampson Low, Son & Co., 1853), 420.

12. Bradburn's report showed "by a startling array of facts, that the existence of slavery not only jeopards, but actually, in many cases, takes away, the rights and liberties of free colored persons." *Eighth Annual Report of the Board of Managers of the Mass. Anti-Slavery Society Presented January 22, 1840* (Boston: Dow & Jackson, 1840), xxvi. Discussion of it is in Weld, *American Slavery as It Is*, 141. Bradburn's efforts are related in Frances H. Bradburn, *A Memorial of George Bradburn* (Boston: Cupples, Upham and Company, 1883). Birdseye's report was New York State Assembly, Select Committee on the Petition of Various Citizens to Prevent Kidnapping, Report No. 341.

13. See the section "Laws to Allow for Rescue of Kidnap Victims" in Chapter 4.

14. See case study of Ignatius Beck.

15. See case studies of George Anderson and Sidney O. Francis. Thomas Lipscomb, of Virginia, was also instrumental in the liberation of Francis and the apprehension and conviction of Francis's kidnappers.

16. See case study of Mary Boyd.

17. See case study of Stephen Dickinson, Robert Garrison, and Isaac Wright.

18. Disapprobation of Barker's efforts was related in "The War at the South," *Emancipator* (August 5, 1841); and *North-Carolina Star* (September 8, 1841): 3. The latter included a suggestion that Barker be "taken before his honor Judge Lynch." Barker's activities are detailed in Jacob Barker, *Incidents in the Life of Jacob Barker of New Orleans, Louisiana* (Washington, DC: The Author (?), 1855), 220ff.; and in "Mass. Legislature. Report on the Deliverance of Citizens Liable to Be Sold as Slaves," *Liberator* (March 29, 1839); and in Massachusetts, General Court, Joint Special Committee on Deliverance of Citizens Liable to Be Sold as Slaves, *Report on the Deliverance of Citizens, Liable to Be Sold as Slaves*, 14ff., available in Samuel J. May Anti-Slavery Collection (Cornell University), http://ebooks.library.cornell.edu/cgi/t/text/pageviewer-idx?c=mayantislavery&cc=mayantislavery&idno=08839218&q1=jacob+barker&view=image&seq=1&size=100 (accessed October 31, 2015). Hazard's efforts are related in "Rowland Gibson Hazard," University of Rhode Island, University Libraries, Special Collections and University Archives, http://www.uri.edu/library/special_collections/exhibits/hazard/Rowland%20G%20Hazard.html (accessed August 4, 2013); *Biographical Cyclopedia of Representative Men of Rhode Island* (Providence, RI: National Biographical Publishing Co., 1881), 269 (which notes he was threatened "with the extremity of 'Lynch law.'"); and Caroline Hazard (ed.), *Essay on Language and Other Essays and Addresses by Rowland Gibson Hazard, LL.D.* (Boston: Houghton, Mifflin and Company, 1889), viii. The latter notes that: "For weeks he allowed himself only five hours sleep, and visited the jails of the city."

19. See case study of John Hight and Daniel Prue.

20. See case study of Frank Jackson.

21. See case study of Hester Jane Carr.

22. See case study of Aaron Cooper.

23. Solomon Northup, *Twelve Years a Slave* (Baton Rouge: Louisiana State University Press, 1968), 228ff.

24. Torrey noted that the numerous contributions showed that "the disposition to extend the hand of relief to abused African strangers, is not at the present period, by any means confined exclusively to the limits of a solitary religious society." Torrey, *A Portraiture of Domestic Slavery in the United States*, 80ff.

25. See case study of Eli Terry.

26. See case study of Stephen Dickinson, Robert Garrison, and Isaac Wright.

27. See case study of Catharine, David, James, and Martha Morris.

28. "Abduction and Enslavement of Two Citizens of New York," *Albany Evening Journal* (January 31, 1857).

CHAPTER 7

1. Sue Eakin noted that an 1830 law in Louisiana provided for the confiscation of slaves from an owner who was abusing them, and she cites one

example where this occurred in central Louisiana. Based on Solomon Northup's descriptions of how slaves were mistreated, however, such an example would appear to be exceptional—ordinarily, owners could treat their slaves as they wished. Sue Eakin, *Solomon Northup's* Twelve Years a Slave *and Plantation Life in the Antebellum South* (Lafayette: University of Louisiana at Lafayette, 2007), 449.

2. See Philip G. Zimbardo, *The Lucifer Effect: Understanding How Good People Turn Evil* (New York: Random House, 2007).

3. See case studies of Abby Guy, Patience Hicks, Alexina Morrison, and Salome Muller.

4. William Jay's letter to the mayor, in regard to the kidnapping of Peter John Lee, was printed in: "Annals of Kidnapping," (Cincinnati, OH) *Philanthropist* (March 3, 1837).

CHAPTER 8

1. This was a neighborhood in which many slave dealers operated. See the discussion of Washington, D.C., slave traders in Chapter 3.

2. "Lost Boy," *Daily National Intelligencer* (July 16, 1827): 1.

3. "Kidnapping," (Richmond) *Dispatch* (January 23, 1858).

4. Ibid., 1.

5. "The Kidnapping Case before the Mayor," *New York Evening Express* (February 4, 1858): 4.

6. "Kidnapping," (Richmond) *Dispatch* (January 25, 1858): 1; and "An Interesting Case of Alleged Kidnapping," *New York Herald* (February 3, 1858), which says Peterson had been teaching at the school since the 1830s. A "John Peterson" is listed as a teacher at Colored School No. 1 in 1853: *Manual of the Board of Manual of the Board of Education of the City and County of New York, September, 1853* (New York: W. C. Bryant and Co., 1853), 158.

7. Richmond mayor Joseph Mayo noted that Anderson was literate, but also said, "He is a weak, silly negro, easily imposed on, about twenty years old, not more than five feet high, and has a very downcast look." See "An Interesting Case of Alleged Kidnapping." His "idiocy" is also noted in: "Kidnapping," (Richmond) *Dispatch* (January 25, 1858): 1; "New York Items," *Brooklyn Daily Eagle* (April 9, 1858): 2; *New York Herald* (April 9, 1858): 4; and "The New York Kidnapping Case," (Richmond) *Daily Dispatch* (April 12, 1858): 1 (which noted that, because he could not understand the concept of an oath, he could not testify at the trial of his kidnapper).

8. "Kidnapping," (Richmond) *Dispatch* (January 23, 1858); "Kidnapping," (Richmond) *Dispatch* (January 25, 1858): 1; and "An Interesting Case of Alleged Kidnapping" (which gives the "Graham" spelling).

9. Thomas may have been in Missouri, but he was not from there. He reportedly was well known to the New York authorities. "Requisition on the Governor," (Richmond) *Daily Dispatch* (February 13, 1858): 1. He is one of the Sing Sing Prison inmates listed in the 1860 census, where his birthplace

is given as New York: 1860 Federal Census, Town of Ossining, Westchester County, New York, 99. He appears to have lived in Chemung and Schuyler Counties in the 1850s and likely worked with his father as a merchant: 1850 Federal Census, Town of Catharine, Chemung County, New York, 64; and an advertisement for a store in Havana, Schuyler County, run by "E. H. Thomas & Son," *Havana* (NY) *Journal* (July 9, 1853). Upstate newspapers, in articles about Thomas's sentencing, noted he had previously resided in the town of Havana: *Havana* (NY) *Journal* (May 29, 1858); and *Geneva* (NY) *Courier* (June 2, 1858). He committed suicide in the town of Catlin, Chemung County in 1881: "Suicide of Oscar M. Thomas," *Havana* (NY) *Journal* (July 30, 1881).

10. Possibly Anderson was sold twice, but he seems to have definitely been sold to "Raglan," since a deposition from a "Mr. Raglan, of Petersburg, Va." was used as evidence at the trial: "The New York Kidnapping Case," 1 (which mentions that a Mr. Davis witnessed the transaction). Another article gives this buyer's name given as "Rufin Raglan," "Court of General Sessions," *New York Herald* (April 11, 1858). The man likely was Reuben Ragland, from Petersburg, Virginia, who had a slave-trading brother named John Davis Ragland. See [Carl von Loesch], "Who Was Reuben Ragland?" The Ragland Mansion, http://www.raglandmansion.com/ragl.en.html (accessed January 30, 2015).

11. "Kidnapping," (Richmond) *Dispatch* (January 23, 1858).

12. "An Interesting Case of Alleged Kidnapping."

13. (Washington, DC) *Evening Star* (February 13, 1858); and "Case of Anderson, the Kidnapped Negro," *New York Herald* (February 12, 1858): 3.

14. "An Interesting Case of Alleged Kidnapping."

15. "Case of Anderson, the Kidnapped Negro," 3; and *Evening Star* (February 13, 1858).

16. "An Interesting Case of Alleged Kidnapping." Trimble's affidavit is given in "The Kidnapping Case before the Mayor," *New York Evening Express* (February 4, 1858): 4.

17. "The Alleged Kidnapping Case," (Richmond) *Dispatch* (February 17, 1858).

18. (New Haven) *Columbian Register* (February 20, 1858): 2; and "Return of the Kidnapped Negro (Anderson) and the Kidnapper," *New York Evening Express* (February 15, 1858): 3. Both articles inexplicably describe Thomas as a "Frenchman."

19. Thomas's aliases were mocked in "Court of General Sessions—Saturday," *New York Sun* (May 24, 1858), and in "Return of the Kidnapped Negro (Anderson) and the Kidnapper," 3, where he was called "the man with all the *aliases*."

20. "Court of General Sessions," *New York Herald* (February 16, 1858): 1.

21. "Return of the Kidnapped Negro (Anderson) and the Kidnapper," 3.

22. "Court of General Sessions," *New York Herald* (April 11, 1858).

23. Chatfield and Stuart at least handled the appeal following Thomas's conviction: *New York Times* (April 26, 1858): 2; and "Legal Intelligence," *Morning Courier and New-York Enquirer* (April 10, 1858). Chatfield had been

impeached for malfeasance, and resigned as attorney general in 1853. *Journal of the Assembly of the State of New-York; at Their Seventy-Sixth Session*, Vol. 2 (Albany, NY: Charles Van Benthuyse, 1853), 1388ff.; and *Manual for the Use of the Legislature of the State of New York, 1921* (Albany, NY: J. B. Lyon Company, 1921), 391. Stuart had been tried for bribery in 1855, and though acquitted, resigned his position: "The Trial of Judge Stuart," *Brooklyn Daily Eagle* (November 21, 1855); "City Judge of New York," (Little Falls, NY) *Journal* (January 3, 1856); and "The Death of Ex-Judge Stuart," (New York) *Evening Post* (September 16, 1871).

24. Anderson may not have been allowed to testify due to his inability to understand what it meant to take an oath. "The New York Kidnapping Case," 1.

25. "Court of General Sessions," *New York Herald* (April 11, 1858); and "The New York Kidnapping Case," 1. "Rufin Raglan" was probably Reuben Ragland, of Petersburg, Virginia.

26. The most detailed accounts of the trial and the Recorder's charge to the jury are in "Legal Intelligence," *Morning Courier and New-York Enquirer* (April 10, 1858); and *New York Herald* (April 11, 1858).

27. *New York Times* (April 26, 1858): 2.

28. "The Negro-Kidnapping Case," *New York Times* (May 24, 1858): 3.

29. Ibid. See also the case study of Sarah Taylor.

30. His commitment to prison was recorded at Ancestry.com. New York, Governor's Registers of Commitments to Prisons, 1842–1908 (database online; Provo, UT: Ancestry.com Operations, Inc., 2014, page 321). He is among the inmates at Sing Sing Prison in 1860. 1860 Federal Census, Town of Ossining, Westchester County, New York, 99.

31. *Seventeenth Annual Report of the Inspectors of State Prisons of the State of New York* (Albany, NY: Charles Van Benthuysen, 1865), 36; and New York, Executive Orders for Commutations, Pardons, Restorations and Respites, 1845–1931, page 482 (database online), Ancestry.com; and New York, Executive Orders for Commutations, Pardons, Restorations and Respites, 1845–1931, page 690 (database online), Ancestry.com.

32. "Suicide of Oscar M. Thomas," *Havana* (NY) *Journal* (July 30, 1881).

33. "Imitating Solomon Northrup," (Washington, DC) *Evening Star* (June 30, 1860). John "Bull" Frizzell (or Frizzle) was a troublesome secessionist during the Civil War. "Arrests of Secessionists," *National Republican* (June 13, 1861): 3. He was involved in a failed plot to kidnap Abraham Lincoln. Thomas Nelson Conrad, *The Rebel Scout: A Thrilling History of Scouting Life in the Southern Army* (Washington, DC: National Publishing Co., 1904), 122ff.

34. Armstrong was likely the 18-year-old black man listed in the household of his sister, Hannah, in Watertown, New York in 1855. 1855 New York State Census, Watertown, Jefferson County, New York, Household #185. In the 1865 census, a "Geo. Armstrong" lived in Watertown with his mother, Pamelia Armstrong, and was serving in the army at the time. 1865 New York State Census, Watertown, Jefferson County, New York, Household #241. The *Watertown Business and Residence Directory for 1855* (Watertown, NY:

J. D. Huntington, 1855) contains a listing for Mrs. P. Armstrong, a widow who was black.

35. When the District of Columbia slave trader who had purchased the kidnapped Northup was put on trial, a local newspaper reported that "it was pretty well proved that he [Northup] was himself a principal party to the fraud." "Kidnapped," *Alexandria* (VA) *Gazette* (January 21, 1853): 2; *Boston Herald* (January 24, 1853): 1 (both attributing the information to the *Washington Republic*). Speculation that Northup had been complicit in his kidnapping surfaced again after the case against his kidnappers was dropped in 1857: "it is more than suspected that Sol. Northup was an accomplice in the sale, calculating to slip away and share the spoils," *Syracuse Daily Courier* (July 3, 1857), attributed to the *Saratogian's* report of an investigation by the *Albany Evening Journal*; a variation appeared in the *Lowell Daily Citizen and News* (June 17, 1857). See also the case study of Solomon Northup.

36. "A Fugitive Slave Case—a Free Negro Kidnapped and Sold—Requisition from Gov. Morgan," *New York Evening Express* (July 9, 1860), 4. (Attributed to the *Albany Journal*.) Haddock was a Watertown newspaper publisher and author, and something of an adventurer—his participation in a balloon ascension in 1859 appeared in: John Wise, *Through the Air: A Narrative of Forty Years' Experience as an Aeronaut* (Philadelphia: To-Day Printing and Publishing Company, 1873), 543ff. His life was summarized in Dave Shampine, "Times Gone By: The Misadventures of Watertown's John Haddock," *Watertown Daily Times* (September 27, 2009).

37. "The Case of George Armstrong," (District of Columbia) *Evening Star* (July 11, 1860).

38. "Return of the Fugitive," *Syracuse Daily Journal* (July 17, 1860).

39. Ibid.

40. William Williams testified that " 'Nashe' (Ignatius Beck)" had belonged to Joseph Beck. P. W. Chandler, *The Law Reporter*, Vol. 2 (Boston: Weeks, Jordan and Company, 1840), 106.

41. Terry Buckalew, "A Hero Buried on Queen Street," Friends of Bethel Burying Ground (May 1, 2014), http://preciousdust.blogspot.com/2014/05/a-hero-buried-on-queen-street.html (accessed January 21, 2014). More information on Beck's manumission, including a citation to its record in the Prince George's County, Maryland, Land Records is given in Terry Buckalew, "Ignatius Beck," Southwark Historical Society (January 29, 2013), http://www.southwarkhistory.org/ignatius-beck/ (accessed January 21, 2014). Abolitionist Isaac T. Hopper wrote that, according to a letter he received concerning Beck, he had been "duly manumitted in the city of Washington," and Hopper was able to obtain authenticated copies of the paperwork from a Samuel Brooks in that city. See Isaac T. Hopper, "Tales of Oppression," *National Anti-Slavery Standard* (January 20, 1842): 130.

42. See Terry Buckalew's articles, *op. cit.*

43. Probably around 1805, according to Buckalew.

44. Isaac T. Hopper, "Tales of Oppression," *National Anti-Slavery Standard* (January 20, 1842): 130.

45. Beck's enslavement may have lasted as long as three years, since he later testified that, beginning in 1810, he had been away from Philadelphia for two to three years. Chandler, *The Law Reporter*, Vol. 2, 110.

46. Martin Robison Delany, *The Condition, Elevation, Emigration, and Destiny of the Colored People of the United States* (N.p., 1852.), Chapter 8. Text available from Project Gutenberg, http://www.gutenberg.org/files/17154/17154-h/ 17154-h.htm (accessed January 22, 2015). The 1840 Census includes in Moyamensing (today, a neighborhood in South Philadelphia) an Ignatius Beck household with two free black persons, one male between the ages of 35 and 55, and one female, aged 10 to 24. There is either an age discrepancy (since Beck would have been about 65 in 1840), or this individual may have been a relative of Beck. 1840 Federal Census, Moyamensing, Philadelphia County, Pennsylvania, 99.

47. "Colored People in Philadelphia," *The Genius of Universal Emancipation*, No. 2, Vol. 1, 3rd series (February 1831): 163.

48. Joseph A. Borome, "The Vigilant Committee of Philadelphia," *Pennsylvania Magazine of History and Biography*, Vol. 92, No. 3 (July 1968): 320–31, 339.

49. Chandler, *The Law Reporter*, Vol. 2, 110.

50. "Pennsylvania, Philadelphia City Death Certificates, 1803–1915," index and images, FamilySearch, https://familysearch.org/pal:/MM9.1.1/JK98 -RYZ (accessed January 22, 2015), Igantious Beck, 14 Oct 1849; citing Philadelphia City Archives and Historical Society of Pennsylvania, Philadelphia; FHL microfilm 1,906,952; "Mortuary Notice," (Philadelphia) *Public Ledger* (October 17, 1849): 2 (which gave his age as 72).

51. Buckalew, "Ignatius Beck"; Buckalew, "A Hero Buried on Queen Street"; Valerie Russ, "Queen Village Burial Ground a Hot Topic," *Philadelphia Daily News* (May 5, 2014).

52. "Outrageous Cases of Kidnapping," *Jamestown* (NY) *Journal* (November 2, 1860).

53. For a well-researched article on Boyd, see H. Scott Wolf, "The Fate of Jeremiah Boyd: A Tale of Kidnapping and Murder in Old Galena," *Illinois Heritage*, Vol. 7, No. 3 (May–June 2004): 10–16. Boyd's occupation in 1850 was "drayman," and he was head of a household of five people, including a woman (probably his wife) named Milly who was born about 1815 in Tennessee. 1850 Federal Census, Galena, Jo Daviess County, Illinois, 277. In 1860, his occupation was given as "miner," and his apparent wife then was Mary, born about 1830 in Virginia. 1860 Federal Census, Galena, Jo Daviess County, Illinois, 473.

54. "Disgraceful Outrage in Illinois," *New York Times* (November 6, 1860).

55. "Murder and Supposed Kidnapping," *New York Times* (October 24, 1860), attributed to the *St. Louis News*.

56. *Liberator* (October 19, 1860).

57. "Escape of a Murderer and Kidnapper—The Murderer Still at Large," (Oskaloosa, KS) *Independent* (October 31, 1860).

58. Wolf, "The Fate of Jeremiah Boyd," 10–16.

59. Joseph Tate, *Digest of the Laws of Virginia Which Are of a Permanent Character and General Operation; Illustrated by Judicial Decision: To Which Is Added, an*

Index of the Names of the Cases in the Virginia Reporters, (Richmond, VA: Smith and Palmer: 1841), 221.

60. Benjamin Watkins Leigh, *Reports of Cases Argued and Determined in the Court of Appeals, and in the General Court of Virginia*, Vol. 1 (Richmond, VA: Samuel Shepherd & Co.: 1830), 588–97.

61. For an account of Carr's story, based largely on her freedom suit, see Greg Crawford, "To Be Sold: Hester Jane Carr's Story," *Out of the Box: Notes from the Archives @ The Library of Virginia*, http://www.virginiamemory.com/blogs/out_of_the_box/2014/10/22/to-be-sold-hester-jane-carrs-story/ (accessed December 7, 2014).

62. According to a footnote in *The First Annual Report of the New York Committee of Vigilance for the Year 1837, Together with Important Facts Relative to their Proceedings* (New York: Piercy & Reed, 1837), 56–57.

63. Carr's petition, referenced in Greg Crawford's article, said the woman's name was Nancy Daws, or Nancy Donald. Parker's letter, printed in the Committee of Vigilance report, gives her name as Nancy Haws, and suggests she was a woman of "bad fame." She was called "Mrs. Davies alias Haws" in "City Recorder—Kidnapping—and Free People of Colour in New York," *The Friend* (Seventh Day, Tenth Month, 1836): 21–22.

64. Beasley was partners with William H. Wood. Crawford, "To Be Sold: Hester Jane Carr's Story."

65. In Parker's letter, printed in the Committee of Vigilance report, he said the man used the name Timothy Collins.

66. Parker was probably the same William C. Parker who represented defendants in the Nat Turner case. See Kenneth S. Greenberg. *Nat Turner: A Slave Rebellion in History and Memory* (Oxford: Oxford University Press, 2003).

67. Cockcroft prepared one, as did Mary Crippen of Brooklyn, a black relative of Carr's. Crippen's affidavit references one from Mrs. Elizabeth Johnson, though it is not included with the other documents. *The First Annual Report of the New York Committee of Vigilance for the Year 1837*.

68. "City Recorder—Kidnapping—and Free People of Colour in New York," *The Friend* (Seventh Day, Tenth Month, 1836): 21–22.

69. Crawford, "To Be Sold: Hester Jane Carr's Story."

70. "Enslavement of a British Subject," *New York Times* (August 10, 1857). Information from the *Times* article was reprinted in various publications, including "Dimmock Charlton and His Grandchild," *Anti-Slavery Reporter* (January 1, 1858); and Mary L. Cox, *Narrative of Dimmock Charlton, a British Subject, Taken from the Brig "Peacock" by the U.S. Sloop "Hornet," Enslaved while a Prisoner of War, and Retained Forty Five Years in Bondage* (London: Forgotten Books, 2013). E-book of a work originally published in 1859.

71. In addition to being a jurist, Judge Charlton served as mayor of Savannah and was in the state legislature: I. J. Hofmayer and Harry S. Strozier (eds.), *Report of the Thirty-fourth Annual Session of the Georgia Bar Association* (Macon, GA: J. W. Burke Company, 1917), 261.

72. Perhaps the James Kerr listed in Chatham County, Georgia: 1850 Federal Census, District #13, Chatham County, Georgia, 327. The 1850 Slave

Census shows that he owned 13 slaves. 1850 Federal Slave Census, District #13, Chatham County, Georgia.

73. Charlton's reasoning is related in "Enslavement of a British Subject," *New York Times* (August 10, 1857).

74. "Slave Case in Westchester County," *New York Tribune* (August 13, 1857).

75. Ibid.

76. "The Slave, Demock Charlton," *New York Times* (July 23, 1857).

77. "Dimmock Charlton—His Story Confirmed," *Anti-Slavery Bugle* (February 13, 1858); and Cox, *Narrative of Dimmock Charlton*.

78. Cox, *Narrative of Dimmock Charlton*.

79. "Enslavement of a British Subject," *New York Times* (August 10, 1857).

80. "Dimmock Charlton," *Frederick Douglass' Monthly* (August 1859).

81. "A Curious History," (San Francisco) *Daily Evening Bulletin* (August 27, 1857).

82. "Custody of a Child," *Boston Evening Transcript* (February 10, 1860); and "Court Calendar," *Boston Daily Advertiser* (February 14, 1860).

83. Paul Heinegg, *Free African Americans of North Carolina, Virginia, and South Carolina, from the Colonial Period to about 1820*. Vol. 1, 5th ed. (Baltimore: Clearfield Company, 2007), 285.

84. In 1820, Arthur owned eight slaves. 1820 U.S. Census, Pittsylvania, Virginia, 75.

85. The reports of Arthur's appeal from the original verdict appear in *Virginia Reports, Annotated, Jefferson—33 Grattan. 1730–1880* (Charlottesville, VA: Michie Company, 1904), "Arthur v. Chavis," 642–48; and Peyton Randolph, *Reports of Cases Argued and Determined in the Court of Appeals of Virginia: To Which are Added, Reports of Cases Decided in the General Court of Virginia*, Vol. 6 (Richmond, VA: Samuel Shepherd & Co., 1829), "Arthur v. Chavis," 142–58.

86. The reports of Arthur's appeal from the original verdict appear in: *Virginia Reports, Annotated, Jefferson—33 Grattan. 1730–1880* (Charlottesville, VA: Michie Company, 1904), 645.

87. Ibid., 646.

88. Paul Heinegg, *Free African Americans of North Carolina, Virginia, and South Carolina, from the Colonial Period to About 1820*, Vol. 1, 5th ed. (Baltimore: Clearfield Company, 2007), 285.

89. "Kidnapping in Caroline County," *Frederick Douglass' Paper* (May 18, 1849): 2; and "Kidnappers in Caroline County," *Albany Evening Journal* (April 19, 1849) specifically identify the victims as being free.

90. "Kidnapping in Maryland," *Baltimore Sun* (April 18, 1849): 4. Attributed to the *Denton Journal* (as were all the newspaper reports). The *Sun* said it had occurred "Thursday night week," (April 5), and *Frederick Douglass' Paper* (May 18, 1849) also gave that date. New York's *Commercial Advertiser* (April 18, 1849) specified that the "attrocious outrage" occurred on the night of April 6.

91. Michael J. Gall, Glenn R. Modica, and Tabitha Hilliard, "Navigation and Negotiation: Adaptive Strategies of a Free African American Family in Central Delaware" (presented at the Middle Atlantic Archaeological

Conference March 2014, Langhorne, PA), http://www.academia.edu/ 6983465/Navigation_and_Negotiation_Adaptive_Strategies_of_a_Free_African _American_Family_in_Central_Delaware_Presented_at_the_Middle_Atlantic _Archaeological_Conference_March_2014_Langhorne_PA_ (accessed February 6, 2015); and Todd A. Herring, "Kidnapped and Sold in Natchez: The Ordeal of Aaron Cooper, a Free Black Man," *Journal of Mississippi History*, Vol. 60, No. 1 (1998): 343–44. An "Aron Cooper" was listed as the head of a family of four nonwhites in 1800: 1800 Federal Census, Kent County, Delaware, 121. In 1810, he had a family of six nonwhites: 1810 Federal Census, Murder Kill Hundred, Kent County, Delaware, 10.

92. Herring, "Kidnapped and Sold in Natchez," 344–45.

93. Cooper's story is detailed in Herring, "Kidnapped and Sold in Natchez," 341–53. It is summarized in Calvin Schermerhorn, *Money over Mastery, Family over Freedom: Slavery in the Antebellum Upper South* (Baltimore: Johns Hopkins University Press, 2011), 41–42.

94. Herring, "Kidnapped and Sold in Natchez," 351.

95. In 1820, he was the head of a family of five free blacks, with one person, probably Cooper, engaged in agriculture—possibly his work on Briscoe's plantation led him to a new occupation after his return. 1820 Federal Census, Camden, Kent County, Delaware, 37.

96. The incident is described in "State v. Abram M. Weaver," in Perrin Busbee, *Reports of Cases at Law Argued and Determined in the Supreme Court of North Carolina* (Raleigh, NC: W. W. Holden, 1853), 9–15.

97. Quote from Busbee, *Reports of Cases at Law Argued and Determined in the Supreme Court of North Carolina*, 10.

98. "Abram M. Weaver" (Greensboro, NC) *Patriot* (September 25, 1852): 3; and "Kidnapping—Abram M. Weaver," (Baltimore) *American and Commercial Daily Advertiser* (October 6, 1852): 5.

99. Busbee, *Reports of Cases at Law Argued and Determined in the Supreme Court of North Carolina*, 13.

100. (Winston-Salem, NC) *People's Press* (May 10, 1851): 3. "Habeas Corpus," *Carolina Watchman* (May 29, 1851): 1.

101. "Superior Court," *Greensboro Patriot* (April 30, 1853): 2.

102. His surname was sometimes given as Dickenson or Dickerson. A summary of his story appears in: Carol Wilson, *Freedom at Risk: The Kidnapping of Free Blacks in America, 1780–1865* (Lexington: University Press of Kentucky, 1994), 59. His personal account originally appeared in "Narrative of Stephen Dickenson [*sic*]," *National Anti-Slavery Standard* (October 8, 1840) and was reprinted in John W. Blassingame (ed.), *Slave Testimony: Two Centuries of Letters, Speeches, Interviews, and Autobiographies* (Baton Rouge: Louisiana State University Press, 1977), 690–95.

103. One account said they lived in Hackensack, New Jersey, just across the river from Manhattan. "Annals of Kidnapping, Case 4th" (Cincinnati, OH) *Philanthropist* (August 28, 1838).

104. "Narrative of Stephen Dickenson [*sic*]," *National Anti-Slavery Standard* (October 8, 1840).

105. "Annals of Kidnapping, Case 4th" (Cincinnati, OH) *Philanthropist* (August 28, 1838).

106. Inward Slave Manifests for the Port of New Orleans, Roll 12, 1837–1839. Transcriptions available online at http://www.afrigeneas.com/slavedata/Roll.12.1837-1839.html (accessed March 15, 2015).

107. "Narrative of Stephen Dickenson [*sic*]," *National Anti-Slavery Standard* (October 8, 1840).

108. "Annals of Kidnapping, Case 4th," (Cincinnati, OH) *Philanthropist* (August 28, 1838).

109. "Narrative of Stephen Dickenson [*sic*]," *National Anti-Slavery Standard* (October 8, 1840).

110. This may well have been a native northerner, Charles H. Langdon-Elwin, who had been assigned by the governor of New Hampshire to carry out certain legal tasks in New Orleans. John Farmer, *The New-Hampshire Annual Register and United States Calendar, No. 15* (Concord, NH: Marsh, Capen and Lyon, 1836), 34.

111. He reached New York on July 7, 1840. "Stephen Dickerson [*sic*]," *The Colored American* (July 18, 1840).

112. "Narrative of Stephen Dickenson [*sic*]," *National Anti-Slavery Standard* (October 8, 1840).

113. Coffin's letter is printed in *Memorial Biographies of the New-England Historic Genealogical Society, Volume VI, 1864–1871* (Boston: New-England Historic Genealogical Society, 1905), "Joshua Coffin," 1–9; and William B. Trask, "Necrology," *New England Historical and Genealogical Register*, Vol. 20, No. 3 (July 1866): 268–70. Coffin's role in the rescue later cost him his position as a letter carrier in Philadelphia: To the Public," *Liberator* (September 10, 1841). Wright, around 1850, left for the West Coast, and many adventures at sea, and eventually planned to reconnect with his family in New York. "Black and White, an Ex-Slave Restored to his Family after Thirty Years' Absence," *Sacramento Daily Union* (February 14, 1885).

114. Simpson probably had an idea that Wright was a free man, since his ad stated: "He was originally from New York, and no doubt will attempt to pass himself as free." See *Liberator* (March 29, 1839).

115. "Narrative of Stephen Dickenson [*sic*]," *National Anti-Slavery Standard* (October 8, 1840).

116. Ruggles's significant activity on the case, which included his making a trip to New Bedford, is detailed in Graham Russell Hodges, *David Ruggles: A Radical Black Abolitionist and the Underground Railroad in New York City* (Chapel Hill: University of North Carolina Press, 2010), 128ff.

117. Ruggles appealed to the public for information: "Kidnapping and Arrest," *The Colored American* (June 23, 1838).

118. Wilson apparently claimed to have been ill, and not on board the boat when the men were taken off. "Annals of Kidnapping, Case 4th," (Cincinnati, OH) *Philanthropist* (August 28, 1838). Ruggles claimed that though Wilson may not have been aboard, he "shared in the avails." See "David Ruggles and the Daily Papers," *Emancipator* (August 30, 1838). Wilson's arrest was

noted in "Bringing Slaves to the United States," *Liberator* (August 10, 1838). Wilson's name appears as the master of the *Newcastle* on slave manifests: Inward Slave Manifests for the Port of New Orleans, Roll 12, 1837–1839. Transcriptions are available online at http://www.afrigeneas.com/slavedata/Roll.12.1837-1839.html (accessed March 15, 2015). The charges against him do not appear to have impacted his career. Newspaper shipping advertisements made note of a number of vessels commanded by Wilson (as "J. Dayton Wilson"), including the *Newcastle, Oconee,* and *General Parkhill,* of which he was part owner: "Ship Building—a Launch," *New York Herald* (December 10, 1838). He also captained the steamship *Sierra Nevada* in the 1850s and died aboard her, near Panama in 1853. "Obituary, Death of Capt. Jonathan Dayton Wilson," *New York Herald* (March 16, 1853).

119. Ruggles sought donations to help with the rescue efforts. *The Colored American* (July 21, 1838).

120. The arrest and incarceration of Lewis was noted in *Albany Evening Journal* (August 13, 1838); "Annals of Kidnapping, Case 4th," (Cincinnati, OH) *Philanthropist* (August 28, 1838); and "David Ruggles and the Daily Papers," *Emancipator* (August 30, 1838). He probably was not in jail for long, since a New Bedford directory listed him as a mariner in 1841: Henry Howland Crapo, *New Bedford Directory* (New Bedford, MA: Benjamin Lindsey, 1841), 90. He may have been the "Capt Thomas Lewis" whose death in Louisiana was noted by a New Bedford newspaper: "Died," *New Bedford Register* (September 13, 1843).

121. "Denoument [*sic*] of the Case of the Colored Man, Henry Dixon," (Auburn, NY) *Daily American* (June 29, 1857).

122. "An Appeal to the Benevolent and Liberal Citizens of Rochester and Western New York," *Albany Evening Journal* (December 8, 1856).

123. "A Nut for the Abolitionists to Crack," *Charleston Courier* (July 23, 1857); "Result of an Effort to Liberate a 'Citizen of New York Held in Unlawful Bondage!' " *Macon Telegraph* (June 6, 1857).

124. "A Nut for the Abolitionists to Crack," *Charleston Courier* (July 23, 1857).

125. Biographical sketch of Seymour, in Joel H. Monroe, *Historical Records of a Hundred and Twenty Years, Auburn, N.Y.* (Geneva, NY: W. F. Humphrey, Printer, 1913), 148–49.

126. Abby Maria Hemenway (ed.), *The Vermont Historical Gazetteer: A Magazine Embracing a History of Each Town, Civil, Ecclesiastical, Biographical and Military,* Vol. 3 (Claremont, NH: Claremont Manufacturing Company, 1877), 957. Sampson's information on Dixon's case is in "An Appeal to the Benevolent and Liberal Citizens of Rochester and Western New York," *Albany Evening Journal* (December 8, 1856); and *Documents of the Assembly of the State of New-York, Eightieth Session—1857,* Vol. 1, Report No. 47.

127. "An Appeal to the Benevolent and Liberal Citizens of Rochester and Western New York," *Albany Evening Journal* (December 8, 1856).

128. Dean was a Macon slave trader. Saul S. Friedman, *Jews and the American Slave Trade* (New Brunswick, NJ: Transaction Publishers, 1998), 166.

Census records show he was a planter, and owned 63 slaves in 1850. 1850 Federal Census, Georgia, Bibb County, Macon, 150; 1860 Federal Census, Georgia, Bibb County, Vineville District, 569; and 1850 Federal Slave Census, Georgia, Bibb County, 303.

129. Sampson's statement was printed in: *Documents of the Assembly of the State of New-York, Eightieth Session—1857*, Vol. 1, Report No. 47.

130. "Result of an Effort to Liberate a 'Citizen of New York Held in Unlawful Bondage!' " *Macon Telegraph* (June 6, 1857); and "A Nut for the Abolitionists to Crack," *Charleston Courier* (July 23, 1857). Some support for this scenario is provided in "The 'Boy' Henry Dixon Obstinately Refuses His Freedom," *New York Herald* (July 26, 1857), which says that Dixon was sold as a slave according to the laws of a slave state. James Dean perhaps made it a practice to obtain slaves in this manner, since he had, by the same process, obtained possession of a free man named Wesley Ford, convicted of a crime in Maryland in 1853. Ford showed his documentation to a newspaper reporter after the end of the war: "The Labor Question in Central Georgia, Immense Supplies of Cotton in the State," *New York Times* (December 10, 1865).

131. *Documents of the Assembly of the State of New-York, Eightieth Session—1857*, Vol. 1, Report No. 47; "An Appeal to the Benevolent and Liberal Citizens of Rochester and Western New York," *Auburn Journal* (December 3, 1856); and "An Appeal to the Benevolent and Liberal Citizens of Rochester and Western New York," *Albany Evening Journal* (December 8, 1856). Austin's service as an agent is mentioned in the December 3, 1856 *Auburn Journal* article, and in "Denoument [*sic*] of the Case of the Colored Man, Henry Dixon," (Auburn, NY) *Daily American* (June 29, 1857). Austin was listed as an alderman of the city of Auburn in (Auburn, NY) *Daily American* (November 5, 1858).

132. "An Appeal to the Benevolent and Liberal Citizens of Rochester and Western New York," *Albany Evening Journal* (December 8, 1856).

133. *Documents of the Assembly of the State of New-York, Eightieth Session—1857*, Vol. 1, Report No. 47; and "Result of an Effort to Liberate a 'Citizen of New York Held in Unlawful Bondage!' " *Macon Telegraph* (June 6, 1857).

134. "Denoument [*sic*] of the Case of the Colored Man, Henry Dixon," (Auburn, NY) *Daily American* (June 29, 1857). Under the provisions of the 1840 law, Austin was entitled to reimbursement of his expenses from the state of New York, and presumably he obtained it. Altogether, $1,200 had been expended on the attempt to rescue Dixon.

135. *Documents of the Assembly of the State of New-York, Eightieth Session—1857*, Vol. 1, Report No. 47.

136. "An Appeal to the Benevolent and Liberal Citizens of Rochester and Western New York," *Auburn Journal* (December 3, 1856).

137. "Result of an Effort to Liberate a 'Citizen of New York Held in Unlawful Bondage!' " *Macon Telegraph* (June 6, 1857); and "A Nut for the Abolitionists to Crack," *Charleston Courier* (July 23, 1857).

138. "Result of an Effort to Liberate a 'Citizen of New York Held in Unlawful Bondage!' " *Macon Telegraph* (June 6, 1857).

139. "Case of Henry Dixon," *Anti-Slavery Bugle* (August 20, 1857).

140. Porter supported much charity work in Rochester and was a principal in an Anti-Slavery Society there: William F. Peck, *Semi-Centennial History of the City of Rochester* (Syracuse, NY: D. Mason & Co., 1884), 168.

141. "The 'Boy' Henry Dixon Obstinately Refuses His Freedom," *New York Herald* (July 26, 1857).

142. "Case of Henry Dixon," *Anti-Slavery Bugle* (August 20, 1857).

143. See, for example, "A Nut for the Abolitionists to Crack," *Charleston Courier* (July 23, 1857); and "The 'Boy' Henry Dixon Obstinately Refuses His Freedom," *Memphis Daily Appeal* (August 2, 1857).

144. "Refuses to Be Freed," *Providence Daily Post* (June 25, 1857).

145. Molyneux's letter is given in "The Dixon Case Again," (Auburn, NY) *Weekly American* (May 12, 1858), though his first initial is incorrectly given as "L." Molyneux was at the Consulate for many years, speculated in cotton, and married a slave-owning Georgian woman. He "apparently came to accept the basic political philosophy of most slave-owning Georgians." See: Robert H. Welborn, "The British Consulate in Georgia, 1824–1981," *Proceedings and Papers of the Georgia Association of Historians* (1982):105–11; page 106.

146. "The Dixon Case Again," (Auburn, NY) *Weekly American* (May 12, 1858).

147. (Auburn, NY) *Daily American* (May 17, 1859).

148. Dredden may have been a former slave, since Sussex County records show that in 1816 William Huffington Jr. purchased from Ephraim Tull "a certain negro man named Stephen Dredden for 5 years then to go free which he served and was discharged by William Huffington, Jr." See J. M. Huffington, *Huffington Family History* (The Author, 1968), 138.

149. The text of Dredden's affidavit detailing the incident was given in "Communicated for the Watchman, Kidnapping!" (Wilmington, DE) *American Watchman* (July 23, 1817); "Kidnapping!" *Trenton* (NJ) *Federalist* (August 4, 1817); and *Boston Recorder* (August 5, 1817). An abbreviated version appeared in "Kidnapping," (Petersburg, VA) *American Star* (July 31, 1817): 3. Dredden's story is summarized in Schermerhorn, *Money over Mastery, Family over Freedom*, 42.

150. "Communicated for the Watchman, Kidnapping!"(Wilmington, DE) *American Watchman* (July 23, 1817); "Kidnapping!" *Trenton* (NJ) *Federalist* (August 4, 1817); and *Boston Recorder* (August 5, 1817). An abbreviated version appeared in: "Kidnapping," (Petersburg, VA) *American Star* (July 31, 1817): 3.

151. The Dredden family remained in Broad Creek Hundred after the kidnapping. The 1820 census shows Dredden as the head of a household consisting of six free blacks: 1820 Federal Census, Broad Creek Hundred, Sussex County, Delaware, 390–91.

152. 1850 Federal Census, Shawneetown Precinct, Gallatin County, Illinois, 395. The listing shows that the two oldest children were born in Mississippi prior to 1833. The next two were born in the early 1830s in Alabama, and the two youngest were born in Illinois in the 1840s.

153. "Kidnapping," *Illinois State Journal* (April 23, 1849). The children's names and ages were listed in an ad placed by Benjamin: "$300 Reward! Arrest the Villains" (advertisement), *Illinois State Journal* (April 23, 1849).

154. "Kidnapping," *Illinois State Journal* (April 23, 1849).

155. "The Gallatin County Kidnappers," *Illinois State Journal* (July 10, 1849).

156. Author and researcher Jon Musgrave located court records. See Musgrave's post on a genealogy page, available at the ILGALLAT-L Archives, http://archiver.rootsweb.ancestry.com/th/read/ILGALLAT/2004-01/1074554661 (accessed April 21, 2015).

157. "Kidnapping," *Illinois State Journal* (April 23, 1849).

158. 1850 Federal Census, Shawneetown Precinct, Gallatin County, Illinois, 395. (Emily is listed as "Emeline.")

159. This case of kidnapping was widely reported in newspapers (much of them attributing the information to some Worcester publications, including *The Christian Reflector* and the *National Aegis*. The victim's name is usually give as Sidney O. Francis, but his middle name is given in *The Liberator*, which printed it as "Orison" in "Kidnapping in Worcester," *The Liberator* (October 4, 1839): 2, and as "Orrison" in "Trial of the Kidnappers," *The Liberator* (February 7, 1840): 1. Details provided here rely on testimony given during the trial of the kidnappers, for which some of the best sources are: "Trial for Kidnapping," *Massachusetts Spy* (February 5, 1840): 3; "Trial of the Kidnappers," *The Liberator* (February 7, 1840): 1; P. W. Chandler (ed.), *Law Reporter*, Volume II (May, 1839–April, 1840, Inclusive). (Boston: Weeks, Jordan and Co., 1840), 342–43, for the case "Commonwealth v. Dickinson Shearer and Elias M. Turner"; and an affidavit by Sidney's mother, which was prepared less than two weeks after Sidney had left home with the men, was printed in "Kidnapping in Worcester," *The Liberator* (October 4, 1839): 2. Sidney's own testimony provided information on the trip to Fredericksburg, and that of Thomas H. Lipscomb detailed how his suspicions were aroused there, and Lipscomb's noble efforts on Sidney's behalf.

160. "Trial for Kidnapping," *Massachusetts Spy* (February 5, 1840): 3.

161. "A less known area slave dealer was Thomas H. Lipscomb, who had been a Fredericksburg municipal officer, and a captain in the War of 1812." See Ruth Coder Fitzgerald, *A Different Story: A Black History of Fredericksburg, Stafford, and Spotsylvania, Virginia* (Greensboro, NC: Unicorn, 1979), 29. An ad for a runaway slave named Judy said that she "belonged to Mr. Charles Lewis, and was sold by Mr. T. H. Lipscomb, both of Fredericksburg." *Richmond Whig* (February 9, 1841): 3. Lipscomb's occupation was listed as "slave dealer" in the 1860 Federal Census, Fredericksburg, Spotsylvania County, Virginia, 279.

162. See case study of Nahum G. Hazard.

163. Sources for the text of Clark's letter are "Kidnapping in Worcester," *The Liberator* (October 4, 1839): 2 (which has it addressed to the Worcester postmaster, citing the *Christian Reflector*); and "Extraordinary Abduction," *Cleveland Observer* (October 9, 1839): 75; and "Extraordinary Abduction," *Morning Courier and New York Enquirer* (September 28, 1839): 1 (the latter two, citing the *National Aegis*, a newspaper published in Worcester, say the letter was addressed to the mayor of Worcester. At the trial, one of the witnesses

was M. L. Fisher, Esq., postmaster, who was identified as the recipient of the letter, "Trial of the Kidnappers," *The Liberator* (February 7, 1840): 1. The letter is quoted and paraphrased in "Kidnapping," *The Friend* (Seventh Day, Tenth Month [i.e., October 7], 1839): 7, which said it was received in Worcester on September 23, citing the *Massachusetts Spy* as its source.

164. "Extraordinary Abduction," *Cleveland Observer* (October 9, 1839): 75.

165. See Diana Francis's affidavit in "Kidnapping in Worcester," *The Liberator* (October 4, 1839): 2.

166. A copy of the indictment was forwarded to Virginia governor David Campbell, available in Virginia Governor's Office, Executive Papers of Governor David Campbell, 1837–1840 (bulk 1837–1839), Accession 43151, State Records Collection, The Library of Virginia.

167. The brothers spoke "in praise of the kindness they met with on their journey, and especially among Virginians." See "The Kidnappers," *New Hampshire Patriot and State Gazette* (October 14, 1839): 3. The two men were compensated for their rescue mission: George received $57.62, and Benjamin $48.70, as reimbursement for expenses, as per Chapter 12 of laws enacted in 1840, approved by the governor on February 28, 1840, *Acts and Resolves Passed by the Legislature of Massachusetts, in the Year 1840* (Boston: Dutton and Wentworth, 1840), 248.

168. His arrival in New York City was reported in "Extraordinary Abduction," *Cleveland Observer* (October 9, 1839): 75; and in *Saturday Morning Transcript* (Boston) (October 5, 1839): 6, which says that the *New York Commercial* described him as "a bright intelligent little fellow." He was back in Worcester by mid-October. "Massachusetts," *Emancipator* (October 17, 1839).

169. John Adams Vinton, *The Richardson Memorial: Comprising a Full History and Genealogy of the Posterity of the Three Brothers, Ezekiel, Samuel, and Thomas Richardson* (Portland, ME: Brown, Thurston & Co., 1876), 688.

170. A Fredericksburg newspaper reported that the criminal case there was delayed in order that "requisition" (that is, extradition) papers—which were "in the hands of the sheriff of Worcester county, who was in town yesterday"—could be presented to Virginia Governor David Campbell. The requisition paperwork, completed on October 5 by Governor Everett, sought extradition of Shearer and Turner, as well as three men suspected in the kidnapping of Nahum Gardner Hazard (though not all of them were in Virginia). A copy of the signed and sealed requisition is among Campbell's papers: Virginia Governor's Office, Executive Papers of Governor David Campbell, 1837–1840 (bulk 1837–1839), Accession 43151, State Records Collection, The Library of Virginia.

171. "The Kidnapping Case," *Commercial Advertiser* (October 14, 1839): 2 (attributed to the *Fredericksburg Arena*).

172. "The Kidnappers," *Portsmouth Journal of Literature and Politics* (October 19, 1839): 3. Another account gives the officers' names as Phillips and Hinds, and explains how provisions of Virginia law had delayed extradition (in spite of the desires of Virginia officials) and that Wilkinson may have avoided being extradited as a result of a technicality. "The Kidnappers and

Their Victims," *Liberator* (October 18, 1839) (attributed to the *Massachusetts Spy*).

173. "Massachusetts," *Emancipator* (October 17, 1839).

174. A letter from Phillips to Everett, dated November 28, 1839, notes that he had returned that morning with Dickinson Shearer. Virginia Governor's Office, Executive Papers of Governor David Campbell, 1837–1840 (bulk 1837–1839), Accession 43151, State Records Collection, The Library of Virginia.

175. Phillips reported Shearer's belief, and wrote that "Shearer says that the friends of Wilkinson are determined to rescue him." Letter from Phillips to Everett, dated November 28, 1839, Virginia Governor's Office, Executive Papers of Governor David Campbell, 1837–1840 (bulk 1837–1839), Accession 43151, State Records Collection, The Library of Virginia.

176. All were prominent attorneys: Merrick, Barton, and Chapman were judges during their careers. Bates had been a U.S. Congressman and was elected to the U.S. Senate just over a year after the trial. D. Hamilton Hurd, *History of Worcester County, Massachusetts with Biographical Sketches of Many of Its Pioneers and Prominent Men*, Vol. 2 (Philadelphia: J. W. Lewis & Co., 1889), 1445.

177. "Trial for Kidnapping," *Massachusetts Spy* (February 5, 1840): 3.

178. Lipscomb is referred to as "J.P. Libscomb" in "Trial for Kidnapping," *Massachusetts Spy* (February 5, 1840): 3. He was called a "noble-minded gentleman" in "The States," *Emancipator* (February 8, 1840): 162; and "Trial of the Kidnappers," *Liberator* (February 7, 1840): 1 (both relying on reporting by *The Christian Reflector*). The *Emancipator* article even said he was "prompted by motives which do him the highest honor."

179. "Trial for Kidnapping," *Massachusetts Spy* (February 5, 1840): 3.

180. Ibid.

181. Ibid.

182. Ibid. Theron Metcalf, *Reports of Cases Argued and Determined in the Supreme Judicial Court of Massachusetts*, Vol. 3 (Boston: Little, Brown and Company, 1866), 19–26, has the discussion and decision for Turner's appeal. Hurd, *History of Worcester County, Massachusetts, with Biographical Sketches of Many of its Pioneers and Prominent Men*, Vol. 2, 1445, gives Turner's sentence as 18 months, but a news item printed not quite so many years later said it was only 10 months (though it also incorrectly states that Shearer had been sentenced to only six years). "Common Pleas Court Record," *Springfield Republican* (March 21, 1856): 2.

183. *Massachusetts Vital Records, 1841–1910*, Vol. 50, 155.

184. John E. Paige, "Taverns and Early Hotels of Southbridge," *Quinebaug Historical Society Leaflets*, Vol. 3, No. 6 (no date, but "Delivered at Meeting of Society, January 30, 1914"): 67; E. M. Turner, a "hotel keeper," is listed in the 1860 Federal Census for Southbridge, Massachusetts, 164; *Massachusetts Vital Records 1841–1910*, Vol. 375, 511; Orrin Peer Allen, *Inscriptions from the Two Ancient Cemeteries of Palmer, Mass.* (Palmer, MA: Cemetery Commissioners, 1902), 64.

185. Horace Gray Jr., *Reports of Cases Argued and Determined in the Supreme Judicial Court of Massachusetts*, Vol. 6 (Boston: Little, Brown and Co., 1859),

427–28, which says Shearer had left Massachusetts and had not returned by 1856. He may have been the Dickinson Shearer (which is not a very common name) who was listed as a passenger on the steamship *Constitution*, bound for Monterey, California "Passengers," *Daily Alta California* (April 27, 1851); "Common Pleas Court Record," *Springfield Republican* (March 21, 1856): 2.

186. Abby Guy's story has been related in the following books and articles: Robert S. Shafer, "White Persons Held to Racial Slavery in Antebellum Arkansas," *Arkansas Historical Quarterly*, Vol. 44, No. 2 (Summer 1985); 134–55; Teresa Zackodnik, "Fixing the Color Line: The Mulatto, Southern Courts, and Racial Identity," *American Quarterly*, Vol. 53, No. 3 (September 2001): 420–51; John Bailey, *The Lost German Slave Girl: The Extraordinary True Story of Sally Miller and Her Fight for Freedom in Old New Orleans* (New York: Atlantic Monthly Press, 2005); and Ariela Julie Gross, *What Blood Won't Tell: A History of Race on Trial in America* (Cambridge, MA: Harvard University Press, 2008).

187. A 13-year-old black named Wilson Hays, born in Ohio, lived in the household of James Boswell and his wife (both black) in Warren County, Ohio. Warren County borders Hamilton County, in which Cincinnati is located. 1850 Federal Census, Deerfield, Warren County, Ohio, Dwelling #669. Subsequent censuses do not show a black man named Wilson Hays in Ohio.

188. Per Doy's Narrative: John Doy, *The Narrative of John Doy, of Lawrence, Kansas* (New York: Thomas Holman, 1860), 24. It has not been possible to reliably document Smith's previous residency, given that his name is such a common one.

189. Doy, *The Narrative of John Doy, of Lawrence, Kansas*, 24. A shorter version of the incident was given in a letter Doy wrote from jail. *Liberator* (March 18, 1859).

190. Doy, *The Narrative of John Doy, of Lawrence, Kansas*, 24. It is conceivable that Doy, in order to avoid accusations of aiding fugitives, lied about the free papers, but if so, why would he not lie and say that all 13 people bore them? It is apparent from Doy's book that he held back nothing about his adherence to abolition, and probably was not concerned enough about being seen as a violator of the Fugitive Slave Law that he would alter facts to hide his antislavery leanings.

191. Doy, *The Narrative of John Doy, of Lawrence, Kansas*, 26.

192. "Thirteen Negroes Captured in Kansas," *Liberty* (MO) *Weekly Tribune* (February 4, 1859).

193. Local newspapers reporting on the incident noted that both Hays and Smith said they were free: "Thirteen Negroes Captured in Kansas," *Liberty* (MO) *Weekly Tribune* (February 4, 1859).

194. Doy, *The Narrative of John Doy, of Lawrence, Kansas*, 50.

195. Ibid.

196. Ibid., 51.

197. Ibid.

198. Ibid., 52.

199. Ibid., 52n.

200. His surname is sometimes given as "Hazzard," or even "Hassard." In an affidavit submitted in connection with his military pension, however, Hazard notes he used the "Hazard" spelling, though a brother spelled his surname as "Hazzard." Elizabeth Tennessee, *The Story of Nahum: Tracing a History of Black Life in America* (Devens, MA: Freedom's Way Heritage Association, 2001), 26.

201. Per George Bradburn's letter: "More Kidnapping," *Liberator* (October 11, 1839): 162.

202. Shearer operated a store in Palmer, Massachusetts, in the 1830s. *Finding Aid for James Shearer Daybook, 1836–1838*, Special Collections and University Archives, University of Massachusetts Amherst Libraries, MS 418, http://scua .library.umass.edu/ead/mums418.pdf (accessed September 18, 2014).

203. "The Kidnapping Case," (Boston) *Atlas* (October 15, 1839); and "Massachusetts," *Emancipator* (October 17, 1839). The newspapers gave the surname as Tate, but it was undoubtedly Bacon Tait, who operated a Richmond slave jail in the 1830s (which later became Lumpkin's jail). Maurie D. McInnis, *Slaves Waiting for Sale: Abolitionist Art and the American Slave Trade* (Chicago: University of Chicago Press, 2011), 100.

204. Per an account of Hazard's story that may have been based on an interview with him, though the writer has seemingly intermingled details from the separate case of Sidney O. Francis. Ethel Stanwood Bolton, *Shirley Uplands and Intervales: Annals of a Border Town of Old Middlesex, with Some Genealogical Sketches* (Boston: George Emery Littlefield, 1914), 76ff. This flawed account is apparently relied on by Tennessee, *The Story of Nahum*.

205. The letters are referenced in "More Kidnapping," *Liberator* (October 11, 1839): 162.

206. In 1839, Bradburn was a member of the Massachusetts House of Representatives and made a report about the kidnapping of state residents in March. See Theodore Dwight Weld, *American Slavery as It Is: Testimony of a Thousand Witnesses* (New York: American Anti-Slavery Society, 1839), 141; and *Eighth Annual Report of the Board of Managers of the Mass. Anti-Slavery Society* (Boston: Dow & Jackson, 1840), Proceedings, xxvi.

207. Per Bradburn's memorandum dated September 26, 1839. Frances H. Bradburn, *A Memorial of George Bradburn* (Boston: Cupples, Upham and Company, 1883), 140; Bradburn's response to Clark, in "More Kidnapping," *Liberator* (October 11, 1839): 162; and a slightly abbreviated version that appeared in "The Worcester Kidnappers," *Emancipator* (October 10, 1839): 94.

208. Brown, who also lived on Flat Hill, was an officer in the state militia, a church deacon, and also served as a municipal officer. George A. Cunningham, *Cunningham's History of the Town of Lunenburg*, Vol. 2, 98, available from Internet Archive, https://archive.org/details/cunninghamshistoad00cunn (accessed March 19, 2015). Brown was reimbursed for his expenses for his trip to retrieve Hazard, which amounted to about $116, including fares, meals, shoes and a vest for Hazard, and $28 for Brown's service from September 30 to October 15. See documents reproduced in Tennessee, *The Story of Nahum*, 18–19.

209. The indictment of William Little, James Shearer, and Francis L. Wilkinson, for kidnapping, and the requisition from Massachusetts governor Edward Everett to Virginia governor David Campbell, October 5, 1839, are in Campbell's papers. Virginia Governor's Office, Executive Papers of Governor David Campbell, 1837–1840 (bulk 1837–1839). Accession 43151. State Records Collection, The Library of Virginia.

210. "The Kidnappers and Their Victims," *Liberator* (October 18, 1839).

211. See case study of Sidney O. Francis.

212. Phillips felt that the jail could be broken into in less than a half-hour, without being detected. Letter from Ivers Phillips to Edward Everett, November 28, 1839. Clark wrote to Everett that he had told Phillips "my greatest fear was that they would receive assistance from some friends and make their escape." Letter from Clark to Everett, November 25, 1839. Everett commended "the efficient interest" given to the surrender of Dickinson Shearer, and requesting "its continuance, in reference to the other individuals charged" in a letter from Everett to Campbell, December 2, 1839. All these letters are available in Virginia Governor's Office, Executive Papers of Governor David Campbell, 1837–1840 (bulk 1837–1839), Accession 43151, State Records Collection, The Library of Virginia.

213. Bradburn, *A Memorial of George Bradburn*, 141; and "Another Trial with Acquittal," *Liberator* (February 7, 1840).

214. "Another Trial with Acquittal," *Liberator* (February 7, 1840). The author has found nothing documenting the apprehension of James Shearer. He was undoubtedly the man by that name, identified as a former merchant from Palmer, Massachusetts, who went to Canada, and then relocated to Minnesota around 1849. In Minnesota, he was a farmer and held a number of official positions: W. H. C. Folsom, *Fifty Years in the Northwest: With an Introduction and Appendix Containing Reminiscences, Incidents and Notes* (St. Paul, MN: Pioneer Press Co., 1888), 367; and 1880 Federal Census, Denmark, Washington County, Minnesota, 184.

215. Letter from Ivers Phillips to Edward Everett, November 28, 1839, available in Virginia Governor's Office, Executive Papers of Governor David Campbell, 1837–1840 (bulk 1837–1839), Accession 43151, State Records Collection, The Library of Virginia.

216. In 1850, Hazard lived with his mother and stepfather in Townsend, Massachusetts; 1850 Federal Census, Townsend, Middlesex County, Massachusetts, 82. In 1855, he lived in the Townsend household of William Dix. 1855 Massachusetts State Census, Townsend, Middlesex County, Dwelling #94. Hazard was also enumerated in 1865 Massachusetts State Census, Townsend, Middlesex County, Dwelling #108; 1870 Federal Census, Leominster, Worcester County, Massachusetts, 299; 1880 Federal Census, Leominster, Worcester, Massachusetts, 528; 1900 Federal Census, Leominster, Worcester County, Massachusetts, 247; and 1910 Federal Census, Leominster, Worcester County, Massachusetts, 84. His military service is mentioned in Ithamar B. Sawtelle, *History of the Town of Townsend, Middlesex County, Massachusetts: From the Grant of Hathorn's Farm, 1676–1878* (Fitchburg, MA: The Author, 1878), 279; and Charles

Barnard Fox, *Record of the Service of the Fifty-fifth Regiment of Massachusetts Volunteer Infantry* (Cambridge, MA: J. Wilson and Son, 1868), 141.

217. "Liberated from Slavery," (Augusta, GA) *Chronicle* (August 31, 1859).

218. See John W. Shepherd, *Reports of Cases Argued and Determined in the Supreme Court of Alabama during January and June Terms, 1860*, Vol. 36 (Montgomery, AL: Montgomery Advertiser Book and Job Office, 1861), 97.

219. "Liberated from Slavery," (Augusta, GA) *Chronicle* (August 31, 1859).

220. Shepherd, *Reports of Cases Argued and Determined in the Supreme Court of Alabama during January and June Terms, 1860*, Vol. 36, 95.

221. "White Slaves Seeking Freedom," *Massachusetts Spy* (September 28, 1859).

222. Shepherd, *Reports of Cases Argued and Determined in the Supreme Court of Alabama during January and June Terms, 1860*, Vol. 36, 95.

223. "White Slaves Seeking Freedom," *Massachusetts Spy* (September 28, 1859).

224. "Liberated from Slavery," (Augusta, GA) *Chronicle* (August 31, 1859).

225. Shepherd, *Reports of Cases Argued and Determined in the Supreme Court of Alabama during January and June Terms, 1860*, Vol. 36, 97.

226. "White Slavery in Alabama," *National Era* (September 15, 1859).

227. In 1855, Hight was a 16-year-old servant, living in Seneca, New York, whose place of birth was given as the District of Columbia. 1855 New York State Census, Town of Seneca, Ontario County, Family #195. He was probably the son of Jesse "Hite," who was listed in the household of General Thomas Jessup: 1850 Federal Census, Washington, District of Columbia, 97.

228. 1855 New York State Census, Town of Seneca, Ontario County, Family #217.

229. "A Rascal Caught," *Ohio State Journal* (December 9, 1857). Until 1872, Geneva was included in the town of Seneca. Charles F. Milliken, *A History of Ontario County, New York and Its People*, Vol. 1 (New York: Lewis Historical Publishing Co., 1911), 465–66.

230. 1855 NYS Census, Penn Yan, Yates County, Family #268.

231. "A Rascal Caught," *Ohio State Journal* (December 9, 1857).

232. "A Case of Kidnapping," (Cleveland, OH) *Morning Leader* (December 5, 1857); and "The Kidnapped Negro Restored to Freedom," *Cleveland Plain Dealer* (December 19, 1857).

233. "The Kidnapping Case," *Geneva Courier* (December 16, 1857).

234. "The Kidnapped Negro Restored to Freedom," *Cleveland Plain Dealer* (December 19, 1857); and "The Trial of Van Tuyl—His Conviction and Sentence," *Geneva Gazette* (April 22, 1859), which says that Prue "made tracks for the north, not waiting to confront in Court his kidnapper."

235. "Dan Prue Is Dead," *Geneva Advertiser* (July 23, 1895). The letter may have been written by Prue, as implied in Kathryn Grover, *Make a Way Somehow: African-American Life in a Northern Community, 1790–1965* (Syracuse, NY: Syracuse University Press, 1994), 34. Or it may have been prepared on his behalf by a lawyer from Franklin, Ohio. "A Model Black Republican," *Charleston Courier* (December 10, 1857).

236. "The Kidnapped Negro Restored to Freedom," *Cleveland Plain Dealer* (December 19, 1857).

237. "The Kidnapping Case," *Geneva Courier* (December 16, 1857). Though it may not have been Grave's intention in this case (as he afterward showed no interest in being involved with kidnapping), "serial selling" was a way to make it harder for a kidnap victim to be located by rescuers. "It was reported that he [Hight] had been 'shoved' through several hands in Kentucky in order to thwart any efforts that night be made for his recovery." "The Kidnapped Negro Restored to Freedom," *Cleveland Plain Dealer* (December 19, 1857).

238. "The Kidnapped Negroes—Further Facts in the Case," *Buffalo Courier* (December 7, 1857).

239. "A Requisition from New-York for Kidnappers," *New-York Daily Tribune* (December 7, 1857).

240. See published statement by Walker and Lay: "The Geneva Kidnapping Case," *Albany Evening Journal* (January 4, 1858).

241. "The Geneva Kidnapping Case," *New-York Daily Tribune* (December 12, 1857).

242. Ibid.

243. Ibid.; and "The Kidnapping Case," *Geneva Courier* (December 9, 1857).

244. "Van Tuyl, the Kidnapper," (Syracuse, NY) *Daily Journal* (April 1, 1858).

245. "Arrest of a Kidnapper," *New York Times* (February 17, 1858). According to an overview of the whole case, charges against Van Tuyl in Kentucky were dropped, as the kidnapping had not happened there, but rather in New York. "The Trial of Van Tuyl—His Conviction and Sentence," *Geneva Gazette* (April 22, 1859). Van Tuyl made an unsuccessful escape attempt at Memphis, Tennessee. "Mr. Van Tuyl a Slippery Customer," *Geneva Gazette* (March 17, 1858).

246. *Springfield* (MA) *Republican* (September 29, 1858); and *Utica Morning Herald* (November 15, 1858).

247. "The Trial of Van Tuyl—His Conviction and Sentence," *Geneva Gazette* (April 22, 1859); and *Utica Morning Herald* (November 15, 1858).

248. "Could Not Agree," *Albany Evening Journal* (January 28, 1859).

249. "The Trial of Van Tuyl—His Conviction and Sentence," *Geneva Gazette* (April 22, 1859).

250. "Van Tuyl," *Albany Evening Journal* (April 21, 1859).

251. *New York Governors Registers of Commitments to Prisons, 1842–1908*, 239; and "The Trial of Van Tuyl—His Conviction and Sentence," *Geneva Gazette* (April 22, 1859).

252. Grover, *Make a Way Somehow*, 36. An 1881 article noted that, though Van Tuyl was dead, Walker and Prue still resided in Geneva. "An Old Event Revived," *Geneva Advertiser* (July 26, 1881).

253. A Geneva newspaper made reference to his kidnapping at the time of the death of his mother, Mary Ann Hight, in 1893: "Home Matters," *Geneva Advertiser* (November 14, 1893); and "A Bit of History," *Geneva Advertiser* (November 14, 1893). Though a local history book mentions that he served

as a soldier during the Civil War, the author was unable to find any record of such service. Milliken, *A History of Ontario County, New York and Its People*, Vol. 1, 200.

254. "Dan Prue Is Dead," *Geneva Advertiser* (July 23, 1895); Military Service Records, National Archives and Records Administration.

255. The two main sources for Houston's narrative differ in certain details. In "Romantic Suit for Freedom," *Albany Evening Journal* (June 11, 1850), which took it from the *New Orleans Delta* of June 1, 1850, the captain's name is given as Davis. In "Adventures of a British Subject Sold into Slavery," *Sabbath Recorder* (April 29, 1852), the name is M'Coy. Both versions of the story were reprinted by various newspapers at the time, and the 1852 version is included in Blassingame, *Slave Testimony*, 284–86. Houston is briefly discussed in: Ulrich Bonnell Phillips, *American Negro Slavery: A Survey of the Supply, Employment and Control of Negro Labor as Determined by the Plantation Regime* (New York: D. Appleton, 1929), 445.

256. The 1852 version of the story inexplicably says it was "Tricupo," and confused St. Martin Parish as "St. Matthew county."

257. Quote from "Romantic Suit for Freedom," *Albany Evening Journal* (June 11, 1850).

258. The bar's name is given as the Western Exchange, run by a man named Burdon, in "Romantic Suit for Freedom," *Albany Evening Journal* (June 11, 1850). The man's name was given as Henry Boardman in "Adventures of a British Subject Sold into Slavery," *Sabbath Recorder* (April 29, 1852).

259. See Bennett H. Young, *A History of Jessamine County, Kentucky* (Louisville, KY: Courier-Journal Job Printing Co., 1898), 234–37. Willis was killed in action.

260. Instead of Richardson, the rather unusual surname of Rustno is given in "Adventures of a British Subject Sold into Slavery," *Sabbath Recorder* (April 29, 1852).

261. Or Lapiere; "Adventures of a British Subject Sold into Slavery," *Sabbath Recorder* (April 29, 1852). This account also has him being sold to an Irishman named Gardner, a lawyer named John Howard, and a Natchez man named Barber, prior to coming into "Lapiere's" possession.

262. Mure was the consul at this time. James J. Barnes and Patience P. Barnes (comp.), *The American Civil War through British Eyes: Dispatches from British Diplomats*, Vol. 1, November 1860–April 1862 (Kent, OH: Kent State University Press, 2003), 53n. His name is inexplicably given as Mayhew in "Adventures of a British Subject Sold into Slavery," *Sabbath Recorder* (April 29, 1852).

263. As the consul told him would be the case: "Adventures of a British Subject Sold into Slavery," *Sabbath Recorder* (April 29, 1852).

264. Houston was declared to be free by a judge in the Fourth District Court of New Orleans on November 29, 1851. Judith Kelleher Schafer, *Becoming Free, Remaining Free: Manumission and Enslavement in New Orleans, 1846–1862* (Baton Rouge: Louisiana State University Press, 2003). The court documents (cited by

Schafer, but which the author was unable to consult) are filed as *Houston, f.m.c. v. Lapice*, #3729, Fourth District Court of New Orleans.

265. "Adventures of a British Subject Sold into Slavery," *Sabbath Recorder* (April 29, 1852).

266. The story, published in the *New Orleans Delta*, was reprinted in "Romantic Suit for Freedom," *Albany Evening Journal* (June 11, 1850).

267. "A Queer Hoax," *Times-Picayune* (April 15, 1852).

268. *Times-Picayune* (May 2, 1852). A search for the *Broad Oak* in the Irish Shipwrecks database shows that she was a bark, built in 1832, whose home port was Liverpool. She wrecked on December 29, 1852, when returning to Liverpool from Pernambuco, in Brazil, loaded with sugar and cotton. http://www.irishshipwrecks.com/shipwrecks.php?wreck_ref=382 (accessed March 24, 2015).

269. Evidence presented in court proved that he was born free. "Moore Superior Court," (Fayetteville, NC) *Observer* (August 30, 1858). His military enlistment paperwork indicated he was born in Mercer County, Pennsylvania, in about 1828. War Department records for Company A, 41st Regiment, United States Colored Troops, National Archives and Records Administration.

270. One newspaper said: "He had all along protested his freedom, but without effect." "Colored Items," *Springfield* (MA) *Republican* (September 13, 1858). Jackson's contention that he was free could account for his being sold so many times, since slaveholders were leery of owning kidnapped freemen and sought to unload the problem onto someone else.

271. Possibly a South Carolina slave trader, since a report of the court session relating to Jackson's status says he was "sold on the block in Richmond, Va. to a South Carolina trader." "Moore Superior Court," (Fayetteville, NC) *Observer* (August 30, 1858). It was also said that he was locked up in a jail in Fincastle, Virginia. Samuel J. May, *The Fugitive Slave Law and Its Victims* (New York: American Anti-Slavery Society, 1861), 18.

272. The abortive rescue is related in Samuel W. Durant and Pliny A. Durant, *History of Lawrence County, Pennsylvania: With Illustrations Descriptive of Its Scenery, Palatial Residences, Public Buildings Fine Blocks, and Important Manufactories* (Philadelphia: L. H. Everts & Co., 1877), 33. Jackson's enslavement and escape attempt is briefly mentioned in "Slavery," *Liberator* (July 4, 1851).

273. Durant and Durant, *History of Lawrence County, Pennsylvania*, 33; and "The Kidnapping and Recovery of Frank Jackson; Two Underground Stations in New Castle, Lawrence County," *New Castle Daily News* (March 5, 1897).

274. Benjamin Briggs, "Set Thy House in Order: George C. Mendenhall's New Order of Carolina Quakerism," *The Southern Friend*, Vol. 28, No. 2 (2006): 32.

275. In 1860, Swann was a 44-year-old farmer; 1860 Federal Census, Moore County, North Carolina, 142. The 1860 Slave Census shows that he owned 17 slaves in 1860. Jackson had been sold to Swann by McInnis and Murtchison, slave traders in Wilmington, North Carolina. "Moore Superior Court," (Fayetteville, NC) *Observer* (August 30, 1858).

276. Durant and Durant, *History of Lawrence County, Pennsylvania*, 33. His phony title fooled some newspapers, who referred to him as "Col. Geo. C. Morgan." "A Case of Kidnaping [*sic*]," *North Carolina Standard* (October 13, 1858), which got the story from the *National Intelligencer*.

277. Jackson may have also been locked up in the Randolph jail, a place where he also was visited by Mendenhall, according to "Frank Jackson," *Anti-Slavery Bugle* (September 18, 1858).

278. A writer reported seeing Jackson in Philadelphia, as he made his way home: *National Era* (September 16, 1858). His homecoming was noted in "A Free Slave Liberated," *St. Albans* (VT) *Messenger* (September 30, 1858); and "A Free Colored Man Rescued from Slavery," (Richmond, VA) *Daily Dispatch* (September 8, 1858).

279. Durant and Durant, *History of Lawrence County, Pennsylvania*, 33; Samuel P. Bates, *History of Pennsylvania Volunteers, 1861–5* (Harrisburg, PA: R. Singerly, 1871), 997; and Military Record for Francis Jackson, Company A, 41st Colored Infantry, United States Colored Troops, National Archives and Records Administration.

280. "The Kidnapping and Recovery of Frank Jackson; Two Underground Stations in New Castle, Lawrence County," *New Castle Daily News* (March 5, 1897).

281. "It appears by the account given by his distressed wife, now residing in this city, that they were driven from Northampton, Va., some years ago, by the violence of the slaveholders of that place, who were determined to expel all free colored persons." From *The First Annual Report of the New York Committee of Vigilance for the Year 1837*, 16–17. He was described as a "free colored man" in "A Northern Freeman Enslaved by Northern Hands," *The American Anti-Slavery Almanac for 1839* (New York and Boston: American Anti-Slavery Society, 1838).

282. William Jay, in a letter to the mayor of New York City, said that: "Lee is supposed to have been" a free man. "Annals of Kidnapping," (Cincinnati, OH) *Philanthropist* (March 3, 1837).

283. Some years later, when Lee and other blacks left Virginia again, some of the men said Lee had led *that* venture. "Peter John Lee, the Man Who Stole Himself," *Emancipator* (December 4, 1844).

284. The text of the warrant appears in "Kidnapping by Authority," *Emancipator* (April 8, 1841); and *State of New York. In Supreme Court. Seth W. Benedict, ads. Daniel D. Nash* (N.p., n.d.), 34–35.

285. "More Legalized Kidnapping," (Warsaw, NY) *American Citizen* (April 19, 1837). According to a letter from William B. Smead, a man named Isaac was to have been hung on January 10, 1834, but was reprieved and "sent to the penitentiary to be transported. So he is now a slave to some one."

286. "Peter John Lee, the Man Who Stole Himself," *Emancipator* (December 4, 1844); and "Outrage and Kidnapping," *New York Sun* (November 23, 1836), reprinted in *State of New York. In Supreme Court. Seth W. Benedict, ads. Daniel D. Nash*, 40–41.

287. "Outrage and Kidnapping," *New York Sun* (November 23, 1836), reprinted in *State of New York. In Supreme Court. Seth W. Benedict, ads. Daniel D. Nash*, 40–41, which says the man who lured Lee to Rye received $1.50 for doing so.

288. There were four, according to "Peter John Lee, the Man Who Stole Himself," *Emancipator* (December 4, 1844). A tavern keeper recalled years later that a party consisting of Boudinot, Nash, a man named Lyon, and one or two others had stopped at his place before the incident, and returned several hours later with a black man. Affidavit of Amos F. Hatfield, in *State of New York. In Supreme Court. Seth W. Benedict, ads. Daniel D. Nash*, 43–44. Gilbert Lyon, a resident of Rye, said there were 10 to 12 "ruffians." See "Outrage and Kidnapping," *New York Sun* (November 23, 1836), reprinted in *State of New York. In Supreme Court. Seth W. Benedict, ads. Daniel D. Nash*, 40–41.

289. Nash sued for libel because a publication had called him a kidnapper: "Abolition Libel—Heavy Damages," *Morning Courier and New-York Enquirer* (March 24, 1841). Nash was awarded $1,500 in damages: *State of New York. In Supreme Court. Seth W. Benedict, ads. Daniel D. Nash*, 46. Nash was removed from his position in New York after a confrontation in Savannah, Georgia, in which he wrongfully accused a man of being an abolitionist. *Liberator* (May 19, 1837). According to that *Liberator* article, after his dismissal, Nash told David Ruggles, "I'll make a business of it now. It don't require a warrant from the mayor to catch niggers." Boudinot and Nash, along with John Lyon, Edward R. Waddy, and F. H. Pettis, worked with City Recorder Richard Riker to "retrieve runaways and seize free blacks." They were called the "New York Kidnapping Club." See C. Peter Ripley (ed.), *The Black Abolitionist Papers: Volume III: The United States, 1830–1846* (Chapel Hill: University of North Carolina Press, 1991), 180n.

290. New York mayor Cornelius W. Lawrence verified that Boudinot was a constable in the third ward: "Annals of Kidnapping," (Cincinnati, OH) *Philanthropist* (March 3, 1837). During a confrontation, Josiah Hopper denounced Boudinot as a kidnapper and a "negro catcher": "Police, A Case," *Morning Courier and New-York Enquirer* (March 30, 1837); and "City Occurrences, Fugitive Case Resumed," *New-York Daily Express* (March 31, 1837).

291. Affidavit of Amos F. Hatfield, in *State of New York. In Supreme Court. Seth W. Benedict, ads. Daniel D. Nash*, 43–44.

292. "It is true they did not condescend to bring their victim before a judge, fearing probably the production of free papers." *The First Annual Report of the New York Committee of Vigilance for the Year 1837*, 16.

293. "Peter John Lee, the Man Who Stole Himself," *Emancipator* (December 4, 1844).

294. He was said to have been the man named merely as "Henry" in Marcy's warrant.

295. In the case of George Thompson, another man arrested under Marcy's warrant, *habeas corpus* proceedings were conducted for several days before he was officially sent back to Virginia.

296. "Peter John Lee, the Man Who Stole Himself," *Emancipator* (December 4, 1844).

297. Estimates of the number of slaves Helm brought to New York ranged from 40 to 100, with 60 being a reasonable number. Bob Rolfe, "Bath Was Center of Slave Trade; Captain Helm Cracked the Whip," *Steuben Courier and the Steuben Advocate* (November 24, 1960), 1, 4. A local historian wrote that Helm had about 40 slaves. Harlo Hakes, *Landmarks of Steuben County, New York* (Syracuse, NY: D. Mason & Company, 1896), 59. Rev. B. W. Swain, who extensively researched Bath slaves, named 15 who belonged to Helm, but knew there were others. "The African M. E. Zion Church," *Bath* (NY) *Advocate* (June 14, 1893). The 1810 Federal Census shows Helm in possession of 31 slaves, so if he had indeed had more, some had already been sold or had escaped. 1810 Federal Census, New York, Steuben County, Bath, 41.

298. Irvin W. Near, *A History of Steuben County, New York, and Its People*, Vol. 1 (Chicago: Lewis Publishing Co., 1911), 101; and Rolfe, "Bath Was Center of Slave Trade; Captain Helm Cracked the Whip," 1, 4.

299. For Helm's troubles in New York, see Austin Steward, *Twenty-two Years a Slave, and Forty Years a Freeman: Embracing a Correspondence of Several Years, while President of Wilberforce Colony, London, Canada West* (Canandaigua, NY: The Author, 1867), 116. Some of Helm's sales of slaves are detailed in "Reminiscences," *Bath* (NY) *Plaindealer* (February 7, 1885).

300. Apparently slaves were being sold, counter to state law: "It would seem from these transactions which were open and notorious, either that the foregoing law was a dead letter, or the Courts had given some construction that virtually nullified it." The quote is from "Reminiscences," *Bath* (NY) *Plaindealer* (February 7, 1885), which mentions a number of such sales. According to one article, the successful escape of one large group of slaves encouraged others. Rolfe, "Bath Was Center of Slave Trade; Captain Helm Cracked the Whip," 1, 4. Steward was advised that, because Helm had hired him out to someone else, he was thereby a free man. Steward, *Twenty-two Years a Slave, and Forty Years a Freeman*, 109.

301. Steward, *Twenty-two Years a Slave, and Forty Years a Freeman*, 116–19.

302. Some accounts say 1818, and some 1820. The latter seems more likely, because it is closer to the time of his kidnapping trial, which clearly took place in June 1821. *The American (For the Country)* (July 4, 1821).

303. The question arises as to whether Helm was kidnapping free blacks or stealing slaves. Since many of his slaves had "self-liberated," some of his victims may have technically been slaves. Steward, who as one of Helm's former slaves would have been acquainted with most of these victims, says: "They had basked for a short season in the sunshine of liberty, and thought themselves secure from the iron grasp of Slavery." Steward, *Twenty-two Years a Slave, and Forty Years a Freeman*, 120–21. In regard specifically to the Lucases, Harry had been purchased at a sheriff's sale on June 20, 1818, for $120. "Reminiscences," *Bath* (NY) *Plaindealer* (February 7, 1885). Buyers, realizing that under the gradual emancipation process then underway in New York State, their ownership of slaves at this time was not permanent, sometimes

arranged for slaves purchased to serve them for a limited amount of time, after which they were to be freed. This is what happened with Harry Lucas. A. L. Underhill, in a historical address, said that Samuel S. Haight had promised to liberate Harry after two years, which he did in July 1820 (though Harry's first name is incorrectly given as "Harvey"). "Bath Board of Trade," *Steuben Courier* (April 10, 1891). The 1820 Federal Census lists Harry "Lucus" as the head of a household of free blacks. 1820 Federal Census, New York, Steuben County, Bath, 234. Regardless of whether Harry Lucas and family were legally free at the time of Helm's escapade, they probably enjoyed *de facto* freedom, and, since they probably did not belong to Helm, his abduction of the children was nonetheless a crime.

304. See account of the incident in Steward, *Twenty-two Years a Slave, and Forty Years a Freeman*, 120–22. A man named Ansel Searl, a regular patron of a Bath tavern, was probably the driver. "He was a teamster. He was engaged with Capt. Helm in kidnapping Harry Lucas and furnishing the transportation to Olean in 1818. He never returned to Bath but went on to Kentucky with the two children of Lucas'. He escaped prosecution by taking up his abode in the West." The cost and effort to extradite him were not made, "so he went scott [*sic*] free." "Reminiscences," *Bath* (NY) *Plaindealer* (January 20, 1894). Searl's first name appeared in an earlier article: "Reminiscences," *Bath* (NY) *Plaindealer* (December 30, 1893), but it may instead have been James, since there was a Kentucky resident named James Searl, who was from Steuben County, New York. *History of Fulton County, Illinois* (Peoria, IL: Chas. C. Chapman & Co., 1879), 928. He moved to Illinois in the 1830s. Federal census records for Kentucky show a James Searle (1820 Federal Census, Kentucky, Campbell County, Covington, 30), and a James Surl (1830 Federal Census, Kentucky, Campbell County, Covington, 258). The man with the whip was "a powerful ruffian by the name of Cummons." "Reminiscences," *Bath* (NY) *Plaindealer* (February 14, 1885).

305. Steward, *Twenty-two Years a Slave, and Forty Years a Freeman*, 121–22.

306. "The children were sold in Kentucky but no one seems to know what became of them." In "Reminiscences," *Bath* (NY) *Plaindealer* (February 14, 1885). William and Peggy were "taken off and never heard of." In "Emancipation Day," *Bath* (NY) *Plaindealer* (August 3, 1889).

307. His conviction was noted in *The American (For the Country)* (July 4, 1821), which, in regard to the fine, reported that Helm was "to remain in prison until paid." A number of sources say he never paid the fine: "Emancipation Day," *Bath* (NY) *Plaindealer* (August 3, 1889); Near, *A History of Steuben County, New York, and Its People*, Vol. 1, 101; and "Reminiscences," *Bath* (NY) *Plaindealer* (February 14, 1885).

308. *The American (For the Country)* (August 8, 1821).

309. Rolfe, "Bath Was Center of Slave Trade; Captain Helm Cracked the Whip," 1, 4. He died in 1825 or 1826. "The African M. E. Zion Church," (Bath, NY) *Advocate* (June 14, 1893).

310. Isaac's age is given in: "Colored Boy Kidnapped," *Brooklyn Daily Eagle* (August 9, 1858); and "A Colored Boy Kidnapped," *Morning Courier*

and New-York Enquirer (August 9, 1858). He reportedly lived with his mother. "The Late Kidnapping Case," *New York Herald* (August 10, 1858).

311. The newspapers possibly got the name of the vessel wrong, as there is no apparent evidence of a schooner by that name visiting New York at the time. Perhaps they meant the *Ann Eliza*, since the shipping columns show several New York arrivals of that ship from Virginia in 1858 (but no clearances or departures). Its arrivals at New York were recorded in the *New York Times* (June 28, 1858; July 28, 1858; September 4, 1858; and October 20, 1858) and the *New York Herald* (October 29, 1858). The name of the master was Matthews, though beginning in October, it changed to Jones. The *Ann Eliza's* arrival at Norfolk, Virginia, from New York was noted in (Baltimore) *Daily Exchange* (June 21, 1858).

312. "The Late Case of Kidnapping," *Morning Courier and New-York Enquirer* (August 10, 1858).

313. He jumped onto a ship, then onto a canal boat—"The Late Kidnapping Affair," *New York Daily Tribune* (August 9, 1858)—onto a ship, then onto the pier—"The Late Kidnapping Affair," *New York Evening Express* (August 9, 1858); or into the water: "The Late Kidnapping Case," *New York Herald* (August 10, 1858).

314. "The Late Kidnapping Affair," *New York Evening Express* (August 9, 1858); "The Late Case of Kidnapping," *Morning Courier and New-York Enquirer* (August 10, 1858); and "The Late Kidnapping Affair," *New York Daily Tribune* (August 9, 1858).

315. "The Late Kidnapping Affair," *New York Evening Express* (August 9, 1858).

316. O. J. Page, *History of Massac County, Illinois, with Life Sketches and Portraits, Part One* (Metropolis, IL: ca. 1900), 167–68; James A. Rose, "The Regulators and Flatheads in Southern Illinois," *Transactions of the Illinois State Historical Society for the Year 1906* (Springfield: Illinois State Journal Co., 1906): 108–21 (page 111); and Jon Musgrave, "Black Kidnappings in the Wabash and Ohio Valleys of Illinois," Hickory Hill Plantations/Old Slave House Preservation Project, created May 10, 1997, http://illinoishistory.com/blackkidnappings.html (accessed January 1, 2015).

317. "Kidnappings," (Cincinnati, OH) *Daily Enquirer* (May 1, 1843). Page (*op. cit.*) says some notices appeared at once, and additional ones months later.

318. Page, *History of Massac County, Illinois*, 168.

319. As researcher Jon Musgrave has noted, some writers gave the name of the plantation owner as William Dowdy, from the state of Mississippi, and others say it was a man named Dorsey, in Mississippi County, Arkansas. Musgrave, "Black Kidnappings in the Wabash and Ohio Valleys of Illinois."

320. Page, *History of Massac County, Illinois*, 168, 169–70.

321. The indictments (which the author was not able to consult) are discussed in Musgrave, "Black Kidnappings in the Wabash and Ohio Valleys of Illinois." The Pope County case files are: *People v. Peyton Gordon, William G.W. Fitch, Caleb Slankard, Joshua Hanly, John Simpkins, and Joseph Lynn*, 1844 —CC—065, Office of the Circuit Clerk, Pope County, Golconda, Illinois;

People v. Peyton H. Gordon, Joshua Hanly, Caleb Slankard, 1844-CC-102; and *People v. Peyton Gordon, William G. W. Fitch, Caleb Slankard, Joshua Hanly, John Simpkins, and Joseph Lynn*, 1844-CC-106, Office of the Pope County Circuit Clerk, Golconda, Illinois. These citations are from: Scott Heerman, "Kidnapping and Capitalism: Human Trafficking in Antebellum America," posted January 13, 2015, Historians against Slavery web page, http://www.historiansagainstslavery.org/main/2015/01/kidnapping-and-capitalism-human-trafficking-in-antebellum-america/ (accessed January 23, 2015).

322. Rose, "The Regulators and Flatheads in Southern Illinois," 111.

323. Ibid.

324. O. J. Page, *History of Massac County, Illinois, with Life Sketches and Portraits, Part One* ([Metropolis, Ill.], [ca 1900]), 171; and Rose, "The Regulators and Flatheads in Southern Illinois," 111.

325. For a good analysis of Morrison's court cases, see Walter Johnson, "The Slave Trader, the White Slave, and the Politics of Racial Determination in the 1850s," *Journal of American History* (June 2000): 13–38. For contemporary accounts, see "An Arkansas White Girl Sold as a Slave," *National Era* (June 9, 1859); and "Successful Suit for Freedom by a White Girl," *Bedford* (PA) *Inquirer* (June 10, 1859).

326. Johnson, "The Slave Trader, the White Slave, and the Politics of Racial Determination in the 1850s," 24.

327. S. F. Glenn, *Reports of Cases Argued and Determined in the Supreme Court of Louisiana, Vol. XVI: For the Years 1861–1862* (New Orleans, LA: Bloomfield & Steel, 1866), 102.

328. Ibid.

329. Johnson, "The Slave Trader, the White Slave, and the Politics of Racial Determination in the 1850s," 36.

330. According to a story in the *Boston Atlas*, which was carried in various newspapers, including "The Story of Ida May," *Lewis County* (NY) *Republican* (January 24, 1855).

331. Slaves in Louisiana could bring freedom suits, unlike other southern states, where a white "next friend" was necessary to begin legal proceedings. Carol Wilson, "Sally Muller, the White Slave," *Louisiana History: The Journal of the Louisiana Historical Association*, Vol. 40, No. 2 (Spring 1999): 151.

332. "To the Public," *New Orleans Picayune* (May 31, 1844).

333. "A Happy Meeting," *Daily Saratoga* (NY) *Republican* (July 17, 1845).

334. *A Narrative of the Case of Salome' Muller, a German Girl Who Came to This Country with Her Parents in 1818, at the Age of Five—Was Reduced to Slavery in Louisiana, and Sold and Kept as an African Slave for More Than Twenty-five Years* (New Orleans, LA [?]: Publisher not identified, circa 1845).

335. For example: *New York Tribune* (July 11, 1844); "Remarkable Case," *Rutland* (VT) *Herald* (May 2, 1844); "An Unparalleled Case of Cruelty and Oppression,"(Brandon, VT) *Voice of Freedom* (May 9, 1844); "Freedom Gained," *American Republican and Baltimore Clipper* (July 1, 1845); "Sally Miller," *Daily Saratoga* (NY) *Republican* (July 17, 1845); "Sally Miller,"(Batavia,

NY) *Republican Advocate* (July 22, 1845); and "Case of Salome Muller," *Anti-Slavery Bugle* (December 12, 1845).

336. See Wilson, "Sally Muller, the White Slave," 148–49; and Carol Wilson, *The Two Lives of Sally Miller: A Case of Mistaken Racial Identity in Antebellum New Orleans* (New Brunswick, NJ: Rutgers University Press, 2007), 89ff.

337. *Sunbury* (PA) *American* (June 10, 1848).

338. Originally published in the *Boston Atlas*, it was reprinted in: "The Story of Ida May," *Trenton State Gazette* (January 8, 1855); "The Story of Ida May," *Onondaga* (NY) *Gazette* (January 20, 1855); and "The Story of Ida May," *Lewis County* (NY) *Republican* (January 24, 1855). The work of fiction was Mary Langdon, *Ida May: A Story of Things Actual and Possible* (Boston: Phillips, Sampson and Co., 1855).

339. Wilson, "Sally Muller, the White Slave," 133–53; Bailey, *The Lost German Slave Girl*; and Wilson, *The Two Lives of Sally Miller*.

340. Solomon Northup, Joseph Logsdon and Sue Eakin (eds.), *Twelve Years a Slave* (Baton Rouge: Louisiana State University Press, 1968).

341. The African American presence in Saratoga is discussed in Chapter 8 of Theodore Corbett, *The Making of American Resorts* (New Brunswick, NJ: Rutgers University Press, 2001).

342. Norman Prindle testified that they had been in Saratoga for a few days. *New York Daily Tribune* (July 14, 1854).

343. Frank Jackson's rescuer encountered difficulty when taking him back to Pennsylvania. See case study of Frank Jackson.

344. See David Fiske, Clifford W. Brown, and Rachel Seligman, *Solomon Northup: The Complete Story of the Author of Twelve Years a Slave* (Santa Barbara, CA: Praeger, 2013), chap. 8.

345. In 1853, a newspaper reported that "it was pretty well proved that he [Northup] was himself a principal party to the fraud." "Kidnapped," *Alexandria* (VA) *Gazette* (January 21, 1853): 2; *Boston Herald* (January 24, 1853): 1 (both attributing the information to the *Washington Republic*). Such speculation surfaced again at the conclusion of legal proceedings against Merrill and Russell: "it is more than suspected that Sol. Northup was an accomplice in the sale, calculating to slip away and share the spoils," *Syracuse Daily Courier* (July 3, 1857), attributed to the *Saratogian's* report of an investigation by the *Albany Evening Journal*; a similar story appeared in the *Lowell* (MA) *Daily Citizen and News* (June 17, 1857). A southern writer said that: "Solomon was one of those cute Yankee niggers who permit themselves to be sold occasionally, pocketing half the proceeds, and then claiming and proving their freedom under the plea of having been kidnapped." In "Letter from Mississippi," *Times-Picayune* (May 26, 1857). In 1894, an acquaintance of Merrill claimed to have heard the story from him. "A Slave Twelve Years," *National Tribune* (October 11, 1894). The tale of complicity was repeated some years later: "Slavery Days Recalled," *Amsterdam* (NY) *Evening Recorder* (December 24, 1902); and "Reminiscences of a Lawyer," *Amsterdam* (NY) *Evening Recorder* (October 30, 1907).

346. "I do solemnly declare before men, and before God, that any charge or assertion, that I conspired directly or indirectly with any person or persons to

sell myself; that any other account of my visit to Washington, my capture and imprisonment in Williams' slave pen, than is contained in these pages, is utterly and absolutely false." In Northup, Logsdon, and Eakin, *Twelve Years a Slave*, 249. For a detailed discussion of the matter, see Fiske, Brown, and Seligman, *Solomon Northup: The Complete Story*, 138.

347. See case studies of Eli Terry and George Armstrong.

348. The incident was reported in "Charge of Kidnapping—a Sheriff under Arrest," (Baltimore) *Sun* (August 25, 1857); "The Kidnapping Case in Maryland—Restoration of the Negro to Liberty," (New York) *Evening Post* (September 2, 1857); "Kidnapping by a Maryland Sheriff," *New-York Daily Tribune* (September 5, 1857); and "Anti-Slavery Items," *The Anti-Slavery Reporter* (January 1, 1859), 24.

349. Information on the documents recovered by Manly are in "The Kidnapping Case in Maryland— Restoration of the Negro to Liberty," (New York) *Evening Post* (September 2, 1857); and "Kidnapping by a Maryland Sheriff," *New-York Daily Tribune* (September 5, 1857).

350. Newspaper accounts do not give his full name, but Stephen H. Manly was the deputy marshal at the time. De Francias Folsom, *Our Police: A History of the Baltimore Force from the First Watchman to the Latest Appointee* (Baltimore: J. D. Ehlers & Co. and Guggenheimer, Weil & Co., 1888), 28.

351. Manly "richly deserves the thanks of every friend of humanity for his timely exertions in rescuing a free man from Slavery," per the *Baltimore Patriot*, reprinted in "Kidnapping by a Maryland Sheriff," *New-York Daily Tribune* (September 5, 1857). Manly received $71.98 for his expenses and services. *Reports of the Majority and Minority Committees in Relation to the Executive Contingency Fund*, Document L. By the [Maryland] House of Delegates, February 20, 1858, 16.

352. His confinement at Towsontown was noted in: "The Kidnapping Case in Maryland—Restoration of the Negro to Liberty," (New York) *Evening Post* (September 2, 1857). His removal to Elkton was mentioned in "Affairs in Cecil County," (Baltimore) *Sun* (December 7, 1857); and "Affairs in Cecil County," (Baltimore) *Sun* (December 21, 1857).

353. "Affairs in Cecil County," (Baltimore) *Sun* (January 4, 1858); "Affairs in Cecil County," (Baltimore) *Sun* (June 14, 1858); and "Reward Offered," (Baltimore) *Sun* (June 25, 1858).

354. "The Kidnapping Case," *New York Evening Express* (March 26, 1858). Descriptions of the couple appear in "New York City: Kidnapping," *New York Times* (March 25, 1858).

355. "Another Kidnapping Case," *New York Herald* (March 25, 1858).

356. "Arrest of Alleged Kidnappers," (Washington, DC) *Evening Star* (March 26, 1858); and "Kidnapping in New York," *Buffalo Courier* (March 26, 1858).

357. "Another Kidnapping Case," *New York Herald* (March 25, 1858).

358. "The Kidnapping Case," *New York Evening Express* (March 26, 1858).

359. *Genesee County Herald* (January 29, 1859); and *New York, Executive Orders for Commutations, Pardons, Restorations and Respites, 1845–1931*. Though the *Herald* gives his sentence as five years, the pardon says it was only two.

360. Augustus Finch Shirts, *A History of the Formation, Settlement and Development of Hamilton County, Indiana* (N.p.: The Author, 1901), 262; John H. B. Nowland, *Early Reminiscences of Indianapolis* (Indianapolis, IN: Sentinel Book and Job Printing House, 1870), 264; and Emma Lou Thornbrough, *The Negro in Indiana: A Study of a Minority* (Indianapolis: Indiana Historical Bureau, 1957), 102.

361. One account says the men stayed in Missouri only a short time. Shirts, *A History of the Formation, Settlement and Development of Hamilton County, Indiana*, 262. Terry's kidnapping is summarized in the history books cited above, but no doubt the most reliable account comes from Thomas Council, one of his rescuers, who surely got many of the details from Terry himself. Thomas W. Council, *An Account of the Rescue from Slavery of Eli Terry* (Indianapolis, IN: Elder & Harkness, 1851), 28ff.

362. Major Edward West was an early settler of Red River County, Texas. He had been sheriff when Texas was a republic. Pat B. Clark, *The History of Clarksville and Old Red River County* (Dallas, TX: Mathis, Van Nort & Col, 1937), 212–13.

363. The text of the note (for $400—apparently the other $200 was paid in cash) appears in James Webb and Thomas H. Duval, *Reports of Cases Argued and Decided in the Supreme Court of the State of Texas, during December Term, 1847*, Vol. 2 (Galveston, TX: The News Office, 1899), 376.

364. Council, *An Account of the Rescue from Slavery of Eli Terry*, 30.

365. West apparently did not completely disbelieve Terry's claim. He refused to pay a note for $400 he had given Carter as part of his payment for Terry, because he said he had been defrauded, and he put up obstacles to Terry regaining his liberty. Council, *An Account of the Rescue from Slavery of Eli Terry*, 30. Council wrote that West's note was given to a man named Reed in exchange for some land, and a Miles Reed is referred to in a court case connected with the note. Webb and Duval, *Reports of Cases Argued and Decided in the Supreme Court of the State of Texas, during December Term, 1847*, Vol. 2, 376.

366. "The Difference between Slaveholders and Abolitionists," (Clarksville, TX) *Standard* (January 12, 1850); and "Restored to Freedom," (Clarksville, TX) *Standard* (February 22, 1851).

367. *History of Dearborn and Ohio Counties, Indiana, from their Earliest Settlement* (Chicago: F. E. Weakley & Co., 1885), 257.

368. "Indiana Yearly Meeting," *Friends' Review* (Tenth Month 26, 1850), 88–89.

369. Nowland, *Early Reminiscences of Indianapolis*, 262ff. An obituary for Council mentioned that he was an early abolitionist. *Cincinnati Daily Gazette* (November 6, 1880). In 1860, he was a 50-year-old merchant, born in North Carolina, and living in Marion County, Indiana. 1860 Federal Census, Wayne Township, Marion County, Indiana, 40.

370. Harrison was a Hamilton County farmer: 1850 Federal Census, Clay Township, Hamilton County, Indiana, 39.

371. As Council wrote, the mission was "shrouded in grave uncertainties." Council, *An Account of the Rescue from Slavery of Eli Terry*, 5.

372. Council, *An Account of the Rescue from Slavery of Eli Terry*, 30.

373. Most likely Amos Morrill, a native of Massachusetts, who practiced law in Clarksville and later became a noted jurist. James D. Lynch, *The Bench and Bar of Texas* (St. Louis, MO: Nixon-Jones Printing Co., 1885), 151ff.

374. Council, *An Account of the Rescue from Slavery of Eli Terry*, 31.

375. Probably John T. Mills, who was praised for his impartiality. Richard B. Marrin and Lorna Geer Sheppard, *The Paradise of Texas: Clarksville and Red River County, 1846–1860*, Vol. 1 (Westminster, MD: Heritage Press, 2007), 129.

376. Council, *An Account of the Rescue from Slavery of Eli Terry*, 32.

377. There was "no opposition to his removal, nor not a particle of excitement . . . raised by the suit." "The Difference between Slaveholders and Abolitionists," (Clarksville, TX) *Standard* (January 12, 1850).

378. "The Difference between Slaveholders and Abolitionists," (Clarksville, TX) *Standard* (January 12, 1850).

379. "Restored to Freedom," (Clarksville, TX) *Standard* (February 22, 1851).

380. Somewhat curiously, Council wrote nothing about any interaction with Terry during the long trip back to Indiana and, in his narrative, refers to him simply as "the negro."

381. Council, *An Account of the Rescue from Slavery of Eli Terry*, 36.

382. "Indiana, Marriages, 1780–1992," index, FamilySearch, https://familysearch.org/pal:/MM9.1.1/XF8F-63D (accessed January 10, 2015).

383. *Swartz & Tedrowe's Annual Indianapolis Directory, 1874* (Indianapolis, IN: Sentinel Company, 1874), 390; and *Swartz & Tedrowe's Indianapolis City Directory, 1875* (Indianapolis, IN: Sentinel Company, 1875), 215. This Eli Terry reportedly relocated to Chicago. "About People," *Indianapolis Sentinel* (May 21, 1875). None of these sources make any mention of Terry being a man of color, however.

384. 1920 Federal Census, Clarksville, Red River County, Texas, Sheet 4B; and Death Certificate #9382, "Texas, Deaths, 1890–1976," index and images, FamilySearch, https://familysearch.org/ark:/61903/1:1:K3C8-G9C (accessed February 6, 2015).

385. Basic information on the Thompson family is given in the report of *Commonwealth v. Alberti, et al.*, printed in A. V. Parsons, *Select Cases in Equity and at Law, Argued and Determined in the Court of Common Pleas of the First Judicial District of Pennsylvania, from 1842 to 1851*, Vol. 2 (Philadelphia: T. & J. W. Johnson, 1851), 495–502. Additional details, especially from a statement by the owner of Mrs. Thompson, are in P. A. Browne, "A Review of the Trial, Conviction and Sentence of George F. Alberti, for Kidnapping," in Paul Finkelman, *Fugitive Slaves and American Courts: The Pamphlet Literature*, Vol. 2. (New York: Garland Publishing, 1988), 27–50, which is also available online in the Library of Congress's American Memory digital collection.

386. Catharine's owner claimed that both she and William were already married to others, back in Maryland. Browne, "A Review of the Trial, Conviction and Sentence of George F. Alberti, for Kidnapping," 50.

387. Browne, "A Review of the Trial, Conviction and Sentence of George F. Alberti, for Kidnapping," 30. The 1850 census lists William and Catherine

[*sic*] Thompson, both born in Delaware, and one son, two-year-old Billy, born in New Jersey: 1850 Federal Census, Chester, Burlington County, New Jersey, 91.

388. Reports of the judicial proceedings do not reveal Price's race, but an item published years afterward said he was "a colored man." "George F. Alberti," *New York Times* (July 27, 1869).

389. Browne, "A Review of the Trial, Conviction and Sentence of George F. Alberti, for Kidnapping," 40.

390. Parsons, *Select Cases in Equity and at Law*, Vol. 2, 497.

391. He used a "billy" on her, according to Parsons, *Select Cases in Equity and at Law*, 497. It was a "mace," per "Kidnapping Case," (Philadelphia) *Dollar Newspaper* (March 5, 1851).

392. Parsons, *Select Cases in Equity and at Law*, Vol. 2, 497.

393. Ibid.

394. Ibid., 495.

395. "Message of the Governor of Maryland," (Baltimore) *Sun* (January 13, 1852); and William Uhler Hensel, *The Christiana Riot and the Treason Trials of 1851: An Historical Sketch* (Lancaster, PA: New Era Printing Co., 1911), 8.

396. The jury took just a few minutes to reach a decision. "Kidnapping Case," (Philadelphia) *Dollar Newspaper* (March 5, 1851).

397. Browne, "A Review of the Trial, Conviction and Sentence of George F. Alberti, for Kidnapping," 33. "Think for a moment," Judge Parsons told the kidnappers, "how great the magnitude of stealing an infant, born in a free State, and binding it in the galling chains of slavery for a little money."

398. "The End: The Anti-Slavery Society of Pennsylvania," (Philadelphia) *Evening Telegraph* (May 5, 1870); Wilson, *Freedom at Risk*, 51; and "Pardon of Alberti," (Baltimore) *Sun* (February 3, 1852).

399. Reprinted in "George F. Alberti," *New York Times* (July 27, 1869).

400. There are discrepancies in the number and names of victims. A newspaper listed: Stephen, age 12; Jacob, 19; Hannah, 23; Mink, 18; Mary, 8; Harvey, 10; Henry James, 20; Caty, 29, and Ann Freedland. "Kidnapping," *Albany Argus* (July 1, 1817). In the record of the court case, Freedland's surname is given as Freeland, and the following names of victims are given: Stephen Neros, Mingo Smith, Catharine Daniels, and David Treadwell. It also says there were two children, whose names were not given. Daniel Rogers, *The New-York City-Hall Recorder, for the Year 1817* (New York, Clayton & Kingsland, 1817), 120ff.

401. "Kidnapping," *Albany Argus* (July 1, 1817).

402. "Kidnappers Taken," *New-York Daily Advertiser* (June 30, 1817).

403. Ibid.

404. Nichols kept a brothel, according to "Kidnapping," *Albany Argus* (July 1, 1817). His establishment was described as both a gambling house and a brothel in "Kidnappers Taken," *New-York Daily Advertiser* (June 30, 1817).

405. "Kidnapping," *Albany Argus* (July 1, 1817).

406. Rogers, *The New-York City-Hall Recorder, for the Year 1817*, 126.

407. "Kidnapping," *Albany Argus* (July 1, 1817).

408. "Kidnappers Taken," *New-York Daily Advertiser* (June 30, 1817).

409. Details of the two trials are available in Rogers, *The New-York City-Hall Recorder, for the Year 1817*, 120ff.

410. Rogers, *The New-York City-Hall Recorder, for the Year 1817*, 125, 126.

411. The court records do not give the mayor's name, but in 1817, former jurist Jacob Radcliff held the office. "Jacob Radcliff," Historical Society of the New York Courts web page, http://www.nycourts.gov/history/legal-history-new-york/luminaries-supreme-court/radcliff-jacob.html (accessed June 8, 2015).

412. Rogers, *The New-York City-Hall Recorder, for the Year 1817*, 126n.

413. Daniel Rogers, *The New-York City-Hall Recorder, for the Year 1819* (New York: Clayton & Kingsland, 1819), 173.

414. Ibid., 173. The arrival of the *Sarah Ann* (from Havana) was noted in "Arrived Last Evening," *New-York Evening Post* (November 22, 1819). Her clearance was noted in "Evening Post Marine List Cleared," *New-York Evening Post* (November 27, 1819). Luckily, Underhill was not aboard, contrary to Pulford's plans for her.

415. A newspaper praised Glasshune for his actions, and also Hassey, Gillen, and George Wooldridge for their "spirited exertions" in the case. *New-York Daily Advertiser* (December 18, 1819). An advertisement for the Eagle Tavern, on Water Street, gave Wooldridge's name as the proprietor, and identified him as the son-in-law of Henry J. Hassey. *New-York Daily Advertiser* (May 20, 1818). Gillen was a constable in the 2nd Ward. *Minutes of the Common Council of the City of New York, 1784–1831*, Vol. 8, July 6, 1814 to January 27, 1817. (New York: City of New York, 1917), 96.

416. Rogers, *The New-York City-Hall Recorder, for the Year 1819*, 173.

417. Colden was mayor from 1818 to 1820. Charles H. Haswell, *Reminiscences of an Octogenarian of the City of New York (1816 to 1866)* (New York: Harper & Brothers, 1896), 101. Haswell also notes, on page 78, that he had been president of the Manumission Society.

418. Rogers, *The New-York City-Hall Recorder, for the Year 1819*, 174.

419. Ibid.

420. Ibid., 174. Pulford's sentencing was also noted in "A Kidnapper Caught," (Cortland, NY) *Republican* (January 6, 1820).

421. Rogers, *The New-York City-Hall Recorder, for the Year 1819*, 174.

422. George Washington Smith, *A History of Southern Illinois* (Chicago: Lewis Publishing Company, 1912), 473; George W. Smith, "The Salines of Southern Illinois," *Transactions of the Illinois State Historical Society for the Year 1904* (Springfield: Phillips Brothers, 1904), 258. Walter White may have been the man by that name, born around 1821, who lived in Equality in 1860: 1860 Federal Census, Equality, Gallatin County, Illinois, 2. The incident appears not to have been reported in the antislavery newspapers at the time of its occurrence.

423. Crenshaw had previously been tried, and acquitted, for kidnapping. John Drury, *Old Illinois Houses. Occasional Publications of the Illinois State Historical Society* (Springfield: Illinois State Historical Society, 1948), 30–31, which

references an article by Barbara Burr Hubbs for the *Illinois Journal of Commerce*. Crenshaw's home came to be known as "The Old Slave House." Crenshaw's possible involvement in kidnapping is discussed in Amy Musser, "Old Slave House," *Scholars*, McKendree University Online Journal of Undergraduate Research (Issue 13, Summer 2009), http://www.mckendree.edu/academics/scholars/issue13/musser.htm#_ftnref16 (accessed April 27, 2014); and in Jon Musgrave, *Slaves, Salt, Sex and Mr. Crenshaw* (Marion, IL: illinoishistory.com, 2004). See also Jon Musgrave's web site, illinoishistory.com.

424. 1870 Federal Census, Township 9 Range 8, Gallatin County, Illinois, 358; 1880 Federal Census, Equality, Gallatin County, Illinois, 490; and 1900 Federal Census, Equality, Gallatin County, Illinois, 236.

425. Smith, *A History of Southern Illinois*, 473.

426. Quote from Henry Howe. *Historical Collections of Ohio in Two Volumes, an Encyclopedia of the State*, Vol. 1 (Columbus, OH: Henry Howe & Son, 1889), 418; "Kidnapping," (New York) *Daily Tribune* (December 13, 1842); Stanley Harrold, *Border War: Fighting over Slavery before the Civil War* (Chapel Hill: University of North Carolina Press, 2010), 61.

427. Conversation with Gary L. Knepp, May 1, 2015. Another source also said that a former owner laid claim to the mother and children, even though the latter had been born out of bondage. J. H. Galbraith, "Highlights of Ohio History: Robert Fee," (Canton, OH) *Repository* (July 18, 1931).

428. 1840 Federal Census, Washington Township, Clermont County, p. 74.

429. "From the Ohio Sun," (Georgetown, OH) *Democratic Standard* (December 6, 1842). Other evidence that Fanny was free is cited in Keith P. Griffler, *Front Line of Freedom: African Americans and the Forging of the Underground Railroad in the Ohio Valley* (Lexington: University Press of Kentucky, 2004), 18.

430. "From the Ohio Sun."

431. Griffler, *Front Line of Freedom*, 18; Harrold, *Border War*, 61. Public meetings in support of the victims were held in Washington, Ohio—(Georgetown, OH) *Democratic Standard* (December 6, 1842)—and in Batavia, Ohio—(Georgetown, OH) *Democratic Standard* (December 20, 1842).

432. Gary L. Knepp, *Freedom's Struggle: A Response to Slavery from the Ohio Borderlands* (Milford, OH: Little Miami Pub. Co., 2008), 148–49.

433. Galbraith, "Highlights of Ohio History: Robert Fee."

APPENDIX

1. See case study of George Armstrong.

2. See case study of Stephen Dickinson, Robert Garrison, and Isaac Wright.

3. See case study of Sarah Taylor.

4. As a follow-up to Sarah Nicholson's story, her return to Philadelphia aboard the ship *Hercules* was noted in *American Traveller* (Boston, MA; August 22, 1828).

5. See case study of Solomon Northup.

6. See case study of Joel Henry Thompson.

Further Reading

The current work builds upon earlier research on the kidnapping phenomenon which was reported in:

Carol Wilson, *Freedom at Risk: The Kidnapping of Free Blacks in America, 1780–1865* (Lexington: University Press of Kentucky, 1994).

A book that has some significant material relating to how the kidnapping of freemen was one of the factors causing friction between the North and South before the Civil War is:

Stanley Harrold, *Border War: Fighting over Slavery before the Civil War* (Chapel Hill: University of North Carolina Press, 2010).

A work that deals with efforts by blacks in New Orleans to be freed from slavery is:

Judith Kelleher Schafer, *Becoming Free, Remaining Free: Manumission and Enslavement in New Orleans, 1846–1862* (Baton Rouge: Louisiana State University Press, 2003).

An understanding of the challenges free blacks faced in southern states can be obtained from:

Ira Berlin, *Slaves without Masters: The Free Negro in the Antebellum South* (New York: Pantheon Books, 1975).

An excellent study of the internal slave trade in the United States is:

Robert H. Gudmestad, *A Troublesome Commerce: The Transformation of the Interstate Slave Trade* (Baton Rouge: Louisiana State University Press, 2003).

CONTEMPORARY PUBLICATIONS

Solomon Northup's narrative, originally published in 1853, provides the most detailed firsthand account of a kidnapping victim available. Two annotated editions of his book have been published, over 100 years after it was originally issued:

Solomon Northup, *Twelve Years a Slave*, edited by Joseph Logsdon and Sue Eakin (Baton Rouge: Louisiana State University Press, 1968);

Sue Eakin, *Solomon Northup's* Twelve Years a Slave *and Plantation Life in the Antebellum South* (Lafayette: University of Louisiana at Lafayette, 2007), revised and reissued as *Twelve Years a Slave—Enhanced Edition by Dr. Sue Eakin* (The Woodlands, TX: Eakin Films & Publishing, 2013).

Another edition, with some observations by scholars Henry Louis Gates Jr. and Ira Berlin, is:

Solomon Northup, *Twelve Years a Slave* (New York: Penguin Books, 2013).

An interesting account of a rescue, including the hazards faced by some men who went south to obtain the release of a victim, is:

Thomas W. Council, *An Account of the Rescue from Slavery of Eli Terry* (Indianapolis: Elder & Harkness, 1851).

In addition to newspaper accounts, the story of Dimmock Charlton was related in a pamphlet originally printed in 1859, now available as:

Mary L. Cox, *Narrative of Dimmock Charlton, a British Subject, Taken from the Brig "Peacock" by the U.S. Sloop "Hornet," Enslaved while a Prisoner of War, and Retained Forty Five Years in Bondage* (London: Forgotten Books, 2013).

The personal observations of Dr. Jesse Torrey, as they relate to kidnapping, are especially interesting.

Jesse Torrey, *A Portraiture of Domestic Slavery in the United States*, 2nd ed. (Ballston Spa, NY: The Author, 1818), also published as Jesse Torrey, *American Slave Trade* (London: J. M. Cobbett, 1822).

Index

ABOUT THE AUTHOR

DAVID FISKE, MLS, is a librarian and researcher with extensive experience in African American history. His published works include *Solomon Northup: His Life before and after Slavery* and *Solomon Northup: The Complete Story of the Author of* Twelve Years a Slave. He received his bachelor's degree from Cornell University and his master of library science from the University at Albany.